The Architecture of Europe

Classical Architecture 1420–1800

Also by Doreen Yarwood

Published

English Costume
The English Home
The Architecture of England
The Outline of English Architecture
English Houses
The Outline of English Costume
The Architecture of Italy
Robert Adam
The Architecture of Europe
European Costume
The Architecture of Britain
Encyclopedia of World Costume
Costume of the Western World
The British Kitchen
Five Hundred Years of Technology in the Home
English Interiors
Encyclopedia of Architecture
Chronology of Western Architecture
Fashion in the Western World
The Architecture of Europe
Volume 1 The Ancient Classical and Byzantine
    World 3000 BC–1453 AD
Volume 2 The Middle Ages 650–1550
Volume 3 Classical Architecture 1420–1800
Volume 4 The 19th and 20th Centuries

The Architecture of Europe
Classical Architecture 1420–1800

Doreen Yarwood

Volume 3

B.T. Batsford Ltd, London

© Doreen Yarwood 1992
First published 1992

Typeset by
Servis Filmsetting Ltd, Longsight, Manchester
and printed in Great Britain

for the publishers
B.T. Batsford Ltd
4 Fitzhardinge Street
London W1H OAH

A CIP catalogue for this book is
available from the British Library

ISBN 0 7134 6964 1

Publishers' Note
The figure numbers run consecutively through
Volumes 1 to 3.

Contents

Preface

There are many books available on the architecture of Europe. Most of these cover a specific area or period and a number present the subject in a general way. It is rare for one in the English language to deal with Europe as a whole; generally only western Europe is discussed and, within this context, a carefully chosen selection of western European countries. This is understandable, especially in the light of the older, academic approach to the subject, for it was long considered that only countries such as France, Italy and possibly Germany and the Low Countries had been instrumental in influencing and forming British architectural history.

Since 1945, with increasing leisure time, the expansion of higher education and, above all, a greater facility of travel, the whole of Europe has become opened up to tourists and students and academic study has broadened its base. There are still some difficulties and frustrations in visiting eastern Europe, but it is now easier for people to visit the Soviet Union and the satellite countries. In the light of these factors, the publishers and I decided that I should write a book which would narrate simply and chronologically the history of European architecture within the geographical boundaries of modern Europe, showing the architectural development and interdependence of the 23 countries concerned from the time of Ancient Greece to the present day.

This is an immense canvas even for a work of this size and there can be no pretence of comprehensiveness or detail. The aim is to present as clear a picture as possible of the general evolution of style and taste in different areas, illustrating which trends—whether they be, for example, political, social or climatic, influenced certain areas at certain times. I have given greater space in each chapter to the countries which were of paramount importance in leading certain movements and which produced the finest work of that age. The areas concerned vary from century to century: Greece and Rome in the classical world, France in the Middle Ages, Italy in the Renaissance, Germany and Finland in the twentieth century. I have also given especial coverage to countries in eastern and northern Europe which tend to have been left out of books on European architecture. In this volume predominance is given to the Italian Renaissance, to Italian, German and Spanish Baroque, French Rococo styles and to neo-classicism in England.

Half the space is devoted to illustration, for architecture is a visual subject. My husband, John Yarwood, and I have travelled some 67,000 miles in Europe, mainly by car, visiting each of the countries, many of them several times. My husband has taken over 25,000 photographs from which the illustrations, both line drawings and photographic plates, have been made.

In Europe, as on a small scale in England, great buildings are constantly in process of demolition and alteration. Even today few of the books available on European architecture provide a reliable guide to the present state of such monuments. I hope that at least for a few years, this book will provide an up-to-date guide on the condition and existence of interesting architectural work. In our travels we have encountered many discrepancies from written descriptions; some buildings referred to as intact were totally destroyed in the Second World War, others have been demolished, adapted, restored or altered. This is a continuous process and only constant study can present an accurate overall picture.

I hope that one of the uses of this book may be to encourage readers to go to see buildings *in situ*. With this in mind, I have not followed the common tradition of naming buildings and places according to the time of their construction, but have referred to them by the names used currently in their present countries, names to be found readily in standard atlases and guide books.

The author and publishers wish to acknowledge the kindness of the publishers Chatto and Windus for permitting the reproduction of some of my drawings from my *Architecture of Italy*, published by them in 1970. In the present volume these are Figs 646, 655, 657, 661, 662, 748, 750, 756, 758, 759. All the photographs were taken by Professor John Yarwood.

East Grinstead 1992   *Doreen Yarwood*

I
Renaissance and Mannerism: 1420–1650

The Italians say '*Rinascimento*', the Spaniards '*Renacimiento*', the Portuguese, '*Renascença*'. The Germans and Dutch, like ourselves, use the French term '*Renaissance*'. The nations of Europe so describe this unique force which overwhelmed, like a restless tide, the thought and spirit of Medieval man. The words differ but the meaning is synonymous: re-birth.

The word is a literal description of what occurred at this time. Everyone has heard of the Renaissance, especially in relation to its transformation of the arts. We know that it was a movement towards Humanism from the hierarchical interpretation of Christianity; that there was a leaning towards the classical forms of literature and in the visual arts away from the Medieval. We also know that the movement began in Italy in the fourteenth century and that it spread westwards, first to France, then to Germany, England and the Iberian Peninsula and that its eastward influence, apart from Hungary and Poland, was negligible, due to the strength of the Turkish and Byzantine traditions.

But why did this movement arise in the fourteenth century? Why did it begin in Italy? Why, indeed, did a force of such power and surging life, sweeping all before it, begin at all?

It is impossible to overstress the importance of the effect of the Renaissance on architecture and its sister visual arts. As its ideas took hold in one country after another, the fundamentals of these arts were transformed. To gain an understanding of the character of this metamorphosis, it is essential to try to discover the answers to these questions. Perhaps it would be best to consider first the last query, for this is the essence of the matter. Why did the Renaissance come at all and what was its meaning?

After the collapse of the ancient classical world of Greece and Rome, mankind had slowly emerged from a barbaric state into the Middle Ages. The motivation of the rise in spirit and quality of living was religious, founded on Christianity. As has been described in Volume 2,

Chapters 1 and 2, this religion in Europe, its form differing only marginally from east to west, had been the foundation of all life. Intellectual thought and culture had been provided by the Church.

The seeds of the Renaissance are to be found in the questioning of this Christian dogma by men of high intellectual stature. They questioned, not the importance of Christianity as a faith and way of life, but man's interpretation of it which, until then, had stressed his unimportance and impermanence. These Renaissance scholars, studying with fervour and absorbed interest the literature of ancient Greece and Rome, envisaged a concept of man as an individual human being, important in his own right. This view conflicted with the existing theological ruling that man's life on earth should be secondary to his future life after death. Despite the excitement and fears engendered by the questioning, after hundreds of years, of such established doctrines, the scholars continued their exploration. They set in motion intense desire for knowledge and a realisation of the need for expansion of learning in universities not subject to the jurisdiction of the Church. Their source of study was the ancient classical world. It is not surprising therefore that, rediscovering the greatness of its culture and art buried, often literally in the case of architecture, for 1000 years, they identified the new humanist thoughts with classicism.

The spirit of the Renaissance arose from man's vital spark of curiosity and his need for change which has always been present, and which distinguishes him from the animal world. It also, to a lesser extent, separates the man of intellect from the majority of mankind in whom resides resistance to change. Resistance to these new concepts was expressed, as is usual, most forcibly by older members in the community.

The Renaissance began in the fourteenth century because it was not until this time that the climate of opinion and the studies and understanding of the leaders of thought were ripe for such theories. Medieval society had largely ignored the remains—architectural, artistic and literary—of the classical world. The dissatisfaction with Medieval life, especially in regard to its religious concepts, combined with man's curiosity about himself and his historical development, led to the discovery of what had been. That the beginnings of this interest in the classical past should have manifested themselves first in Italy was a natural corollary of the fact that here had been the centre of the great Roman Empire. It was in Italy that the major part of the remains existed which came to be the basis for the dominant theme of the Renaissance.

The Renaissance began in the world of literature, and bore fruit in the writings of Petrarch, Boccaccio and Dante. It found expression in university expansion and continued in sculpture and painting with the work of artists like Nicola Pisano, Cimabue and Giotto. Architecture came later. Brunelleschi, in Florence, was the first outstanding architect to develop the classical style and this was more Tuscan and Romanesque than of classical Rome. The discovery of a copy of the 10-volume *De Architectura* by Marcus Vitruvius Pollio (usually called Vitruvius) at S. Gall in 1414 led to the later, purer style developed under Bramante in Rome. Vitruvius was a Roman architect and engineer who had lived in the first century B.C. and in his books, which cover a wide field ranging from medicine to painting and mathematics to sculpture are included detailed data on the correct proportions, rules and style of classical architecture as practised in his day. These books were to have a far-reaching influence on the classical architecture of Europe until the end of the eighteenth century. They were translated into many languages and certain architects and schools of architecture relied heavily upon them, notably the Palladian School in England.

Indeed, it was a characteristic of the Renaissance period of architecture and decoration that artisans and architects all over Europe gained much of their information from books of all types, published mainly in Italy and later in France, Flanders and Germany. Medieval craftsmen and designers had passed on their knowledge primarily by word of mouth and by example. In the Renaissance, leading architects and designers published their designs for buildings and ornament in what were termed pattern books. These drawings and descriptions led to a much faster spread of knowledge of the new styles than had ever been possible in the Middle Ages. Architects in England or Spain, for instance, came to erect buildings based on the designs in such books though they had never seen either an ancient classical building or a Renaissance one.

Meanwhile, in Italy, the early fifteenth century works of Brunelleschi and Alberti were followed by the pure High Renaissance designs of Bramante. Christianity was still the basis for designs in art, but the treatment, especially in sculpture and painting, was less hierarchical. Renaissance forms were vigorous, lively interpretations of nature in human and animal shape as well as plant life and landscape.

With the Renaissance, in Florence, came a change in the artist's status and also in his versatility. The artist, whatever his medium, became an important member of society. He was revered for his skill and paid well for his work. He was in demand by wealthy men of rank: to write about them, build churches and palaces for them, and to decorate these in the prevailing mode. The artist recognised this status and would not demean himself by working for a patron who did not follow his advice or appreciate his work. If the artist was good he could pick and choose. At the same time he was expected to produce a remarkably high standard of work in different media. All the great Renaissance artists were practised in more than one visual art form, though they might prefer to work in one rather than another. For instance, Giotto, a painter, was appointed architect to Florence Cathedral. Alberti, the famous Renaissance architect, was also a mathematician, writer and scholar. Michelangelo was not alone in excelling as painter, sculptor and architect, indeed he held the opinion that a complete, mature artist should have proved himself with commissions in all three arts, in that order, so that by the time he was 50–60 years old he might, after such experience, become a good architect. Renaissance artists created works of superb mastery, but they were never narrow specialists.

Italy continued dominant in architecture until the seventeenth century. The great centres of design shifted to Milan, Venice and other cities— but always with Rome to the fore. In the sixteenth century artists, once more seeking change and variety, moved from pure Roman classicism to Mannerism. This word Mannerism, which was coined about 50 years ago, is applied to the transitional type of work which differs from both the purer High Renaissance classicism and the full Baroque of the seventeenth century. It is characterised by a restlessness of feeling and motif and a reluctance to follow too closely the classical rules and traditions. Architects such as Raphael, Peruzzi and Michelangelo used its forms to a greater or lesser degree in different buildings.

Although all Renaissance architecture has fundamental characteristics which render it clearly recognisable wherever it is to be found, outside Italy there were many variations on the theme. These were created partly by national ethos, partly by climate and available building materials, but also by the distance separating the countries from Italy, the source of the style. This factor also governed the period of time which tended to elapse between Italy's fifteenth century work and the first pure examples appearing in England, Spain or Scandinavia as late sometimes as the seventeenth century, by which time Italy had gone on to Baroque.

France was influenced earliest by Italian example and possesses the purest building style. Germany and its neighbouring countries of Poland, Czechoslovakia and Holland based their earlier Renaissance work on pattern books, many of them Flemish in origin. The designs, having been thus copied and transmitted from Italy to France to Flanders, altered *en route* so that the style of building used by German, Dutch and English architects was not like the Italian proto-types. When the national characteristics and building traditions were also incorporated in the work the results became a Flemish Mannerism which is totally different from the Italian one. English work of this type is Elizabethan or Jacobean, characterised by all-over decoration, imperfect understanding of the orders, and build-ings which are still basically Medieval with a clothing of Renaissance ornament superimposed. In few cases is Renaissance structure employed. This effect can be seen also in sixteenth century Polish, German, Dutch and Spanish work. In Spain it took the form of Renaissance Plateresque. This, like its predecessor Gothic Plateresque (see Volume 2, pp. 178–9), is an all-over surface deco-ration of Renaissance forms in rich and intricate manner. Decorative motifs used in such Manner-

ism in all these countries is generally in high relief and includes a bewildering variety of forms: human, animal and plant life, cartouches, strap-work, obelisks and grotesques of all kinds.

None of this Mannerist work is pure Renais-sance. In the past it was often deemed crude and barbaric. It is certainly not to everyone's taste, but it always displays vigour and pulsating life though sometimes it may be vulgar; it has originality and reflects with uncanny accuracy its country of origin. For these reasons it is usually appreciated today on its own merits, not as a derivation, and for its own interest, though it would not be considered of the same high aesthetic quality as S. Peter's in Rome or the Florentine palaces.

Not all the countries of Europe possess remains of pure Renaissance architecture. Some, like the U.S.S.R., Bulgaria and Rumania, largely missed out on this period and retained their Byzantine tradition very strongly till the later seventeenth and eighteenth century. Other countries went direct from Mannerist designs to Baroque, but some, notably France, Spain and England, created, later than in Italy, a pure Renaissance pattern of building. In England this movement was initiated by Inigo Jones and in Spain by architects like Juan de Herrera.

Classical architecture in different guises re-mained the fundamental form of building till after 1900.* There were countless variations but all subscribed to the basic theme: the use of columns as support and/or decoration, the orders and a trabeated form of building allied to a greater or lesser extent to the arcuated one. For the greater part of this 500-year period the inspiration was from ancient Rome but, in the eighteenth and nineteenth centuries, a proportion of the work was based on the civilisation of ancient Greece.

Confusion is sometimes created by the similar terms classical, classicism and classic, all in use to refer to the work of these years. Classical is the adjective describing designs and characteristics of the antique world of Greece and Rome and their later derivations. Classicism is the appro-priate noun. Classic has a wider adjectival mean-ing. It is used to refer to designs of different species, provided that they are based on a proven early, original style; and this might be classical but could equally well be Romanesque or Byzantine.

* *In the nineteenth century, eclecticism also explored Byzantine and Medieval avenues.*

646 *S. Maria Novella, Florence. Façade, Alberti, 1470*
647 *The dome of Florence Cathedral, Brunelleschi,*
    1420–36; lantern, 1461
648 *Interior, S. Lorenzo, Florence, Brunelleschi, from 1420*
649 *Façade, S. Andrea, Mantua, Alberti, begun 1472*

Italy

Early Renaissance: Fifteenth Century Florence

Filippo Brunelleschi (1377–1446) was the first Renaissance architect. He had been both goldsmith and sculptor and had also studied mathematics and spent some time in Rome making measured drawings of ancient Roman buildings. His early work, like the *Ospedale degli Innocenti* (the Foundling Hospital), begun 1419, was Tuscan and Romanesque in derivation. Nevertheless, such designs showed the new classical approach, a desire for symmetry, proportions carefully related in one part to another and the adaptation of the new-found science of perspective to architecture.

In his commission to build a *dome* to the unfinished Medieval *Cathedral*, Brunelleschi had to bring all his knowledge of mathematics and of the structures of ancient Roman vaults (PLATE 75). The practical problem for this date (1404) was considerable; how to construct a dome to span the 138 feet diameter space. This was too great a distance to support on available timber centering. Brunelleschi, like all classical architects, knew that a hemispherical dome would be aesthetically most desirable. He dared not build one on to the existing octagonal drum, which had no external abutment. So he compromised and proceeded carefully, step by step. His dome is constructed on Gothic principles with ribs supporting a later, light infilling. It is taller than a hemisphere to offset the thrust. To retain his exterior and to reduce weight, he made two domes, one inside the other. The lantern, though designed by Brunelleschi, was built after his death. It is weighty and impressive; a fine finial (**647**).

Brunelleschi built several churches and chapels. The outstanding ones are similar; *S. Spirito* (1436) and *S. Lorenzo* (*c.* 1420) (**648**), both of which are basilican and display a feeling of light not found in Medieval churches. His unfinished *S. Maria degli Angeli* (1437) is one of the earliest examples of the centrally planned church; a concept which has intrigued classical architects until the present century. This one is a 16-sided regular polygon; eight chapels open from the octagonal central area. His *Pazzi Chapel* (S. Croce) (1433) contains some magnificent ceramic work by *Luca della Robbia* (1400–82).

Fifteenth century Florence was one of the wealthiest of the city states so it is not surprising that the finest of the early *Renaissance palaces* were commissioned here by the merchants and ecclesiastical families. Because of the early date and the still troubled times, such palaces are distinguished from later examples by their protective lower storeys, which are rusticated and almost undecorated and unpierced by window openings. These lower floors were used as warehouse and shop accommodation, while classical windows lit the living quarters above. A strongly projecting cornice was developed at the roofline. Inside the building was a square, open courtyard, its light elegant arcaded colonnades contrasting with the forbidding exterior elevations. Most of these palaces were astylar. Typical is the *Strozzi* (1489) by *Benedetto da Maiano* (**651**), the *Medici-Riccardi* (1444–60) by Michelozzo, the *Pazzi-Quaratesi* and the later *Gondi* (*c.* 1490) by *Giuliano da Sangallo*. The *Pitti Palace*, begun 1458 and enlarged *c.* 1550, has a vast main elevation and is one of the best known. One or two palaces had façades with orders, such as *Alberti*'s *Palazzo Rucellai* (1446). These are in pilaster form and the vertical strips make an effective break to the horizontal rustication bands. This set a new pattern with was followed increasingly later.

The Fifteenth Century outside Florence

Leon Battista Alberti (1404–72) was the second outstanding architect of this period. A Genoese, he was a different type of man from Brunelleschi; he was more academic and scholarly and his books on architecture spread Renaissance ideas and classical designs far beyond the borders of Italy. Like Brunelleschi though, he had been a sculptor and mathematician. While the former turned his abilities to solving the problems of constructing the Florence Cathedral dome (PLATE 75), Alberti tackled the age-old question of how to reconcile, in church façade design, the differing heights of nave and aisles by an architectural feature. The Medieval period had dealt with this problem by fronting the cathedrals' western end by a façade, unrelated to the structure behind it, as at Orvieto and Siena. Alberti made a feature of it in his prototype, the new façade to *S. Maria Novella* in *Florence*; he inserted side scrolls to mask the junction (**646**). Here is pure Tuscan decoration

RENAISSANCE PALACES IN ITALY

650 Ducal Palace Courtyard, Urbino, Laurana, 1465–9
651 Strozzi Palace, Florence, Benedetto da Maiano, 1489
652 Farnese Palace Courtyard, Rome, Antonio da Sangallo before 1514; after 1546, Michelangelo
653 Doorway, Ducal Palace, Urbino
654 Palazzo Massimi alle Colonne, Rome, Baldassare Peruzzi, from 1532

Plate 75   Dome and eastern apses of Florence Cathedral viewed from the top of Giotto's campanile. Dome by Brunelleschi 1420–36, lantern 1461

655 S. Pietro in Montorio. Chapel in courtyard called 'Il Tempietto', Bramante, 1500–2
656 S. Maria delle Grazie, Milan, Bramante, 1492–7 : (Gothic nave 1470)
657 The Capitol, Rome, including the Palazzo Capitolino, Palazzo Senatore and the Palazzo Conservatori, 1540–1644. Designed by Michelangelo

655

656

657

in coloured marble strips and veneer but correctly classical in its detail and proportions; it is a Renaissance version of the Romanesque S. Miniato al Monte (**281**).

Alberti also designed *S. Francesco* in *Rimini* (1446) and *S. Sebastiano* in *Mantua* (1460), but his masterpiece, also in Mantua, is his *S. Andrea*, begun 1472 (**649**). This is a prototype far ahead of its time, from the triumphal arch façade to the handling of the interior spatial concepts.

Among the palaces of this century outside Florence, the finest is the *Ducal Palace* at *Urbino* (**650** and **653**), set on a hill top. The courtyard especially is elegant and finely proportioned. *Venetian palaces* were still more Medieval than Renaissance in design, differing little from the Ca' d'Oro (**590**), though fenestration and detail slowly changed. The *Palazzo Vendramin-Calergi c.* 1500 by *Lombardo* is typical.

Lombardic work of this time is also apart from the main stream of the Florentine Renaissance. It is nearer to English Mannerism in its rich surface decoration all over the façades. It differs from the English in that the decorative medium is coloured marble rather than carved wood or stone. The *Colleoni Chapel* at *Bergamo* and the *Certosa di Pavia* façade, both of the 1470–80 period and by *Amadeo*, are typical.

The High Renaissance: Sixteenth Century

This century, the *cinquecento*, was the great age of the Renaissance in Italy. Architects of note and stature were numerous and the quality of the work produced in building and decoration was superb. This was the time when the majority of men of high intellect, talent and initiative became artists, for it was in this field that both monetary and human satisfaction were to be gained.

Among the wealth of talented artists, three stand supreme above the others for the originality of their contribution, its quality and their outstanding personalities: Bramante, Raphael and Michelangelo.

Donato d'Agnolo Lazzari (1444–1514), generally called *Bramante*, was born in Urbino and, after some time spent as a sculptor and a poet, began work as an architect in Milan. Here, he quickly established a reputation for Renaissance building, which for the first time was based on the pure Roman form. His *cloisters* at the *Monastery of S. Ambrogio* show this. He reconstructed the tiny *S. Maria presso S. Satiro*. It exists still, overshadowed by towering modern buildings in the centre of Milan. At *S. Maria delle Grazie** he added an eastern arm to the Gothic church (**656**). This had only recently been built, but Bramante's great polygonal drum with its attendant apses is in marked contrast. The feature was imitated widely by other architects.

Early in the new century Bramante went to Rome and here became the leading architect of his day. Like Brunelleschi before him, he was attracted to the classical symmetry of the centrally planned church. In this he was also influenced by Leonardo da Vinci's drawings showing such buildings on Greek cross plan, perfectly symmetrical and with radiating members. Bramante experimented with the theme in a small chapel erected in the courtyard of *S. Pietro in Montorio*. It has achieved a reputation quite disproportionate to its size and is generally regarded as the most perfect monument to the High Renaissance in the world (**655**). Typically Renaissance in his unconcern over combining Christian and pagan influences, Bramante's *tempietto* is built on the supposed site of S. Peter's crucifixion, but in design is based on a circular Roman temple. It is plain, with a Doric peristyle on a stylobate surmounted by a drum and dome within a parapet. Small though it is, the proportions are in such perfect harmony, it could be enlarged greatly without detriment.

Other architects followed Bramante's lead in centrally planned churches. There are many fine examples, notably *S. Maria di Loreto, Rome*, by *Antonio da Sangallo* (1507), *S. Maria della Croce, Crema*, by *Battagio, S. Maria delle Carceri, Prato* by *Giuliano da Sangallo* and, finest and most perfect of all, *S. Maria della Consolazione* at *Todi, c.* 1520.

Bramante carried out a great deal of other work in Rome during his stay there. This included the *cloister* at *S. Maria della Pace*, the *Vatican Courts* and *S. Peter's*. In the famous basilica, Bramante was given his great opportunity to design a large church on centrally planned lines. In 1503, the newly elected Pope Julius II had to face the problem of what to do about the 1200-year-old basilica, founded by the Emperor Constantine, but now in a seriously dilapidated condition. Courageously, he decided to destroy and rebuild

* *Noted for its possession of Leonardo da Vinci's* Last Supper.

the Mother Church of the Roman Catholic faith. Bramante's completely symmetrical design on Greek cross plan, with central dome and apses on each arm of the cross, was approved (658). The first stone was laid in 1506, but when the architect died in 1514, little had been achieved and the four crossing piers proved inadequate to support the enormous projected dome and had to be rebuilt by his successors.

Raphael (Raffaello Sanzio, 1483–1520) had a short life but was responsible for a prodigious quantity of work. In the last decade of his life especially, in Rome, his output as a painter was tremendous. Some of his frescoes decorate the ceilings of the loggia in Peruzzi's beautiful *Villa Farnesina* on the banks of the Tiber (1509–11). In the architectural field Raphael was Surveyor to the fabric of S. Peter's after Bramante and he built a number of palaces and a villa. His earlier work is in Bramante's style, but later he turned to Mannerist forms. Sadly, little of this remains unaltered, though in some cases the building still exists. He built the *Palazzo Vidoni-Caffarelli* (1515) and the *Branconio dell'Aquila*, both in *Rome*, and the *Pandolfini* in *Florence*. His most ambitious and impressive work was the *Villa Madama* on the outskirts of Rome (1516). He based this on Nero's 'Golden House' and designed it for Cardinal dei Medici.

Michelangelo Buonarroti, 1475–1564

In a book devoted to architecture covering 3000 years in the 23 countries of Europe, space does not permit more than a brief mention of any one architect. Michelangelo must always be an exception. More has been written about him than any other artist the world has known, but this giant among Renaissance geniuses was unique. It is not usual for great artists to be praised in or just after their lifetimes. Again, Michelangelo was an exception. In common with a small group of creative artists, his reputation has never wavered nor has the praise abated. While he lived he commanded, despite his prickly, unbending personality, idolatry from his patrons, fellow artists and the public at large. In all three of the visual arts, painting, sculpture, architecture, he led the field while he lived. He himself preferred the medium of sculpture but when, under pressure, he carried out commissions to cover

great walls and ceilings with paintings, the qualities were still of superb genius. The Sistine Chapel ceiling and the wall covered by his Last Judgement bear testimony to this.

Much of Michelangelo's work in architecture was done late in life; S. Peter's and the Campidoglio, for instance. In *Florence* his work came earlier and some of it is in High Renaissance pure style though later, as in Rome, his tendency was towards Mannerism and even Baroque. But, with Michelangelo one cannot apply labels with any accuracy. His work was of his time or slightly ahead of it but it was always so personally Michelangelo that it defies classification. His architecture, like his painting, always possesses a sculptural quality. It is plastic, forceful, controlled, an undefinable mixture of tortured movement and immemorial peace. The contrast between this and Alberti's and Bramante's classicism is very marked. Michelangelo was responsible for two main works in Florence, both in *S. Lorenzo*. The first is his New Sacristy (so-called to differentiate it from Brunelleschi's). This is the *Medici Mausoleum* which Michelangelo designed in 1521, wherein both architecture and sculpture are his. It is a square interior, the walls of which are strongly articulated in High Renaissance manner. Above is a dome supported on pendentives. The tombs of both Lorenzo and Giuliano Medici are here and respectively adorn two sides of the room. They dominate the scheme. Each has a central sculptural portrait figure of the Medici and below are the symbolic designs representing Dawn and Twilight and Night and Day (PLATE 77). In the *Laurenziana Library* nearby, Michelangelo turned further towards Mannerism. This can be seen in the large coupled columns in recesses, bearing no load and flanked by blind windows. The power and tension in the narrow hall is noticeable, contrasting with the controlled, ordered library above. Entrance hall, staircase and library are one complete, complementary unit.

Michelangelo's greatest work is in the *Basilica of S. Peter* in *Rome*. He spent the last 30 years of his life here and himself regarded his work on the basilica as his most important commission, refusing any salary and working on it till his death at the age of 89. He was an admirer of Bramante and liked his plan. He had to modify it for practical reasons, simplifying the small

THE BASILICA OF S. PETER, ROME, 1506-1612

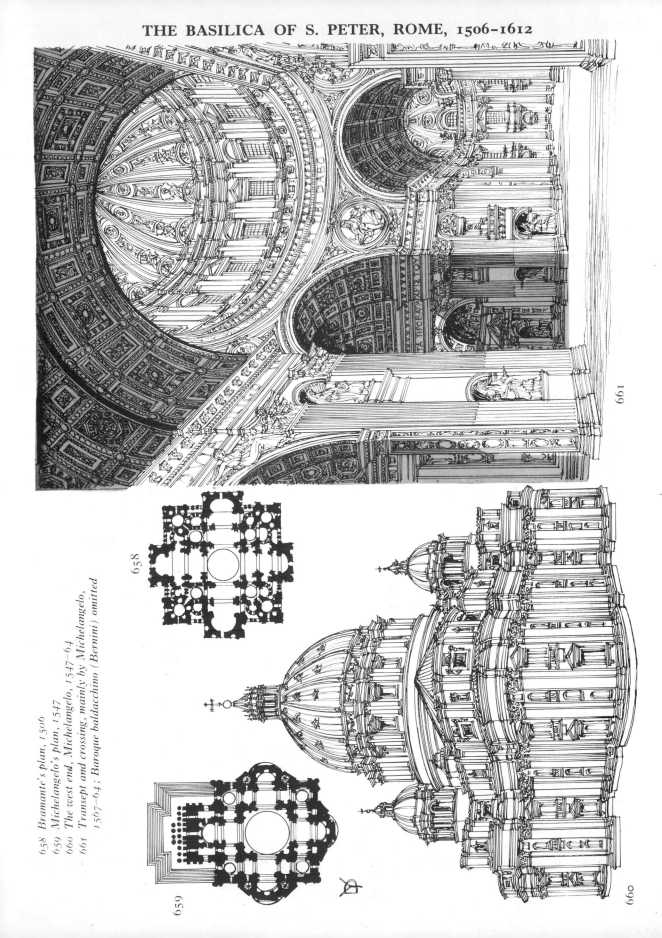

658 Bramante's plan, 1506
659 Michelangelo's plan, 1547
660 The west end, Michelangelo, 1547–64
661 Transept and crossing, mainly by Michelangelo,
       1567–64; Baroque baldacchino (Bernini) omitted

compartments into larger ones and making the building stable by increasing the size of the crossing piers. His plan is shown on p. 11, next to Bramante's (**659** and **658**). Michelangelo's S. Peter's is vast but is so beautifully proportioned that the visitor does not appreciate its size till he compares the height of a pier, for example, with the people in the basilica. Most of the present exterior (apart from the east façade) is Michelangelo's building. It is surrounded by Corinthian order pilasters in giant form, each 100 feet high, surmounted by a 32 feet attic. The whole forms a podium on which the great drum and dome rest. There are three apses, one at the choir (westerly end) and one to each transept. This view of the building, difficult of access because of the Vatican grounds, is shown in Fig. **660**.

About the evolution of the dome of S. Peter's scholars differ. Michelangelo designed a hemispherical one as Brunelleschi had wished to do in Florence and, like him, created an inner shell, but also in hemispherical form. This was based on ancient Roman ideas but, whereas the Romans in the Pantheon had supported the dome on circular walls, Renaissance architects had to raise it on four crossing piers and pendentives. The thrust involved is so great that at that time such a dome was not a feasible structural possibility. When Michelangelo died, the building was largely complete apart from the eastern arm and the dome above the drum. This dome was completed in 1587–90 by Giacomo della Porta and Domenico Fontana, but the exterior form is taller than a hemisphere and is not concentric with the inner one 20 feet lower. The conjecture is whether the final work was based on Michelangelo's altered designs or on those of della Porta and Fontana. Available evidence comprises Michelangelo's one-fifth size scale wooden model of the dome, made in 1561 and in hemispherical form and a taller version shown in a drawing by Michelangelo, now in the Ashmolean Museum in Oxford but not verified as intended for S. Peter's. Historians are divided on this point which is, no doubt, academic. The dome is constructionally sound and on both exterior and interior the most aesthetically satisfying in the world. Its span is 157 feet and the cross rises to 452 feet above the ground.

The interior of S. Peter's as it is seen today is also largely due to Michelangelo. It is archi-tecturally simple. Four arms of the cross are barrel vaulted and decorated by coffers and panels. They meet at the crossing where the drum and dome rise on richly decorated pendentives. Despite the lengthening of the nave in the seventeenth century (Chapter 2) from Greek cross to Latin cross pattern, the interior is basically of one period and design. This is an incredible feat for a building begun in 1506 and completed in 1612. Not a small part of this success is due to the overriding genius of Michelangelo (**661**).

Michelangelo also interested himself in early town planning schemes. His chief contribution here is in the re-designing of *Capitol Hill* in *Rome* (Piazza del Campidoglio). This was designed in 1540. It had been the site for the centre of government since the days of ancient Rome and when, in 1538, the equestrian statue of Marcus Aurelius was moved here (under the impression that it was of Constantine), it was decided to make a worthy setting for this rare Roman monument. Michelangelo designed a piazza on trapezoidal plan, with palaces on three sides and steps approaching the narrow side up the steep hillside from the road below. He designed an oval pavement which was not laid to his design at the time but which, recently, has been relaid to conform to the original pattern. The important feature of the architecture of the palaces is that it is the first recorded use of Michelangelo's giant order, wherein the columns spanned two storeys. This was an innovation, giving dignity and unity to a façade. It was copied extensively later, not only in Italy but in France and England. The whole complex is on Mannerist lines and is one of the few layouts existing from this century which comprises the handling of more than one building in a scheme (**657**).

Sixteenth-Century Palaces, Villas and Churches

The sixteenth century Roman palace differed from its fifteenth century prototype in Florence. Land in the city was costly so wealthy patrons tended to have a town palace on a smaller site, then a more spacious suburban villa in which to relax. The town palace had a High Renaissance street façade and a small courtyard behind. Such palaces were designed by famous architects and tended, during the century, from Renaissance towards Mannerist. Chief among such architects

Plate 76
Florence, Italy
Detail door panel.
Porta di Paradiso.
Baptistery, Ghiberti,
1425–52
Plate 77
'Dawn', from Tomb
of Lorenzo dei
Medici. Medici
Chapel, Church of
S. Lorenzo.
Michelangelo, begun
1531

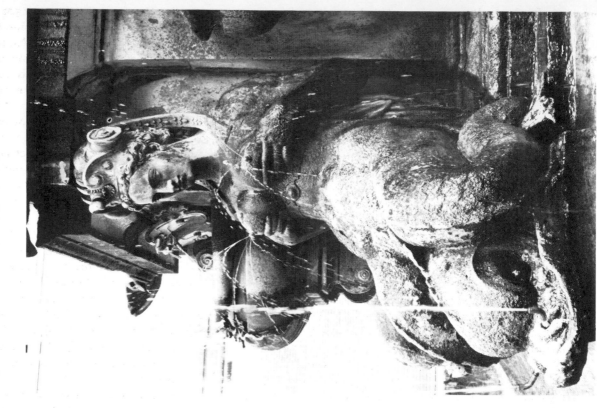

Plate 79
Neptune Fountain detail, Bologna, Italy. Da Bologna, 1563–7

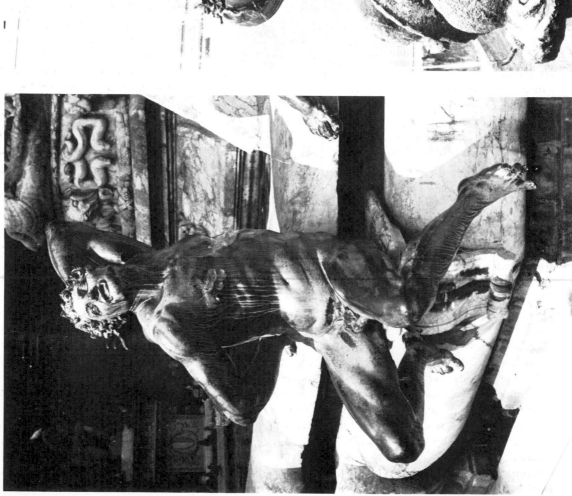

Plate 78
Neptune fountain detail. Piazza della Signoria, Florence, Italy.
Ammanati, 1569–75

were Raphael, Peruzzi, Vignola, Romano and Antonio da Sangallo II. *Baldassare Peruzzi's* Villa Farnesina has already been referred to. Another of his town palaces is the *Palazzo Massimi alle Colonne* (**654**). This, built in 1532, is an early Mannerist work, designed for twin brothers. The façade is subtly curved and breaks many of the classical rules of proportion and the handling of orders, forming a sophisticated elevation, with a fine courtyard behind. The *Farnese Palace* is one of the most magnificent examples. Now the home of the French Embassy, it was built by *Antonio da Sangallo II* on High Renaissance lines. The finely articulated courtyard (**652**) is carefully based on the Colosseum principles with superimposed orders—Doric, Ionic, Corinthian. The top storey was added by Michelangelo.

The second half of the sixteenth century brought a new group of architects: Giorgio Vasari, Giacomo Barocchio (generally called da Vignola after his birthplace), Giulio Romano, Giacomo della Porta, Bartolommeo Ammanati. *Vasari's* famous work is the *Uffizi Palace* in *Florence* (1560–74), now the home of the great art gallery; this is severely Mannerist. *Vignola* worked with Vasari and *Ammanati* on the *Villa Giulia* in *Rome*, built for Pope Julius from 1550 but now the Museum of Etruscan Antiquities. He also designed the fine *villa* at *Caprarola*. *Della Porta* built the *Villa Aldobrandini* at *Frascati* near Rome, a beautiful Mannerist design with fine gardens and fountains.

Giulio Romano is particularly known for his *Palazzo del Te* at *Mantua*, in which city he also worked on the Cathedral and the Ducal Palace. The Palazzo del Te is planned round a central courtyard with a magnificent loggia (**662**) and garden façades.

The Veneto : Sixteenth Century

This area of north-east Italy, under the domination of the Venetian Republic, had always differed from the rest of the country in its artistic expression. Its close mercantile ties with the east gave to its architecture a mixed heritage. Eastern and western influences merged into a unique style. It had been so in Romanesque and Gothic periods; it continued so under the Renaissance. Fifteenth century palaces have been mentioned. In the sixteenth century the pattern continued.

Examples like the *Scuola di San Rocco* (1520–50 and now the City Hospital) and the *Church* of *S. Zaccaria* (1485–1515) illustrate this. But after the collapse of Rome in 1527 several artists came here from elsewhere and the style was brought into line with that of Rome and northern Italy. Two particular architects were Jacopo Tatti, called Il Sansovino (1486–1570) and Michele Sanmichele (1484–1559). *Sansovino* was a Florentine. He was sculptor and architect and a disciple of Michelangelo. Among his outstanding works in *Venice* are the *Library of S. Mark*, the *Mint* (Zecca) and his *Loggia del Campanile*, all in the region of S. Mark's Square. He also built a number of palaces, notably the *Palazzo Cornaro*, now the Prefettura. *Sanmichele* was a Veronese and he returned to his native city after years at Orvieto and Rome. He was in charge of the town's fortification scheme, building town walls and gates, and he designed many *palaces*, for example, the *Canossa*, the *Pompei* and the *Bevilacqua*. Both architects designed in plastic form, showing Michelangelo's influence in their power and chiaroscuro.

The pre-eminent architect of this area in the later sixteenth century was *Andrea Palladio* (1508–80), born Andrea di Pietro della Gondoa. Palladio reverted to the principles of Vitruvius and ancient Rome. He made hundreds of drawings *in situ*, not only in Italy but in Dalmatia and Provence. He published his own designs and ideas in several works of which two, '*I Quattro Libri dell' Architettura*' and '*Le Antichità di Roma*' were translated into many languages and spread his theories all over Europe. The Palladian school of architecture in eighteenth century England is, of course, named after him. Palladio's own work was a mixture of those sources allied to the classicism of Bramante and the Mannerism of Michelangelo and Vignola. Most of his work is in Vicenza and Venice. It comprises churches, palaces and villas, as well as civic works like the replanning of the *town hall* of *Vicenza* (**663**), where he established a pattern in his handling of two superimposed orders (Doric and Ionic) with entablatures broken forward over each column instead of giving the uninterrupted horizontal emphasis as in Sansovino's Library.

In his many palaces and villas he followed what he thought would have been the ancient Roman theme, but as Roman domestic remains are

662 *Palazzo del Te, Mantua, Giulio*
Romano, 1526–34
663 *Town Hall (Basilica*
Palladiana), Vicenza. Re-
clothed by Palladio from 1549

fragmentary, he had to base them on temple design. Two particular examples illustrate his ideas; his *Palazzo Chiericati* in *Vicenza* and the *Villa Capra* (the Rotonda) outside the town. This was copied on at least two occasions in Palladian England, by Lord Burlington at Chiswick House and by Colen Campbell at Mereworth Castle. The Villa Capra is the domestic equivalent to Bramante's 'Tempietto' or S. Maria at Todi. It is the centrally planned villa with central domed hall and the whole *piano nobile* raised on a square podium with four identical porticoes with entrance steps on each side.

In his *churches*, Palladio also used what he thought to be the Roman temple pattern. He developed a type of façade design which incorporated two or more interpenetrating orders differing in scale. He employed this method to solve the old problem of relating the façade to the different height of nave and aisles (see Alberti p.5). Palladio made his nave order larger and higher than that of the aisles. His two outstanding churches are in *Venice*, standing at the water's edge: *S. Giorgio Maggiore*, 1565, and *Il Redentore*, 1577–92 (PLATE 80).

In the second half of the sixteenth century the work of certain artists heralded the Baroque. Michelangelo's contribution at S. Peter's has been mentioned. Also in architecture came *Vignola's* Roman church of *Il Gesù*. This was the Mother Church for the Society of Jesus, which had been founded in 1540. The church design set a pattern for Jesuit churches all over Europe. It was begun in 1568. Vignola's terms of reference were to build a church which could hold a large congregation, all of whom could hear and see the preacher. So the architect must eschew columns, arcades and the nave with aisles pattern. He did so and created a precedent. Il Gesù has no aisles or colonnades; its short broad nave and choir with shallow transepts have side chapels leading off them. To compensate for the lack of side aisle lighting, the large dome has a fenestrated drum which floods the whole church dramatically with light and so gives a unity and space lacking in any Gothic or Renaissance church on the Latin cross plan. Vignola died in 1573 when the church had reached cornice level. Giacomo della Porta built the façade and the interior was altered later in the seventeenth and nineteenth centuries. Despite this it remains the sixteenth century prototype for churches, especially Jesuit ones, all over Europe and marks the crossroads between Mannerism and Baroque. Similarly, in sculpture, *Giovanni da Bologna's* work, as in his *Neptune Fountain* in *Bologna* (1563–7) tends in the same direction (PLATE 79).

Yugoslavia

Remaining buildings of Renaissance style are not numerous. Most of them are in towns bordering the Adriatic coast and show the strong influence from Italy and especially the Venetian Republic. The purest work is in *Dubrovnik*. Two buildings here, in particular (though later restored), have survived the earthquake of 1667 which destroyed so much of the city. The *Rectors' Palace** had been built in the fifteenth century in Gothic style by *Onofrio Giordano della Cava*, but in 1463 the fine Renaissance portico was added. This contains the unusual and varied capitals carved by della Cava, George of Šibenik and Michelozzo (**665** and **666**). Next door is the *Sponza Palace* which served as both custom house and Mint. It was built by Paskoje Miličević and has a fine Renaissance courtyard (**668**). The street façade, like the Rectors' palace, has a ground floor, Renaissance loggia and Gothic fenestration above.

In a less pure, more Mannerist form, are one or two buildings further north. At *Trogir*, opposite to the cathedral in the main square, is an attractive *loggia* with primitive Corinthian style capitals. At one end of the building is a solid square tower. One of the town gateways at *Zadar* has a Renaissance clock tower. This blends with the earlier lower section (**667**).

France

France was the only major European country outside Italy to build in Renaissance form before the seventeenth century. Even here, however, it was not until after 1550 that such work was to be seen. In the earlier sixteenth century buildings erected were basically Gothic in structure and classical only in detail. This ornament was applied without proper comprehension of classical form; buildings were Mannerist. Ecclesiastical structures were especially treated in this way until the early seventeenth century, as at *S. Étienne du Mont* in *Paris* (**670**).

A Rector was elected regularly as head of the city government.

Plate 80   Church of S. Giorgio Maggiore, Venice, begun 1566, Andrea Palladio

RENAISSANCE IN YUGOSLAVIA AND HUNGARY

664 Detail, Chapel of Archbishop Thomas Bakócz, Esztergom
665 Capital and 666 Base of Rectors' Palace, Dubrovnik, Yugoslavia, 1463
667 Porta Marina, Zadar, Yugoslavia; upper part 1571, lower part Roman
668 Sponza Palace (Custom House and Mint), Dubrovnik, 1516–21
669 Chapel of Archbishop Thomas Bakócz in the Cathedral of Esztergom, Hungary, 1507

664

666

665

667

668

669

Though France had close contacts with Italy in the early sixteenth century, both economic and in warfare, and though French designers took easily to using Italianate decorative forms such as orders, scrolls, shells and putti, the Medieval tradition of building persisted. Architecture was slow to follow classical lines until the second half of the century, when architects like De l'Orme and Lescot adopted the new style. Most of this work was in palaces and châteaux where wealthy patrons wished to build in the latest mode. Francis I, almost exactly a contemporary of England's Henry VIII, was the first to show the way. He established a great court, determined to build his culture on Italian lines. He attracted many Italian artists and craftsmen to France, even the great Leonardo da Vinci.

At *Blois*, at *Fontainebleau* and soon in *Paris* (**671** and **677**), Francis built on Renaissance pattern. Others followed suit and French architects, having understood and developed the new

670 *Church of S. Étienne du Mont, Paris, 1517–1618*

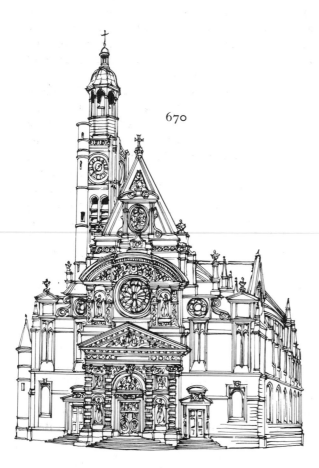

670

style, took to it with pleasure. French Renaissance work is not the same as Italian. It is often more academic, less warm-blooded, monumental or plastic, but much of the later work of the sixteenth century, like Lescot's range in the Cour Carrée in the Louvre (**679**), is of high quality. It quickly established France as a leader of Renaissance design in her own right.

Early Sixteenth-Century Palaces and Châteaux

One of the first instances of Renaissance influence can still be seen in Francis I's wing at the *Château of Blois*. A whole court was planned, but under Francis I's aegis only this range was completed. It contains the famous staircase which, though constructed spirally on Medieval pattern, is classical in appearance and decoration. This range represents the chief contribution of the French court to the early establishment of Renaissance building in France (**677**). It provides an interesting contrast to the adjoining wing of Louis XII, built only a few years earlier but completely Medieval.

Francis' second venture was the immense *Château of Chambord* (**674**). Work was begun in 1519 on a building intended as a hunting lodge. The project grew and was enlarged and altered until the seventeenth century. The original design is thought to have been by the Italian architect *Domenico da Cortona* but, as interpreted by local masons, is very French in character. Chambord is vast, built at the waters' edge and still surrounded by acres of parkland. The château comprises an immense main block with traditional French circular corner towers and with further wings and towers extending at the sides. The wall articulation is simple and Renaissance but the roofline is a riot of chimneys, cupolas, pinnacles and dormers, having much in common (though Gallic in its Mannerist drama) with the Elizabethan great houses of England.

The château interior, based unusually on a Greek cross plan, is noted for the early development in France of the Italian method of arranging the rooms, grouped in suites (*appartements*). These are self-contained and more convenient than the Medieval design of corridor rooms. The double staircase is an outstanding feature of the internal plan. It rises spirally the full height of the building, to a lantern above.

The many châteaux built before 1550 display a varied proportion of Medieval to Renaissance features. Some are entirely Medieval in layout and structure but show classical detail and ornament. They remain fortified, often with moat or surrounding lake, and retain the picturesque French style of roofs, gables and dormers. Very much of this type is the finely situated *Rigny-Ussé*, with its profusion of turrets and chimneys. Also very Medieval is *Amboise*, rebuilt from 1501 by Italian craftsmen. This influence is reflected in the Renaissance detail of dormers and finials in particular. *Azay-le-Rideau*, like Chenonceaux, is among the most picturesque examples, reflected in the encircling spreading waters. It is small, built on simple L-shaped plan, with circular corner towers. The wall articulation and dormer decoration is Renaissance, but Medieval machicolations support the parapets. The frontispiece on the entrance side (**676**) is classical in treatment; a narrow structure with Gothic vertical emphasis. *Chenonceaux*, begun in 1515, based on the Medieval square keep plan, was extended later in the century by *De l'Orme* and *Bullant*. The château is built on the foundations of a mill set by the River Cher and it rises directly from the river. De l'Orme added a terrace across the river upon which Bullant later built his two-storeyed gallery to enlarge the château accommodation. It is interesting to compare the different stages of work from that of the early sixteenth century to the Renaissance and Mannerist style of building (**675**). A merging of Gothic and Renaissance styles can be seen in the two adjacent wings at *Fontaine-Henry* in Normandy. The lower wing is of fifteenth century origin while the taller block added on the left of the façade is Renaissance in its orders and fenestration. An immensely tall roof surmounts this part. A much later example (1606), but still completely Mannerist, is the *Château* at *Brissac*. It has Medieval circular corner towers but a richly articulated Mannerist façade. It is an illustration of how long had to elapse, even in France, before completely classical design replaced Gothic structures.

One of the architectural landmarks between the buildings just described and the more correctly classical ones of the later sixteenth century, is the *Château* at *Ancy-le-Franc*. This is the only surviving building in France by *Sebastiano Serlio*, the Italian architect and writer.

Serlio came to France in 1541 and his influence on French Renaissance design was far-reaching. This was due primarily to his publications (p. 2), which guided French architects on Italian and Roman classical design. His buildings in France were few. The Château at Ancy-le-Franc has been altered and its design is not as Serlio originally intended. His first idea was for a more Italianate structure, with façades of Doric pilasters above a rusticated lower storey. This was too advanced for its time in France and was rejected in favour of the existing, more innocuous scheme of great corner blocks and walls articulated only by low relief Doric pilasters. The entrance porch is richer (**673**) and the internal court displays more variety.

The Palace of Fontainebleau

The building history of Fontainebleau is long and complex. It extends from the Medieval castle to manor house, to a larger château and eventually Napoleon's palace. It has been altered, added to and restored many times. Its importance in Renaissance work lies in its development by Francis I and the architecture and decoration of the Italians Rosso and Primaticcio.

Francis I decided to enlarge the Medieval castle in 1528. The master mason *Gilles Le Breton* was in charge. He refaced the courtyard of the old castle, called the Cour de L'Ovale, and added a fine porch. He built a new entrance to the court, the Porte Dorée. This has three storeys topped by a tall, French style roof. Francis continued his enlargement and alterations and his successors followed on. The Cour du Cheval Blanc was begun. This is the immense entrance courtyard of the present palace. It was enlarged in Napoleon's time and is now called the Cour des Adieux in memory of the Emperor's farewell to his Guard on his departure to exile on the Island of Elba. The original name referred to the copy of the equestrian statue of Marcus Aurelius in the Capitol in Rome (p.12).

The finest views of the exterior work of the sixteenth century are the main entrance forecourt of the Cour du Cheval Blanc (**671**) and the vista across the lake of the Cour de la Fontaine, with its fine wing by Primaticcio, the Aile de la Belle Cheminée.

FRENCH RENAISSANCE CHÂTEAUX

671 *Fontainebleau. Cour du Cheval (later Cour des Adieux), Gilles le Breton, 1528–40*
672 *Gateway, Anet, Philibert de l'Orme, 1548–52*
673 *Entrance doorway, Ancy-le-Franc, Sebastiano Serlio, begun 1546*
674 *Chambord, begun 1519*

Plate 81
Wall decoration. The King's Staircase. Château of Fontainebleau, France. *c.*1541–5, Primaticcio
Plate 82
Detail Outside pulpit. Prato Cathedral, Italy. 1434–8, Donatello

Plate 83
Courtyard, Episcopal Palace, Liège, Belgium. Mannerist. 1525–32
Plate 84
Detail. Schöner Hof, Plassenburg, Kulmbach, Germany, 1551–69

Inside, despite thorough restoration in the nineteenth and twentieth centuries, there still remain some excellent decorative schemes and galleries. The best, dating from the sixteenth century, comprise the Francis I gallery, the King's Staircase and the Henry II Gallery. The Francis I gallery is of typical long gallery proportions: 200 feet in length by only 17 wide. The lower part of the walls is panelled in wood, carved and gilded to the original designs. Above, are stucco sculptured figures and decorations framing the paintings. This type of interior décor was carried out by the two Italians, Giambattista di Jacopo, called *Le Rosso* (1494–1540) and *Francesco Primaticcio* (1505–70). Rosso, a Florentine, came first to Fontainebleau in 1530 and worked on the gallery for nine years, Primaticcio came soon after. He had worked at the Palazzo del Te in Mantua under Romano (p. 15). The decoration of this gallery by these two artists is very fine. It brought a new form of décor to France but, though Italian in origin and in vigour, this mixture of wood carving, stucco sculpture and painting is unmistakably French in its lightness and elegance.

The King's Staircase stands on the site of the bedroom of the Duchess of Étampes, Francis I's mistress. The architect, when he constructed the staircase, retained Primaticcio's magnificent stucco wall groups of slender maidens which frame the frescoes (PLATE 81). The ceiling is deeply coved. This cove is decorated with a riot of Mannerist strapwork and sculpture. The rectuangular centrepiece is painted. The Henry II gallery (or ballroom) is of later construction and has been much restored. It was completed under the architect *Philibert de l'Orme*, and decorated with sculpture and paintings by Rondelet, Primaticcio and others. It is a large, well-proportioned room, beautifully lit with large windows along each side. The walls are painted and panelled, the wood ceiling deeply caissoned and carved. At one end of the hall is a double-stage fireplace; at the other, a musicians' gallery.

Châteaux of the Later Sixteenth Century

After 1550, several architects were developing a more correct Renaissance building style. The chief of these were *Philibert de l'Orme*, Jean Bullant, Jacques Androuet du Cerceau and Pierre Lescot. De l'Orme's work at Fontainebleau has been mentioned. He was Superintendent of the King's Buildings and worked there for some years. He also designed the terrace across the river at Chenonceaux and worked at S. Germain. His principal contribution was at the *Château of Anet* (672) where he worked from 1547 to 1552 for Diane de Poitiers, favourite of Henry II. Much of the château has been destroyed but the gatehouse and chapel exist. The entrance screen and gatehouse provide one of the first Renaissance structures with the orders and proportions correctly understood and utilised.

De l'Orme, born in 1520, was one of France's first professional architects (as Inigo Jones became later to England). He designed, then supervised, the complete construction of a building. The son of a master mason, he studied for some years in Italy, making measured drawings in Rome and becoming fully conversant with the classical theme and grammar. His screen at Anet shows clearly his comprehension. Apart from his buildings, a number of which have now been lost, he published much written work. His major book was '*Premier Livre de L'Architecture*', published in nine volumes in 1569.

Jean Bullant was also born *c.* 1520. He also worked for a number of years in Rome. His style is vigorous, classical but more Mannerist. Typical is his work at the *Château of Écouen*, his bridge and gallery at *Fère-en-Tardenois* and his gallery at *Chenonceaux* (p. 21).

He is thought to have built the *Petit Château* at *Chantilly*, about 1560. This stands on an island in the lake adjacent to the main château, which is of later design due to the destruction at the time of the Revolution. The Petit Château (678) escaped, and illustrates Bullant's Mannerist style. This is not the same type of Mannerism as the early French Renaissance work of the 1520–50 period. Then the classical rules were broken because they were not understood. Bullant adjusted the rules of proportion and handling in a similar manner to the great Italian Mannerist architects like Michelangelo and Raphael.

Du Cerceau (the elder) was the father of a family of architects. He was born *c.* 1520 and also studied in Rome. He published many volumes of engravings both of decoration and of

RENAISSANCE CHÂTEAUX IN FRANCE

675 Chenonceaux, 1515–76
676 Frontispiece, Azay-le-Rideau, 1524
677 Blois, Francis I range and staircase, 1515–24
678 Petit Chateau (left), Chantilly, Jean Bullant, c. 1560

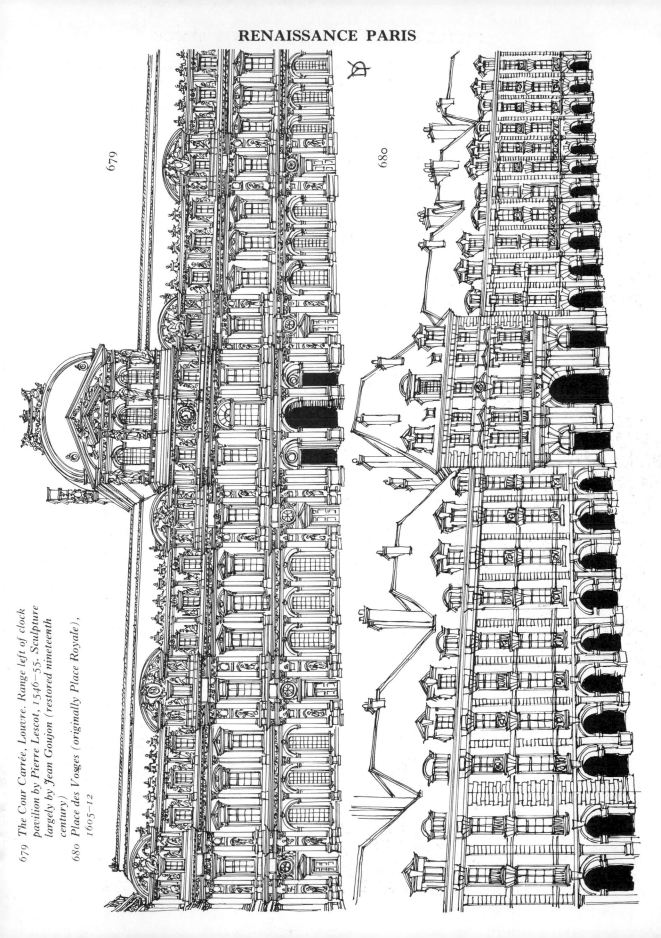

679 *The Cour Carrée, Louvre. Range left of clock pavilion by Pierre Lescot, 1546–55. Sculpture largely by Jean Goujon (restored nineteenth century)*

680 *Place des Vosges (originally Place Royale), 1605–12*

architectural design. Almost nothing of his building work survives.

The fourth of these architects, *Pierre Lescot* (born *c.* 1510 or 1515 *d.* 1578), has become the best known probably because of his work at the Louvre, which is the only one of his major works to survive intact. The initiative for the rebuilding of the Louvre in Paris was due to Francis I. The original thirteenth century royal palace was a *donjon* fortification which existed until the sixteenth century. It had been altered and enlarged but remained Medieval, gloomily brooding over Paris.

Francis commissioned Lescot in 1546 to demolish the tower and court and rebuild on modern lines. Francis died, but his successor Henry II confirmed the commission and Lescot carried out the demolition and built a new west wing (**679**) and part of the south. This west wing of the Cour Carrée, the central courtyard of the Louvre, still remains and the range left of the clock pavilion is Lescot's work. He created here, for the first time in France, elevations on Italian palace courtyard lines. There are three storeys, treated as one façade, broken only by projecting frontispieces. The scheme is Italian but the treatment is French and individually Lescot. Here was a French architect who, though lacking early on-the-spot study in Italy, fully comprehended Renaissance architecture and adapted it to national and personal needs—as Sir Christopher Wren was later to do in England, on a much wider scale. Lescot's façade is correctly classical in proportion and handling; it is not Italianate, as is shown by his use of Composite and Corinthian orders rather than Doric and Ionic and the employment of pilasters throughout the elevation, columns being reserved only for the frontispiece pavilions. Much of the sculptural decoration is by *Jean Goujon*, the great French sculptor of the day. Of particular interest are the exterior ground floor figures and attic reliefs; also, inside, his gallery caryatid figure work. This work was done between 1549 and 1553, though it was extensively restored in the nineteenth century.

Civic Building in Paris and Elsewhere

In the last years of the sixteenth century Henry IV began to reconstruct the centre of Paris after the years of warfare and struggle. The city was impoverished and in need of large-scale development. The king initiated this work and was the first in France to envisage planning by streets and squares rather than solely by individual buildings. Only Italy had built such schemes before, as at Pienza, Venice and Rome (p. 12). Henry's two main achievements were in the area of the Île de la Cité and the Place des Vosges. The *Pont Neuf* (now the oldest bridge in Paris), had been begun in 1578 but left incomplete. Henry simplified the scheme and built a new, wide thoroughfare, paved and—most unusual at that time, without houses upon it—which spanned the western tip of the *Île de la Cité*, thus linking it to the north and south banks of the Seine.

681

681 *Paris: 'Île de la Cité, Pont Neuf, 1578–1604 and Place Dauphine, begun 1607*

The *Place Dauphine*, situated on the triangular piece of ground at this end of the island, was developed as a well-to-do residential neighbourhood and an equestrian statue of the king was set up as a focal centre where the square joins the island section of the Pont Neuf. The Place Dauphine was planned in 1607 and named after Henry's heir. It, and the bridge, still stand, though only house number 14 dates from the original development (**681**).

The king also planned two other squares, the *Place Royale* and the Place de France. The former, begun in 1605 (**680**) and now called the *Place des Vosges*, was completed. It was also intended as accommodation for the wealthy and was a fashionable quarter for many years. The *Place de France* was begun in 1620 but not finished in this period. Henry's town planning on the pattern of squares was in advance of its time in Europe. Covent Garden, developed later in the century under Inigo Jones' direction, was a similar scheme. Other countries followed suit but, in general, not until the later seventeenth or eighteenth centuries.

The town hall of *La Rochelle*, on the western coast of France is an attractive example of provincial civic Renaissance work. Here, the exterior façade is Gothic but the internal courtyard is classical, built 1595–1607.

Churches
The Gothic tradition lingered in ecclesiastical building much later than in secular work. In France so many churches had been built in the Middle Ages that few more were needed and, without the spur provided by the Reformation,* as in England, Holland or Germany, the function remained unchanged and, thus, the design. The usual pattern in the few new churches constructed was that of a Medieval building, especially in the interior, and the introduction of classical motifs and decoration on the façade or chevet. These were applied often haphazardly in Mannerist form, with little understanding of the tenets of classical architecture. *S. Pierre* in *Caen*, built 1530–40 (Volume 2, p. 91), is one of these. It is an almost entirely late Gothic church, but the added eastern apsidal chapels are in Mannerist style. Another, *S. Eustache* in *Paris* was begun in 1532 but completed much later, while its façade is eighteenth century. *S. Michel* in *Dijon* has con-

* *Vigorously suppressed in France.*

siderable Renaissance decoration on its façade but the interior is entirely Gothic. Built 1537–40 the church has a Mannerist quality attractively merged with Medieval work. The most important example of purer Mannerist development is *S. Étienne du Mont* in *Paris* (**670**). This shows mainly on the façade (which was not built till the early seventeenth century) in the entrance portico and frontispiece. In Medieval manner, however, this incorporates, above the portal, a central rose window.

England

During the two centuries from 1420 onwards covered by this chapter, the development of Renaissance building in England was totally dissimilar to that in Italy and had little in common with France. It has been described in Volume 2, Chapter 2 how King Henry VIII, in the 1520s, began to encourage Italian craftsmen to come to England to work and teach local artists and masons the new decoration and architectural forms. This was in line with Francis I's similar efforts in France at the same date. But, whereas Francis was more successful in attracting Italian craftsmen and continued in this pattern, Henry's break with Rome delayed any change of style. The direct link having been cut, the geographical barrier of the Channel, together with the traditional insularity of the English, put off till the early seventeenth century the appearance of pure Renaissance architecture.

Perpendicular Gothic continued till about 1550. Under the Tudor dynasty it acquired slightly different characteristics, like the four-centred arch, an increasing use of brick, larger window openings and flat ceilings rather than open timber roofs. Elizabethan England saw great changes. A form of the Renaissance came to the country; not the pure Italian version based on Bramante or even Brunelleschi, but a Flemish Mannerist type. The design and pattern books which appeared in England, printed mainly in Flanders and Germany, a few in France, presented the English craftsmen with a garbled version of classicism and, since such artisans had never seen a classical building, they tended to accept it as the genuine article.

This Mannerist style was much the same as that employed in Germany and the Low Countries. The orders were used, but decoratively not structurally. The actual buildings, whether in stone, brick or half-timber, were constructed in much the same way as before. But, applied to the surface, often all over exterior façades, were pilasters, columns, strapwork, cartouches, animal and human figure derivations, both caryatid and grotesque. Skylines were a confusion of decorated chimneystacks, cresting and curved gables; the last of these was a specifically Flemish derivative. Building in Elizabethan and Jacobean times, from 1550 to about 1620, was largely domestic. Few churches were built and there was little civic or university work. It was a thriving, bustling age with a rising middle class and a wealthy aristocracy. This wealth was transmitted into the building of great mansions on the country estates throughout the land. Many, like the châteaux of the Loire in France, were built by noblemen to attract the visits of the sovereign and her entourage on the summer tours.

Some of the houses were traditionally English in that the design was monumental, the decoration restrained and the materials of local stone or half-timber. *Longleat House* in Wiltshire (1550–80), *Hardwick Hall* in Derbyshire (1591–7) and *Montacute House* in Somerset (1588–1601 (682) were of this type. Other versions were more striking and original but often over-decorated. The orders were used for entrance porches and for flanking window openings but Flemish strapwork and cresting abounded. The English Perpendicular Gothic form of window design persisted; it was of rectangular shape, divided by mullions and transoms and of casement design. A glorious mixture of styles, such houses were robust, lively, sometimes graceless but never dull. Of this type is *Wollaton Hall* (686), a square pile with turreted corners, surrounding a square court with a taller hall block.

In the Jacobean period in the early seventeenth century came *Audley End* in Essex where, somewhat altered, the hall remains with its fantastic carved screen—a testament to the Flemish pattern book (687). In the grand manner is *Hatfield House*, Hertfordshire, of the same date. This is most impressive, especially on the south, garden front, where the combination of red brick and grey stone is effective. Here the turreted terminal blocks are simple and the rich decoration is reserved for the central porch with its orders and Mannerist ornamentation.

Hatfield is typical, as is Montacute, of the Elizabethan house plan. The old courtyard of the Medieval layout had slowly been abandoned in favour of an 'E' or 'H' shaped plan where there was a central, rectangular block with side wings which projected forwards and backwards in the case of the 'H' and only forwards in the 'E'. The central projecting porch provided the middle stroke of the 'E'.

Half-timber houses were common in stoneless areas. They were picturesque, handsome houses, built in different sizes from cottage to mansion. They had projecting and overhanging gable roofs with carved wooden barge boards and richly decorated porches with corner posts. The same ornamental motifs appeared as in the stone houses. *Little Moreton Hall* in Cheshire is a famous example (683) as is also *Speke Hall* in Lancashire (1598) and *Rumwood Court*, Kent (late sixteenth century).

Three particular features of the house were the long gallery, the staircase and the entrance porch. The long gallery extended along one whole side of the longer elevation of the house. It was a narrow apartment, sometimes more than 150 feet in length and it was lit by windows at the ends and along one whole long side, while fireplaces were set opposite. Especially fine examples can be seen at Montacute House, Hardwick Hall, *Haddon Hall*, Derbyshire and Little Moreton Hall. The staircase was only just beginning to acquire importance in the layout. Elizabethan examples were of richly carved oak, massive and spacious, generally built round a large well. Jacobean staircases, like those at Hatfield, *Knole*, Kent or *Ham House*, Surrey, are magnificent structures, the focal centre of the house interior. Of similar importance outside was the entrance porch, or frontispiece as it was generally called. Set in the centre of the façade, it was the recipient of the main decoration of the building. Orders were superimposed in gay disregard for proportion and suitability.

It was *Inigo Jones* (1573–1652) who brought the Italian Renaissance to England. Although few buildings which he designed survive and much of his work on great schemes, such as Whitehall Palace, never reached fruition or was destroyed, his importance in the history of English architecture is vital. He brought a stylistic revolution to architecture. Before him,

ENGLISH RENAISSANCE

682 *Montacute House, Somerset, 1588–1601*
683 *Little Moreton Hall, Cheshire, half-timber,*
    1559–80
684 *Gateway, Chiswick House, Inigo Jones, c. 1621*
685 *Clare Bridge, Cambridge, Thomas Grumbold,*
    1639–40

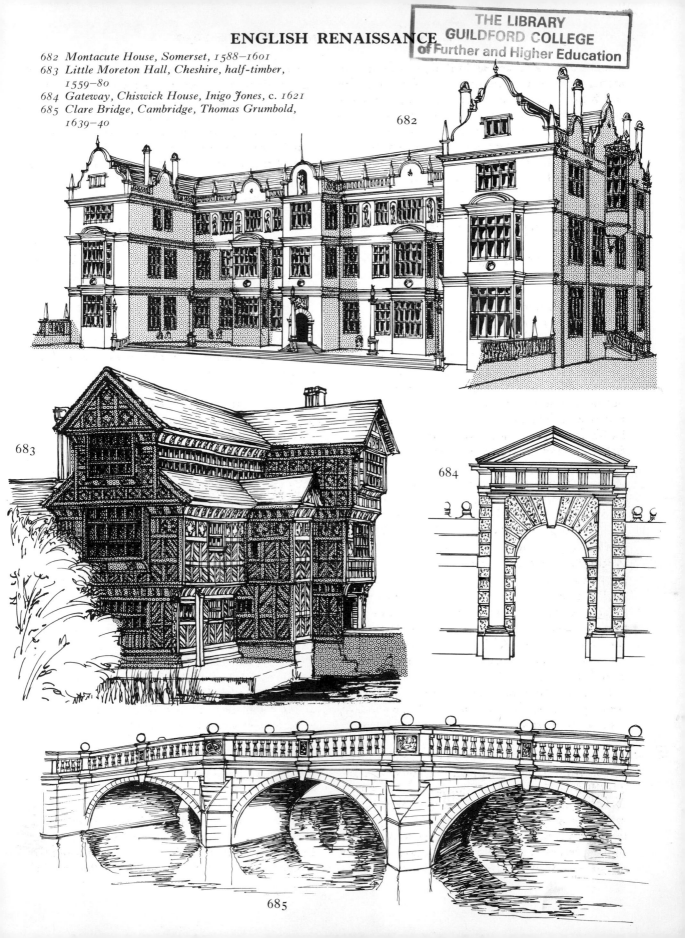

682

683

684

685

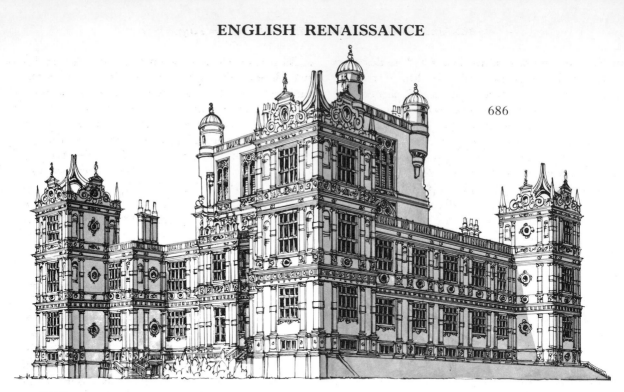

686

686 *Wollaton Hall, Nottinghamshire, 1580–5*
687 *The hall, Audley End, Essex, 1603–16*

687

in England, no one figure had acted as designer and overall supervisor of a building scheme. Each group of artisans—masons, carpenters, glaziers and sculptors—had their own master who was responsible for their section of the work.

Inigo Jones was appointed early in the seventeenth century as Surveyor to the Royal Family. He had the opportunity to travel to France and Italy to study personally Renaissance buildings about which he had read. He was away about 18 months, during which time he made measured drawings of original ancient Roman building remains and Italian and French Renaissance work based upon them. This first-hand study was a revolutionary idea to English builders. They had so far been content to use the second- or third-hand pattern book source.

Inigo Jones had been impressed, while still in England, by Palladio's books and also Vitruvius' works. He was interested, while studying *in situ*, to find himself often in agreement with Palladio's interpretation of ancient classical work. Nevertheless, when he returned home and began to design his own building in Roman classical manner, his schemes were his own, not copies of Palladio or Vitruvius. He was always an original architect.

His two outstanding public buildings still exist: the *Queen's House* at *Greenwich* and the *Banqueting Hall* in Whitehall. One can see immediately, in comparing these (**689** and **688**) with the Elizabethan and Jacobean works, the revolutionary change which he had brought to English architecture. Here, at last, was the pure Roman classicism. The orders were used correctly in proportions laid down and worked out by the ancient civilisations. Decoration is restricted to small specific areas of the elevations. It is in traditional classical form. The Banqueting Hall has two orders, Composite superimposed above Ionic. The building is rusticated and the window openings on the *piano nobile* have alternate round and triangular pediments. The Queen's House is even plainer, with Ionic columns confined to the centre portion and the remainder of the rectangular block broken only by rustication on the lower storey and by simple window openings.

Fragments of two town planning schemes by Inigo Jones exist in London. In *Lincoln's Inn Fields*, Lindsey House is thought to be by him and to illustrate his ideas on terrace town house

architecture. Here is a giant Ionic order spanning two floors. The whole façade is strictly symmetrical. He also designed a piazza for *Covent Garden* with S. Paul's Church and houses with classical elevations round the remainder of the square. The original work has been lost though the church has been rebuilt in the same style.

Towards the end of his life Inigio Jones rebuilt part of *Wilton House* in Wiltshire. He was responsible for the south front and the two cube rooms inside. The Double Cube Room (**690**) is a rich, magnificently proportioned interior. Its superb classical detail in white and gold is in contrast to the modest exterior façade.

Towards the end of his life Inigo Jones redesigned the south front of *Wilton House* in Wiltshire, though we now know that little of Jones' work survived the fire of 1647. The famous Double Cube Room, (**690**), restored and rebuilt after this, was more likely to have been the work of his pupil and nephew *John Webb*, though this superb interior evinces much of Jones' originality, and quality of interior decoration.

Although Inigo Jones brought the Italian Renaissance to England and this had a lasting effect on architectural development, its influence until 1650 was small. Mid-seventeenth century building was plainer than Elizabethan or Jacobean and it was nearer Renaissance forms, but it still reflected Flemish gabling and brickwork more than Italian classicism. Brick was a cheap durable material in great use at this time.

The Low Countries

Although part of the land mass of the continent of Europe, development in this northern region had much in common with that of England. Gothic building continued until the early sixteenth century, after which Renaissance decorative forms were used as all-over surface ornament to structures still fundamentally Medieval. Sources of knowledge for this decoration were the same pattern books used in England, though the results were often more ornate, so illustrating the Flemish love of rich decoration as well as their flat strapwork designs. A strong influence in this field, not only in the Low Countries, but further east as far as Germany and Poland, was *Vredeman de Vries* (1527–1606). He was born in Friesland

688 *Banqueting House, London, 1619–22*

689 *The Queen's House, Greenwich, south side, 1616–35*

690 *Double Cube Room, Wilton House, Wiltshire, 1647–53*

and studied architecture at Antwerp which, in the sixteenth century, was still very much the cultural centre for the region. De Vries published his own books of architectural ornament, based on sources such as Vitruvius and Serlio. The best known of these was his '*Architectura*', published in 1563. It includes designs for orders, strapwork, cartouches and animal and human figure details, including caryatids and grotesques. His designs were widely employed in conjunction with the orders, although, as in England, there was no basic understanding of their classical use.

Typical of the earlier sixteenth century work based on these decorative forms is the *Palais de Justice* at *Bruges* (1535–7). Here are superimposed orders with strange capitals, Gothic style fenestration, rich banded decoration between and tall, ornate, curving gables with high relief tympana and finials in human and animal shape. Of similar date is the vast courtyard of the *episcopal palace at Liège* (**693** and PLATE 83). This is still basically a Medieval court with its finialled pointed gables and widely pointed arched arcade, but the strapwork-decorated fat arcade columns are Flemish Mannerist.

The outstanding building of the sixteenth century is *Antwerp Town Hall*, built 1561–5 by *Cornelius Floris* (**694**). This is the chief monument to Flemish Mannerism. It shows a greater comprehension of classicism than contemporary works such as the *Old Town Hall* at the *Hague* (1564–5) or the Renaissance part of *Ghent Town Hall*, but is still totally unlike Italian Renaissance work. As in the case of such English houses as Longleat and Hatfield, it is indigenous yet has ceased to be Medieval. It is a large rectangular building with an arcade below the roof. It is symmetrical and has an impressive centrepiece, extending the full height of the façade and further into a three-storey gable. This centrepiece has a vertical emphasis contrasting with the horizontal lines of the side portions.

As in England, it was the seventeenth century which brought a purer classical style to the Low Countries, where Dutch architecture began to emerge as the dominant sector while Antwerp as a centre declined in importance. This Dutch architectural prominence was mainly confined to the large towns; the political centre at the Hague and the commercial one at Amsterdam. Two architects particularly are associated with this renaissance: *Lieven de Key* and *Hendrik de Keyser*. De Key (1560–1627) worked mainly at Haarlem and Leyden. He designed the *Leyden Town Hall* in 1597 (**698**) and the *Butchers' Trade Hall* at *Haarlem* in 1602 (**692**). Like Antwerp Town Hall, these are both Mannerist buildings with ornate, curving gables, decorated by obelisks and strapwork, but the windows in the town hall, for instance, are purer Renaissance as is the Ionic entrance portal and rusticated staircase approach. Most of the Dutch building up to this time had been in brick. De Key introduced into these structures the combination of stone decoration and dressings on brick buildings as used at Hatfield in England.

De Keyser (1565–1621) was centred on *Amsterdam*. He developed a Renaissance style of house from the Medieval one. The city was being enlarged and developed in the early seventeenth century when the famous canals—the Herengracht, Prinsengracht, Keizergracht, etc.—were being planned and laid out. The terrace architecture flanking such canals has a specific, individual character. Each house is tall and is surmounted by a lofty gable. Medieval ones had been stepped. Renaissance examples had scrolled sides, strapwork decoration, finials and a pediment at the apex. De Keyser developed a two- and three-stage type of gable, linked by scrolls at each step and with different pilasters to each stage. His façades below were symmetrical, divided into bays and were decorated by orders.

In civic architecture de Keyser designed the *Amsterdam Exchange* (1605) and the *Delft Town Hall* (1618). His most original contribution was in church building. In Amsterdam he built the Zuiderkerk (**695**), the Westerkerk (**697**) and the Noorderkerk. The *Zuiderkerk* was the first church to be built here after the Reformation and de Keyser had to plan a new type of design suitable for a Protestant church. This, like his *Westerkerk*, is a traditional plan, but is very tall and with a lofty tower. De Keyser, like Sir Christopher Wren in England, was noted for the variety of successful, elegant designs for his towers. Apart from these two, the *Mint Tower*, also in Amsterdam, is a landmark (**696**).

In his church design de Keyser shared some characteristics with Brunelleschi in Florence. The relationship and proportion between one part and another, especially in the interior, is

691 *The Mauritshuis, The Hague, Post and Van Campen, 1633, (remodelled, c. 1718)*

692 *Butchers' Guild Hall, Haarlem, de Key, 1602*

693 *Courtyard, Episcopal Palace, Liège, Aart Van der Mulcken*

carefully calculated. His *Noorderkerk* is a small church but interesting as a centrally planned design. He adopted this as appropriate for Protestant needs, just as the Roman Catholics had found it so in Italy. It is on Greek cross plan and quite symmetrical. On the exterior it is a plain brick church, most unpretentious and quite different from the domed Italian counterparts as at Todi or Crema. However, the Noorderkerk proved a successful design and became the prototype of many other Protestant examples throughout northern Europe.

The beginnings of a pure Renaissance style came in the second quarter of the seventeenth century in the *Hague* with the advent of Dutch Palladianism. This, as its name suggests, is strongly influenced by Palladio but, just as Inigo Jones at the same date was introducing Palladianism into England, with his Banqueting Hall, neither the Dutch nor English examples are copies of the Italian architect's work. They are both nationally individual. The chief example in Holland is the *Mauritshuis* at the *Hague* (**691**), designed by *Pieter Post* (1608–69) and *Jacob van Campen* (1595–1657). This, like the nearby *Constantin Huygens' house*, also designed by

Post, in 1633, but later destroyed, had much in common with Inigo Jones' work, and also with the English architect Hugh May's later Eltham Lodge. The plan is simple, in a rectangular block. Giant Ionic pilasters frame the simple, classical windows and swag decorated doorway, which is approached, on the *piano nobile* by entrance steps. The two chief façades have a central pediment and, behind, rises the Dutch style hipped roof.

The Region of Germanic Influence:

Germany, Austria, Switzerland, Czechoslovakia, Hungary, Poland

Germany

The sequence of development in this area was similar to the Flemish and English pattern. Medieval work continued till after 1500. During the sixteenth century buildings were mainly in Mannerist designs with the use of decoration and orders based on pattern books, the classical structure being imperfectly understood. In Germany the work is vigorous and robust. The strapwork and cartouche ornament covers large areas of the building but, though in high relief, is ornamental not structural in character. The

694 Antwerp Town Hall, Cornelius Floris, 1561–5

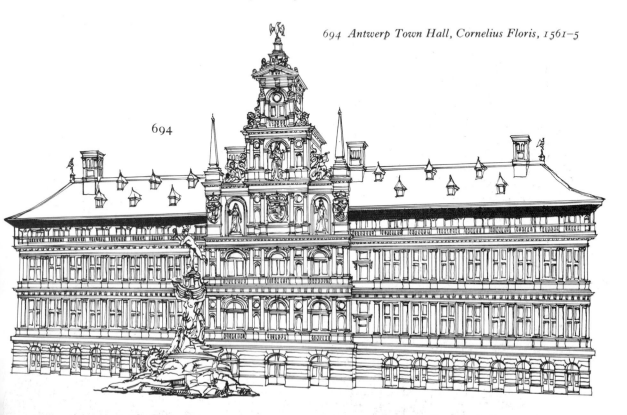

694

695 *Tower, Zuiderkerk, Amsterdam, de Keyser, 1614*

696 *Munttoren (the Mint), Amsterdam, de Keyser, c. 1620*

697 *Westerkerk, Amsterdam, de Keyser, 1620*

698 *Town Hall, Leiden, de Key, 1597–1603*

same motifs appear in carved stone or wood. Much of the considerable quantity of high quality half-timber work possessed by Germany until 1939 was destroyed in the Second World War. This was especially so in cities like Hildesheim, Bremen, Hanover and Frankfurt. In smaller, more remote towns, examples still exist as at Dinkelsbühl and Goslar. The *Bürgerhaus* (Willmann House) at *Osnabrück* (1586) has some typical carved detail, and is an interesting gabled façade.

Like the Flemish, the Germans specialised in the sixteenth century in the tall multi-storey gable, ascending in stages, with scrolls and strapwork, fenestrated and ornately decorated. There are a number of houses in *Lemgo* like the *Hexenbürgermeisterhaus*, 1571 (**700**), which are typical (PLATE 86). The façades of the sixteenth century houses in many German towns were like these. The frontages were narrow but the houses tall, with orders used on five or six storeys, one above the other. The *Town Hall* in *Lemgo* has two very fine such porticoes with both strapwork and sculptured decoration (1565–1612).

With the seventeenth century, as in Flanders and England, came a purer Renaissance style. German *town halls* from about 1500–1700 show this development clearly. Typically German in the sixteenth century style is the façade and courtyard of the town hall at *Konstanz*. The doorway and window openings, in particular, have the typical pattern book decoration in carved stone as well as painted form. A simple, unpretentious example can be seen also at *Heilbronn* (1535–96). There is a different type of sixteenth century design at *Rothenburg-ob-der-Tauber* (**703**). A Renaissance wing was added to the old Medieval town hall about 1572. The Renaissance part, on the corner of the street, is a lower, long elevation with emphasis on the horizontal courses, in contrast to the older tall gabled building with a lofty tower. Here are the beginnings of comprehension of classical principles. Decoration is more restrained and articulation is clearer. The rusticated loggia was added in the seventeenth century. A more advanced design existed in the loggia of the *Cologne Town Hall*, built in 1569 by *Wilhelm Vernuiken*. This was a more Italianate structure, but became a casualty to war-time bombing. It is now rebuilt but in a much simplified form.

The understanding of purer classical design came with *Elias Holl*'s plain, finely proportioned buildings in *Augsburg*, notably the town hall and the arsenal. Both these show first signs of a Baroque quality, particularly the earlier one, the *Arsenal* (Zeughaus) (1602–7) (**705**). This is partly due to the articulation of the central section and the side scrolls, but more especially to the dynamic sculptural group above the portal of S. Michael and the Devil (PLATE 87). This is the work of *Hans Reichle*. No other European country could compete with the quantity and superb quality of sculpture created by Renaissance and Baroque artists in Italy. Sixteenth century Germany, however, developed a talented school of sculptors of whom Reichle was one: an outstanding artist whose style is clearly personal, always vigorous and displaying a powerful clarity.

The *Augsburg Town Hall* was Holl's masterpiece. Built 1615–20, it had a dignified, timeless quality, astylar, finely proportioned and fenestrated. The façade was rebuilt to the original design after damage in the Second World War. Elias Holl had travelled in Italy and was an admirer of Palladio and Sansovino. His own work, though, was much more severe than the approach of either of the Italians. This was perhaps a reaction from the ornate richness of the sixteenth century German façades so that, like Herrera in Spain, his establishment of the purer classical strain was even more restrained in contrast.

Several large scale *castles* and *palaces* were built in the sixteenth and early seventeenth century. These bore no relationship to the fifteenth century Florentine designs, though rather more to the courtyards of later Roman palaces. *Heidelberg Castle*, lying on a shelf of the mountainside above the river Neckar, has a romantic setting. It is very large, partly ruined and most impressive. Built over the period 1531–1612, two wings of the 'schloss', in particular, show a contrast of structural and decorative styles. The Ottheinrichsbau, built in 1556–9 and named after the Elector, its builder, is the earlier and finer part (**701**). Here is rich, powerful German Renaissance building, harmoniously proportioned and with finely carved ornament and sculpture. The whole façade is sculptured but the central, multi-storeyed portal is the focal point of the four-storeyed composition. The range is magnificent, even in ruin. The later, Friedrichsbau range is heavier and more pedestrian, though more correctly classical. This was restored from its ruinous condition in 1900.

The main courtyard, the 'Schöner Hof', at the *Plassenburg* above the town of *Kulmbach*, is a fine example of German palace courts of the mid-sixteenth century. The arcades are in three storeys, of which the upper two are richly sculptured in high relief after the Lombard style of treatment (**704** and PLATE 84). There are some interesting, richly sculptured doorways in this court also, while in the Kasernenhof the main doorway is equally typical of the later bold style in the early seventeenth century.

Aschaffenburg Castle, though a later structure (1605–14), is more Medieval in concept. It is an immense, severe, fortified square block of red sandstone with a tower at each corner (**699**). Its west elevation rises from the banks of the river Main. Inside is a square courtyard, all four sides identical except for a tower set centrally in the wall opposite to the entrance. The whole castle is plain and massive, the walls broken only by Renaissance fenestration. There are no orders, but in the centre of each side is a tall Flemish-style gable. Small staircase towers are set one in each corner of the court. The main entrance is imposing, with rusticated, coupled Doric columns flanking the richly carved strapwork doors.

One of the best examples of pattern book German Renaissance work of the sixteenth century is the entrance gateway to *Tübingen Castle* (**702**). Here is the classic form of orders and ornament of this type with some vigorous and characteristic sculpture and strapwork ornamentation.

One of Germany's largest town palaces is the *Munich Residenz*, built over several centuries from c. 1550 but badly damaged in 1944. In the centre of Munich, many ranges of buildings are grouped around six courtyards. The two Renaissance, early ones suffered least from war damage. These are the Antiquarian Court, built 1559 and altered by *Friedrich Sustris* in 1586–1600 and the Grotto Court (Grottenhof), also by Sustris (1581–6). This is a quiet, restful courtyard in Florentine style with a Perseus fountain in the centre, based on that by Benvenuto Cellini in Florence (**706**). The Munich

fountain is by the Dutch sculptor *Hubert Gerhard*, who carried out so much fine work in Augsburg, especially in the fountains (PLATE 88). The unusual grotto decoration of grotesques and shells is by *Ponzani* (1588) (PLATE 85).

As in Flanders and England, the sixteenth and seventeenth centuries were not years of extensive building of *churches*. There are one or two examples of the earlier German Renaissance style, where the building is fundamentally Medieval, based on the hall church pattern, then decorated with pattern book Renaissance detail all over the façades. A good example of this type is the *Stadtkirche* at Bückeburg (1611–15) (**708**). Another hall church design but with a purer classical façade is the *Hofkirche* (S. Michael) at Neuburg on the Danube (**707**).

A very early Renaissance building is the *Fugger Chapel* in the *Church* of *S. Anna* at *Augsburg*. This, like the Medici Mausoleum in S. Lorenzo in Florence, is the mausoleum for the Fugger family of the city. The chapel was begun in 1509. It was still designed with a Gothic star vault, but on the wall behind the altar are pilasters framing the four relief panels depicting the Fuggers and based on drawings by Dürer. The sculptured *pietà* by *Hans Dancher*, 1518, stands in front. It has survived, though the chapel was badly damaged in the Second World War.

The outstanding Renaissance church in Germany is *S. Michael* in *Munich*. This Jesuit church in the middle of the city was built 1582–97 by *Wolfgang Miller* and *Friedrich Sustris*. The exterior is a mixture of German gable design and Italian orders. It is plain apart from the sculptured figures in niches and the twin doorways on the façade with, between them, *Hubert Gerhard*'s magnificent S. Michael vanquishing the Devil. The interior, damaged during the last war but now restored, is cruciform with shallow transepts. The chancel is narrower than the wide nave and is apsidal-ended. The whole scheme is white and plain. It is classical, with the Corinthian Order used in pilaster form. The Jesuit plan* has the typical three bay nave with chapels leading off it but no colonnade. The barrel-vaulted ceiling is decorated in strapwork bands enclosing panels. The chief focus is the three-tiered high altar, rich in colour and classical decoration (**709**).

* The pattern was set in the first Jesuit Church in Rome, Il Gesit (see page 17).

Plate 86 Oriel window. House in Lemgo, late sixteenth century

Plate 85 Grottenhof, Munich Residenz. Architect: Friedrich Sustris, 1581–6. Grotesques in shell decoration, Ponzani, 1588

GERMAN RENAISSANCE

699 Aschaffenburg Castle, Ridinger, 1605–14
700 Hexenbürgermeister House, Lemgo, 1571
701 Heidelberg Castle, Ottheinrichsbau Wing, 1556–9
702 Tübingen Castle gateway, sixteenth century

GERMAN RENAISSANCE: CIVIC AND DOMESTIC BUILDING

703 Town Hall, Rothenburg-ob-der-Tauber, Gothic
wing (left), Renaissance wing added 1572-8 (right).
Balcony and staircase, Jakob Wolff
704 Doorway, Schöner Hof, Plassenburg, Kulmbach,
1551-79
705 Zeughaus (Arsenal), Angsburg, Elias Holl, 1602-7

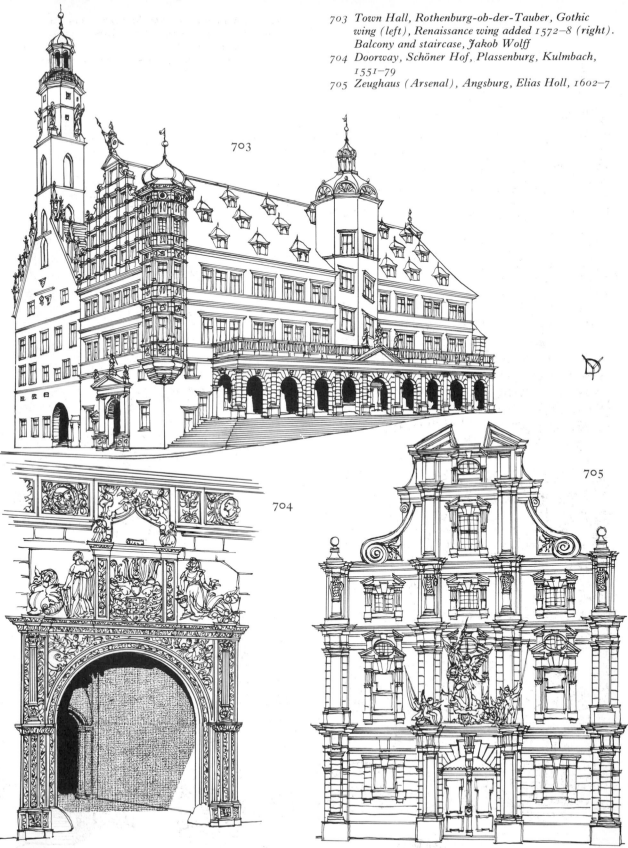

703

704

705

Austria

Not much Renaissance building survives in Austria. The chief examples are some very fine courtyards on a grand scale belonging to castles and civic structures. There is a two-storeyed one with caryatid figures all round the upper arcade at *Schallaborg* (1572–1600) and another, purer Renaissance type in the *Castle Porcia* at *Spittal-an-der-Drau* (c. 1530) which is in the centre of the town. The rectangular courtyard has three storeys of galleries round three sides. The orders used are Ionic on the ground floor, then Composite and Corinthian. On the fourth side the sturdy, decorative Ionic ground floor colonnade is continued unbroken, but above is solid wall pierced only by windows. A staircase in one corner of the court gives sloping balustraded galleries at each level. Another impressive excellent example is the court of the *Landhaus* in the centre of *Graz* (1557–65). This pure classical construction was damaged during the Second World War but is now beautifully restored. A three-storeyed arcade extends round four sides of the central courtyard, supporting a heavy cornice and deep roof with dormers. There is an attractive turreted stairway leading from the court up to the second and third arcade levels (**711**).

Switzerland

Here, the principal surviving building in the purer classical style is the *Spieshof* in *Basle*. This is in four storeys with superimposed orders—Doric, Ionic, Ionic—in engaged column form. The top storey has scrolls instead, supporting the projecting cornice (**710**). Less purely Renaissance, and largely Medieval in structure with sixteenth century detail and fenestration are the *Fribourg Town Hall* and the *Altes Rathaus* in *Lucerne*. The former is of sixteenth century date, the latter seventeenth. The *Basle Town Hall*, in red sandstone, retains its early sixteenth century form, with rectangular, mullioned and transomed windows and tall tower, though it was extensively restored in the late nineteenth century. The paintings all over the façade were restored at the same time.

Czechoslovakia

The Renaissance came late to Czechoslovakia and, since the time was one of strife, only a few buildings have survived unaltered. In *Prague* there are one or two exceptions to this rule. In the early sixteenth century, the Emperor Ferdinand had succeeded in attracting some Italian artisans to his court. The *Royal Summer Palace* (the Belvedere, **712**), was built by Italian

706 The Grottenhof, Residenz, Munich, Sustris, 1581–6. Fountain, Perseus, Gerhard

706

GERMAN RENAISSANCE CHURCHES

707 Church of S. Michael
   (Hofkirche), Neuburg-an-der-
   Donau, Vältlin and Alberthal,
   1607–27
708 Stadtkirche, Bückeburg, Hans
   Wolf, 1611–15
709 Interior, S. Michael, Munich,
   Miller and Sustris, 1582–97

707

708

709

artists and its design clearly derives from Brunelleschi's Foundling Hospital in Florence (p. 5), as can be seen in the simple, round-arched arcade which extends round the building. The *Archbishop's Palace*, also on Castle Hill, was built in 1561, but this was redesigned in 1765 with Rococo decoration. An interesting late instance of Renaissance architecture in the city can be seen in the more Mannerist design of the loggia to the *Valdštejn Palace* (**713**). Also an Italian scheme, this time by *Andrea Spezza*, it derives from Romano's Palazzo del Te at Mantua (**662**). The remainder of the palace in Prague, though of similar date to the loggia, is Baroque in treatment.

The small town of *Tábor*, just south of Prague, is Medieval in the centre but, due to several fires in the sixteenth century, a number of houses in the *Market Square* and the *Pražská Ulice* which leads into it were redesigned or redecorated in Renaissance character. The gabled house shown in Fig. **714** is one of these and there are several houses with ornamental, stepped gables in the Pražská Ulice (Prague Street), numbers 220–3 for example. Others in this street have painted decoration also, number 210 and, with extended, painted relief, pictorial panel, number 157.

Further south, in the centre of the town of *Ceské Budějovice*, the Market Place retains a homogeneity and atmosphere of several centuries ago despite the varied periods of buildings which surround it. The houses are of sixteenth to eighteenth century origin but the round-arched arcades which extend all round this immense square give a coherence to the whole design. The town hall whose façade fronts the square is in Baroque style, as is the Samson fountain in the centre, while the cathedral interior is more neo-classical. The great belfry tower in the north-east corner of the square (from whose gallery a fine view can be obtained) is Medieval, but its gallery is supported on Tuscan columns and the cupola is also of Renaissance design.

Hungary

In *Esztergom*, on the Danube, there is one of the earliest surviving Renaissance works north of the Alps. This is the *Chapel* of *Archbishop Tamas Bakócz*, now part of the interior of the later cathedral. The work dates from 1507 and is based directly on Florentine Renaissance origins

(**664** and **669**). Italian Renaissance forms were established in Hungary at an early date as Italian artists were being employed in Buda from the fifteenth century. Little else survives, unfortunately, and the Italian influence was only short-lived in this turbulent area of Europe. Also of interest are some of the houses, dating from sixteenth and seventeenth centuries in *Beliannisz Square* in *Sopron*, near the Austrian border. This is a picturesque square with simple façades divided by ornamented pilasters and with simple, classical windows and porticoes.

Poland

As in Buda, Italian influence made itself felt early in Poland. Italian artists were employed first in *Cracow*, where some of the earliest Renaissance work outside Italy can still be seen. The *royal castle* on *Wawel Hill*, which had been extended during the Middle Ages, suffered considerable damage by fire in 1499. It was decided to rebuild and King Sigismund commissioned the Italian *Franciscus Italus* to design him a Renaissance palace. On Italus' death in 1516 another Italian, *Bartolomeo Berecci*, took over the work when the courtyard was enlarged into a great quadrangle surrounded on all four sides by a three tiered loggia. This courtyard is immense, about 230 feet square, and is one of the earliest examples of such courts outside Italy. The two lower storeys are arcaded in Florentine Renaissance design but the third floor is characteristically Polish, being unusually high and having distinctive columns and capitals; it is based on national, traditional timber structures (**717**). The room interiors have been restored since the Second World War and there are some fine ceilings of deeply caissoned wood design enriched with gilt and colour, also some interesting frescoes and tapestries. The original building of the Ambassador's Hall dates from 1535 and the southern wing was built from 1565.

Nearby on Wawel Hill at the *cathedral*, the King in 1519 also commissioned the *Sigismund Chapel* as a mausoleum. It adjoins the cathedral on the south side (**720**) adjacent and to the east of the seventeenth century *Vasa Chapel*, which has a similar exterior appearance though its interior is in marbled Baroque. The Sigismund Chapel set the pattern in Poland for Renaissance chapels* as a centrally planned structure with

* *The Royal Palace courtyard similarly set the pattern for palace courts.*

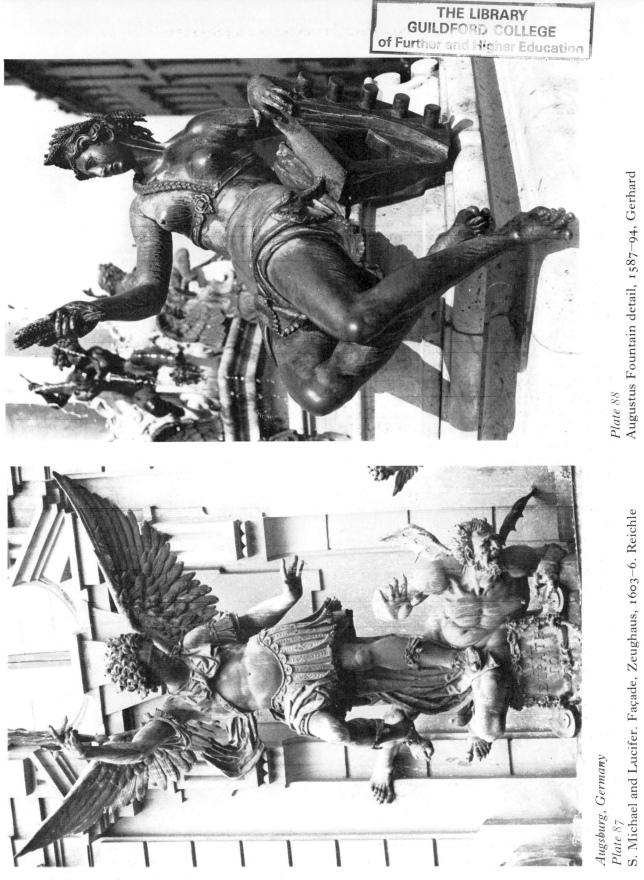

Plate 88
Augustus Fountain detail, 1587–94, Gerhard

Augsburg, Germany
Plate 87
S. Michael and Lucifer. Façade, Zeughaus, 1603–6. Reichle

Plate 89
Doorway cartouche detail. The Armoury, Gdansk, Poland, 1605
Plate 90
Detail, Boim Chapel, L'vov, U.S.S.R., 1609–17

RENAISSANCE IN AUSTRIA AND SWITZERLAND

710 *The Spieshof, Basle, Switzerland, c. 1580*
711 *Courtyard, the Landhaus, Graz, Austria, 1557–65*

710

711

RENAISSANCE IN CZECHOSLOVAKIA

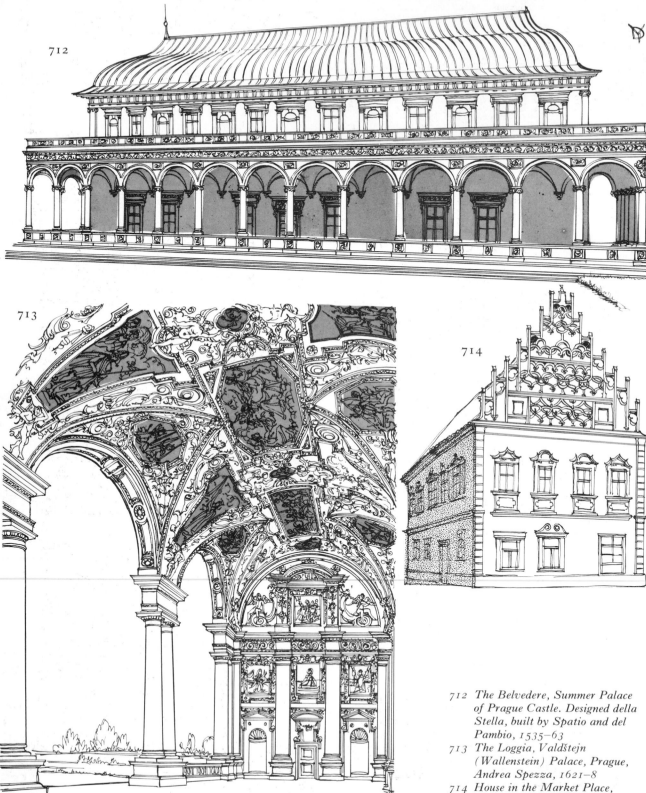

712 The Belvedere, Summer Palace
of Prague Castle. Designed della
Stella, built by Spatio and del
Pambio, 1535–63

713 The Loggia, Valdštejn
(Wallenstein) Palace, Prague,
Andrea Spezza, 1621–8

714 House in the Market Place,
Tábor, mid-sixteenth century

RENAISSANCE IN POLAND

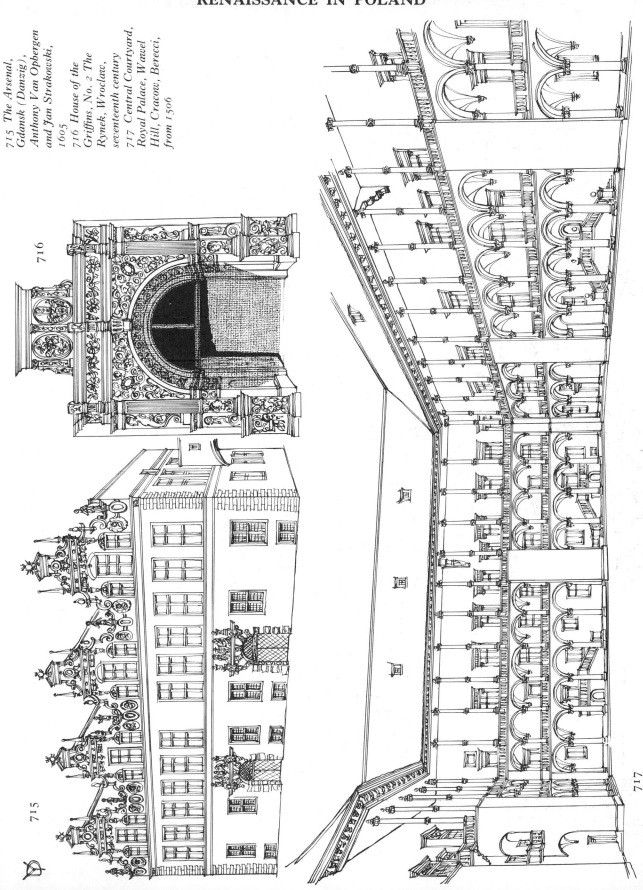

715 The Arsenal, Gdansk (Danzig), Anthony Van Opbergen and Jan Strakowski, 1605

716 House of the Griffins, No. 2 The Rynek, Wroclaw, seventeenth century

717 Central Courtyard, Royal Palace, Wawel Hill, Cracow, Berecci, from 1506

716

715

717

RENAISSANCE IN POLAND

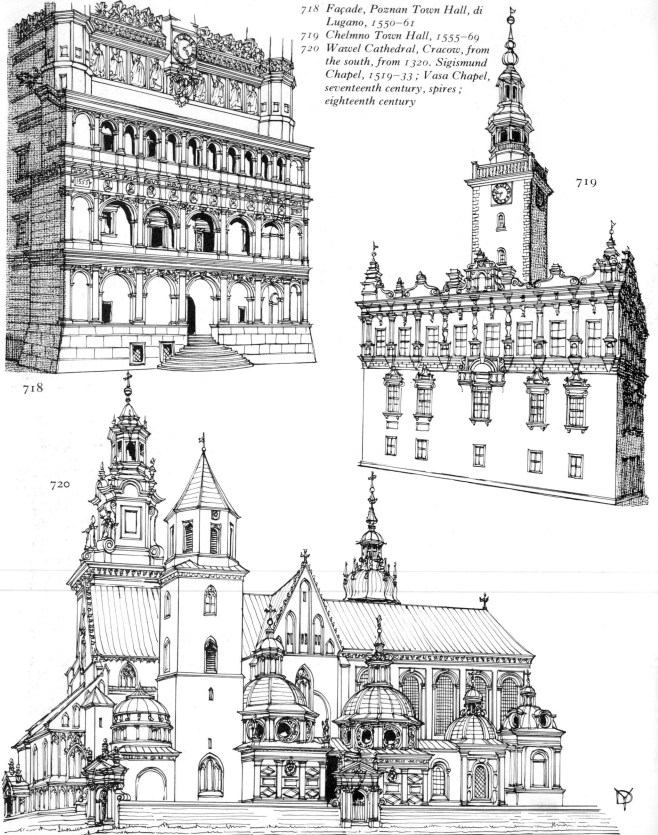

718 *Façade, Poznan Town Hall, di Lugano, 1550–61*

719 *Chelmno Town Hall, 1555–69*

720 *Wawel Cathedral, Cracow, from the south, from 1320. Sigismund Chapel, 1519–33; Vasa Chapel, seventeenth century, spires; eighteenth century*

718

719

720

721 *Doorway, Church of the Benedictines*
722 *Façade, Boim Chapel, 1609–17*
723 *Church of the Benedictines, 1578*

724 *The Anczowski House, Market Place, Peter*
Krasowski, 1577

dome and lantern. Built 1524–33, mainly by Italian artists, it is of stone, with an oak panelled and coffered interior dome supported on brick pendentives; the dome exterior is sheathed in copper. The interior lighting is from the circular windows in the drum. The walls below are articulated with Tuscan order pilasters, with panelling between. Rich sculptured and carved Renaissance tombs surround the walls.

Other chapels which followed, based on this prototype at Cracow, include the Renaissance chapel on the south-east corner of *S. John's Cathedral, Wroclaw* and the *Boim Chapel* at *L'vov* (now U.S.S.R.). The Wroclaw example is on Italian lines but that in L'vov (Lemberg) combines these characteristics with the essential L'vov style of building and decoration. The entire façade is carved in high relief sculpture, depicting scenes at the Crucifixion framed by orders and, below, portrait roundels, strapwork, lions' heads and floral designs, so interwoven that the decorated columns of the order are barely discernable (**722** and PLATE 90).

This blend of Italian Renaissance forms with south-eastern Polish decorative style can be seen elsewhere in L'vov, especially in the buildings grouped round or near the Market Square. The *Black Palace* by *Pietro Krasovsky* is in the same diamond-studded, faceted form as the Palazzo dei Diamanti in Ferrara in Italy (begun 1492) and the Casa de los Picos in Segovia (sixteenth century). The Black Palace in L'vov also has some vigorous, high quality carving on the doorway and window frames (**724**). There are interesting buildings all round the market square. Some are sixteenth century, others seventeenth and eighteenth. The earlier façades are Elizabethan in character.

Nearby is the *Church of the Benedictines*, 1578, which is a mixture of Italian Renaissance and Byzantine form. The domes are Byzantine, but the doorway is richly and beautifully carved in Renaissance style (**721** and **723**). The tall steeple is Italianate. The *Bernadine Church* in the town is typical of the later period in the early years of the seventeenth century. Here is a Gothic interior with a façade in late Renaissance Italianate form. It was mainly designed by *Paolo Romano* with contributions by *Przychylny* and *Bemer*.

There are several Renaissance civic buildings of note in Poland. The *Cloth Hall* at *Cracow* stands in the centre of the large market place. It was first built in the thirteenth century as a street of stone market stalls and about 1400 a market hall was constructed above. Destroyed by fire in 1555, in 1559 *Giovanni Maria Padovano* reconstructed it, adding classical parapets, gables and ornament. Unfortunately the structure has been altered in later years and was comprehensively restored in 1875.

The town halls of Poznan and of Chelmno retain far more of their original form and are more Renaissance in character. The *Poznan Town Hall* was also a Medieval building but, after fire damage in 1536, it was rebuilt from 1550 by *Giovanni Battista Quadro di Lugano* who constructed a Renaissance loggia in front of the Gothic façade (**718**) and added a classical steeple of diminishing stages, extending to 320 feet in height. The upper part was later lost and it was rebuilt to a different design. *Chelmno Town Hall* is a charming, simple Renaissance design (**719**). Symmetrical, with a square central tower and Renaissance steeple, it stands in the centre of the vast market place in this attractive small town.

More in the German and Flemish Mannerist Renaissance style are some of the surviving buildings in *Gdansk* (Danzig) on the Baltic coast. The finest of these which escaped the Second World War devastation of the city, is the *Armoury* (PLATE 89), built 1605. It has characteristic strapwork, sculptured and panelled gables, as well as richly decorated doorways.

There are many *town houses* on Renaissance pattern surviving in Poland, but some of them are now in poor condition. In *Cracow* the usual design was for a central courtyard surrounded by arcaded galleries. Typical are those in Kanonicza Street, built about 1550. Most of the examples in *Warsaw* have been lost but one or two good Flemish style Renaissance houses survive in *Wroclaw*. No. 2 in the main square, the Rynek, is one of these. Called the House of the Griffins, it has a stepped, curved gable, with painted reliefs of animals and birds at each stage of the gable. The doorway is typical of this type of work in Poland (**716**).

The Iberian Peninsula: Spain

Spain is rich in examples of buildings which are influenced decoratively or wholly by Renaissance ideas. A comparatively small proportion of these, however, are in a pure classical style based on Italian development. As in Germany and Flanders, the Roman High Renaissance concepts were slow to penetrate, partly due to the distance separating Italy from Spain but also for religious reasons. In England, the Renaissance was retarded because of the Reformation; in Spain, paradoxically, it was the strength of Roman Catholicism which held back the spread of humanist ideas.

There are three principle stages of Renaissance development between 1500 and 1700 in Spain. These overlap, as different areas adapted themselves to the new forms earlier than others. The first stage is termed *Renaissance plateresque*. This corresponds to the pattern book type of Flemish Mannerism which affected England, Flanders and Germany. Characteristically and similarly, the buildings are still Medieval structurally and only display Renaissance features in their decoration. The Spanish version of this decoration differs from the northern European one. The national love of ornament in Iberia comes to the fore and, exactly as in the Gothic plateresque works of the fifteenth and early sixteenth centuries, the whole surface is covered by carved or stuccoed ornament. The difference is that the motifs are now Renaissance not Medieval. There are many superb examples existing of this style of work in many parts of Spain. They date from any time in the sixteenth century and a few are early seventeenth century. Among the finest of these are the *University façade* at *Salamanca* (1516–29) (PLATE 93), the *Palacio Municipal* at *Baeza* in southern Spain (1559) and the *Casa de las Muertes* (House of the Dead) at *Salamanca*. One of the most successful architects in this style of work was *Enrique de Egas* (d. 1534). He built the great *Hospicio de los Reyes Catolicos* at *Santiago de Compostela* (1501–11), now one of Spain's largest luxury hotels, next to the cathedral (PLATE 92). His masterpiece is the *Hospital of S. Cruz de Mendoza* at *Toledo*, begun in 1504. The entrance portal is a beautiful plateresque feature. The interior court, with its carved stone staircase, is

more Italianate and nearer to purer Renaissance work of the fifteenth century (**726**).

The second stage of Renaissance development was still partly plateresque in its rich surface decoration but shows a tentative comprehension of classical principles and construction. The orders are sometimes used structurally and are more correctly proportioned and detailed. Similarly, many fine examples of this type of work survive in varying districts of Spain. For instance, the *Town hall* (Ayuntamiento) at *Seville* (**728, 729**) by *de Riaño* and the *Luna Palace* (now the Audiencia) in *Zaragoza* (1537–52). This has a simple, Medieval-type façade with an interesting sculptured doorway, but the interior courtyard is reminiscent of Roman palace patios.

Two of the outstanding sixteenth century artists of this stage of development were the sculptor *Alonso Berruguete* (c. 1486–1561) (PLATE 91) and the architect and sculptor *Diego de Siloé* (1495–1563). Both studied in Italy and, on returning to Spain, developed a Spanish style based on Italian High Renaissance themes. One of de Siloé's famous works in his *Escalera Dorada* in *Burgos Cathedral* (1524) which, in its symmetry and handling, shows his appreciation of Michelangelo's Laurenziana Library. He worked for many years on *Granada Cathedral*, especially on the chevet and crossing. He was restrained here from developing a full, classical theme as he had taken over a partly-built Gothic structure begun by Egas. This had a five-aisled nave and chevet with radiating chapels. The result is thus less satisfactory than it might have been. It has power and a Renaissance sense of handling of space but became a hybrid Spanish/Italian composition. For example, inside, Roman orders are used in a Medieval manner. The crossing piers have engaged Corinthian columns on high pedestals, supporting classical entablatures from which, in turn, springs a Medieval lierne vault.

From this middle stage of development came a number of Renaissance courtyards which still exist and show varying stages of understanding of Italian High Renaissance principles. A beautiful example is at the *Tavera Hospital* in *Toledo*, designed by *Bartolomé Bustamente*, a priest who had studied in Italy. It is a vast rectangular building, 350 feet by 260 feet. The entrance façade is plain, with rusticated quoins and window openings and a three-stage classical entrance

RENAISSANCE IN SPAIN

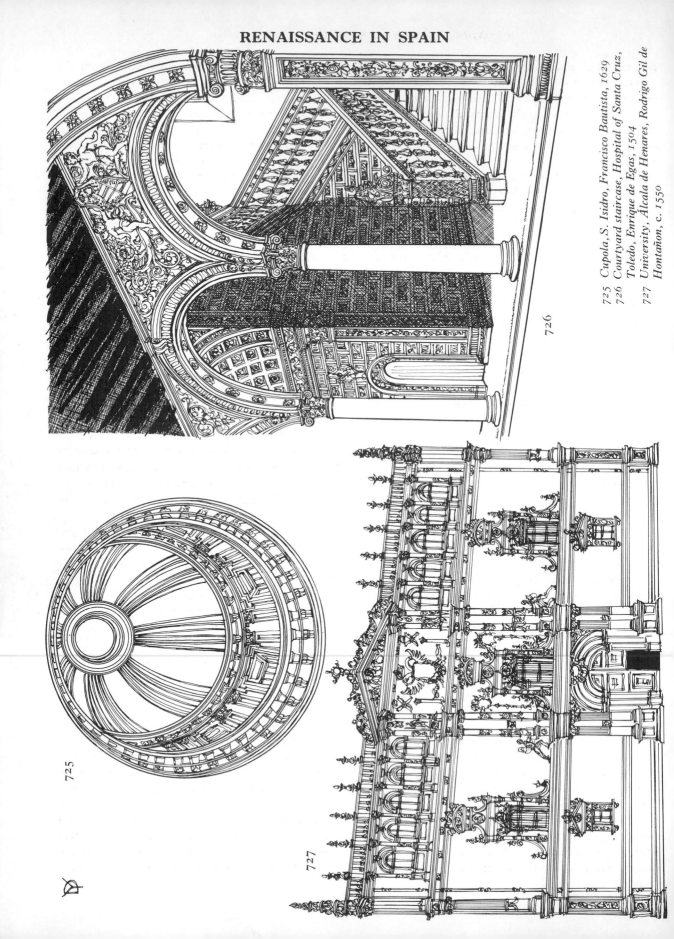

725 Cupola, S. Isidro, Francisco Bautista, 1629
726 Courtyard staircase, Hospital of Santa Cruz, Toledo, Enrique de Egas, 1504
727 University, Alcala de Henares, Rodrigo Gil de Hontañon, c. 1550

726

725

727

portal. The courtyard behind is two-storeyed, Doric below, Ionic above and is divided down the centre by a two-storeyed gallery (**731**). The church is more severely classical, with a giant Doric order all round in pilaster form, broken only by a Corinthian altarpiece. There is a dome over the crossing inside an octagonal tower. The *Alcazar*, also in Toledo, still dominates the town. Enlarged many times from its twelfth century origins, it was built in Renaissance style under Charles V by *Alonso de Covarrubias*. The work was continued by several architects and completed by Herrera. His south front and *de Villalpando's* grand staircase in the patio were outstanding. The Alcazar was left in ruins after the Civil War but is now almost rebuilt.

In 1540, *Rodrigo Gil de Hontañón* was commissioned to rebuild the façade of the *University of Alcalà de Henares*, near Madrid. This is still a middle period Spanish Renaissance work. The symmetrical façade has three storeys, flanked by lower wings. The portal definition is carried up to each storey by coupled columns, but these have more in common with a Jacobean frontispiece than a High Renaissance Roman doorway. The fenestration is classical and the decoration restrained. It is a good 'compromise' achievement (**727**).

The third stage, that of a purer classical style is mainly represented in late sixteenth and in seventeenth century work. There is one early exception. This is the Renaissance part of the *Alhambra Palace* at *Granada*, added by Charles V and built by *Muchaca* (1527–50) (**732**). Based on designs from Hadrian's Villa at Tivoli, the courtyard is circular, surrounded by a two-storeyed pure classical colonnade. It is plain, almost severe, and in strange contrast to the Moorish Palace adjacent to it. The Renaissance palace was never completed and it was many years before such correctly classical building was again attempted in Spain.

The architect who established the genuine classical style was *Juan de Herrera* (c. 1530–97). He studied in Italy and Belgium. His work in Spain is always severe, correct, monumental. There is little ornament and the interiors of his churches, for instance, are chilling. Herrera's influence, however, was considerable. By the later sixteenth century, Spain was ready for a change from over-decoration and a number of

seventeenth century architects followed on the more correct classical lines, though not in Herrera's individualistic style.

Herrera's earliest and most famous work is the *Escorial*. This great monastic palace in the hills near Madrid is a memorial to Philip II. It was his retreat and displays the asceticism and almost fanatical religiosity of the King. He intended a monastery, a royal palace and a mausoleum for Charles V on one site, remote from any other civilisation. This he achieved, though in the twentieth century, civilisation has crept close to the gates of the Escorial in the form of tourist shops, restaurants and villas for wealthy Madrid citizens. The first architect of the Escorial was *Juan Bautista de Toledo*, who designed it in 1559. After his death in 1567, Herrera was commissioned to complete the work, which he did in 1584.

The palace and convent are in the form of a vast rectangle, 670 feet by 530 feet, of grey granite, hewn from the Guadarrama mountains, on whose lower slopes it stands; a magnificent desolate site. The long, severe exterior walls are unbroken save for rectangular window openings and four corner towers. It is an immense structure enclosing the monastery and church and having 16 courtyards (**733**). Philip spared no expense. He supervised every detail of the construction. He told Herrera that the work must be noble, simple and severe, without ostentation. Herrera did as he was asked. The last part of the work was the great *Church of S. Lawrence*. He based it on a central, Greek cross plan, like Michelangelo's S. Peter's, but the nave arm, also like S. Peter's, was later extended, here with an entrance vestibule or narthex. Like the convent, this is also severe. The Doric Order is used throughout; in column form on the pedimented, entrance portico and in pilasters on the twin western towers and in the interior. The church is in grey granite. There is no colour or decoration. The interior is, nevertheless, most effective, though too cold for some tastes. Plain pendentives support the large dome and drum over the crossing. The whole interior is flooded with light from the large windows in the drum, enhanced by the position of the church on the mountain slopes (**734**). The mausoleum, the *Pantheón de los Reyes*, was built in the early seventeenth century for the Hapsburg monarchy by the Italian *Giovanni Battista Crescenzi*. This

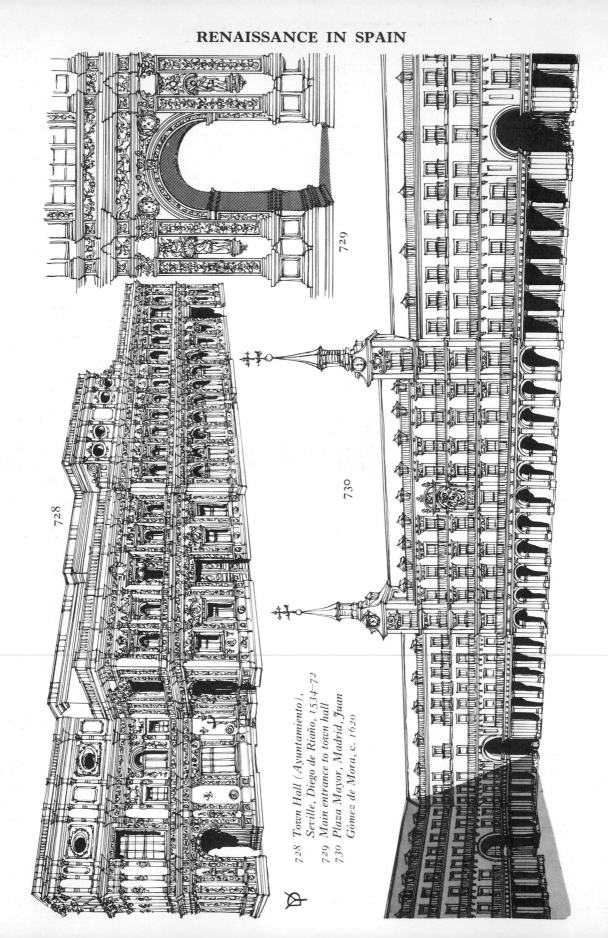

729

730

728

728 *Town Hall (Ayuntamiento),*
Seville, Diego de Riaño, 1534–72
729 *Main entrance to town hall*
730 *Plaza Mayor, Madrid, Juan*
Gómez de Mora, c. 1620

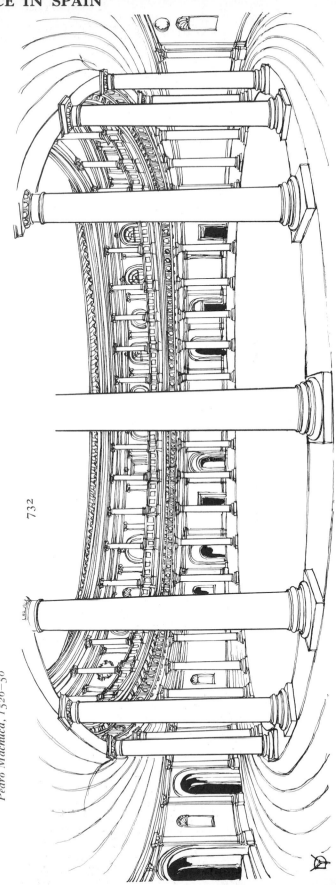

731 *Double patio, Tavera Hospital, Toledo, 1541–79*
732 *Courtyard, Palace of Emperor Charles V, Alhambra, Granada,*
Pedro Machuca, 1526–50

731

732

is a domed octagonal chamber, set under the sanctuary of the church. The whole room is in grey and red marbles, decorated in gilt. The rich colouring is in contrast to Herrera's church above. Coupled Corinthian pilasters are set round the walls, in which are the Hapsburg marble tombs placed on shelves.

Herrera worked on many other projects, though little survives from some of them. At the *Royal Palace* of *Aranjuez*, south of Madrid, he again succeeded Juan Bautista de Toledo. He began a new design in 1567 on Italian High Renaissance villa pattern. The palace was not finished till the eighteenth century and Herrera's designs were considerably altered. His drawings, however, remain. In 1582 he designed the *Seville Exchange* and in 1575 the *Toledo Town Hall*. He worked for many years on *Valladolid Cathedral*. This is typical; plain, large, ascetic.

It is less well lit than his church at the Escorial because it remained incomplete after the architect's death. He intended a huge cathedral on basilican plan of 450 by 300 feet, with equal length nave and choir, corner towers to the façade and a dome over the crossing. At his death only the nave was complete and part of the façade. The latter was finished by Alberto de Churriguera, but the rest was never built so only the unlit, vast, barrel vaulted nave and monumental façade exist.

One of the leading architects of the earlier seventeenth century was *Juan Gómez de Mora* (1586–1647), a follower of Herrera's style and a prolific designer. One of his best known layouts is the *Plaza Mayor* of *Madrid*. This was originally planned by Herrera but de Mora carried out the scheme between 1617 and 1620 (**730**). It is a large square which retains its homogeneity on all

733 The Escorial, near Madrid, south front, Juan de Herrera, 1559–84

733

734

734 *The crossing, Monastery Church of the Escorial,*
Juan de Herrera, c. 1584

four-storeyed sides with arcaded shops on the ground floor and dormers in the roof above. The north side with its twin towers is the focus of the scheme. The square is closed to traffic and reserved for pedestrians, cafés and shops.

Among de Mora's other works are the *Encarnación Church* (1611–16) and *Town Hall*, both in *Madrid*, and the *Jesuit Church* at *Alcalà de Henares* (1625). The Encarnación Church has a simple, narrow, classical façade. Inside it is light and well-proportioned. There is a dome over the crossing and coffered barrel vaults covering the four arms. There are no side chapels to the nave; the walls are articulated with Ionic pilasters with paintings and sculpture between.

Padre Francisco Bautista (1594–1679) based his style on Italian Mannerist examples. His work is to be found in Jesuit churches, chiefly in Madrid and Toledo. His important achievement is the *Cathedral* of *S. Isidro el Real* in *Madrid*. Here he followed Vignola's plan and form of Il Gesù in Rome, but the Madrid example was Herreran in its cool, grey treatment. The cathedral was sacked and the interior damaged by fire in 1936. It has now been rebuilt and re-decorated (**725**).

Among other interesting seventeenth century surviving works are *Sebastian de la Plaza's*

735 Renaissance cloister (Gothic Plateresque church behind), Convent of Christ, Tomar, Diogo de Torralva, 1557

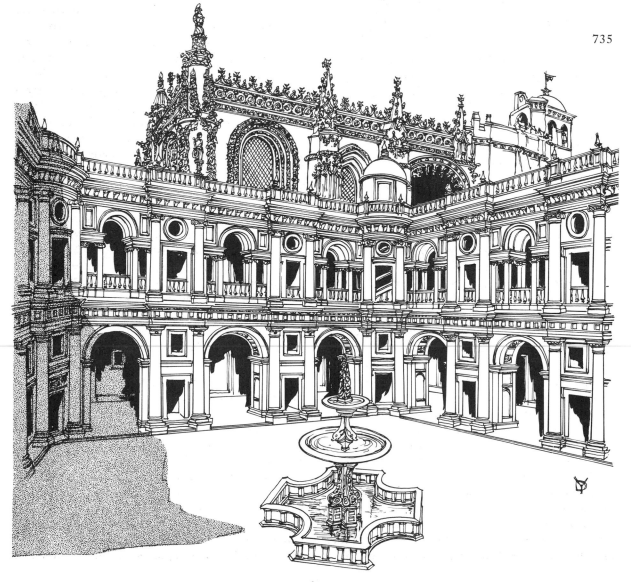

735

Portugal

Unlike Spain, Portugal possesses some pure Italian Renaissance buildings from early in the sixteenth century. This is due to *Diogo de Torralva* (1500–66), for the surviving examples are all by him. His first work was the *Church of La Graça* in *Évora* (1527–37). Though in poor condition externally today, the architect's intentions are clearly visible. Less purely classical than his later work, the façade has Mannerist features, especially in the upper storey of the portico, with its over-sized sculpture breaking the cornice line and giant rosettes set between the over-tall Ionic columns.

At *Tomar*, however, de Torralva surpassed himself. His beautiful, classic Renaissance cloisters at the Convent of Christ are superb. This cloister, the finest of the seven, has giant Ionic columns superimposed over Doric with, between, the smaller scale ordered openings: an insistent reminder of Michelangelo's Campidoglio palaces in Rome (**735**). Part-way up the hill that leads from the present day town of Tomar to the Convent of Christ is his small *Chapel of the Conception* (Conceição), built about 1550. Outside it is unpretentious and of pure classical design. The inside is in the manner of Brunelleschi but is now in poor condition.

Apart from de Torralva's work, most sixteenth century examples in Portugal were of more hybrid form, as in Spain. The *Cathedral* at *Leiria* is typical. A large barn-like building, it has great stone buttresses rising the full height of the façade, and impure, stodgy, windows and doorways.

The late sixteenth century saw a tentative approach towards Italian Mannerism and Baroque. An example is the *Sé Nova* (New Cathedral) at *Coimbra* (**736**). Here are side scrolls and curved and broken pediments. The interior is very plain with stone coffered barrel vaulting and a central dome on Pantheon lines. The plan is a Latin cross and the order throughout, in pilaster form, is Doric. The ornate Baroque altarpieces in the choir and transepts, decorated in gilt and colour, provide a rich contrast to the grey stone interior. *Filippo Terzi* (1520–97) came to Portugal from Italy in 1576 and increased the momentum towards Italian Baroque. He introduced the Jesuit style, based on the prototype, Il

736　*Sé Nova (New Cathedral), Coimbra, façade, Baltasar Alvares, late sixteenth century*

Bernardas Church in *Alcalà de Henares* (1617–26), which presages the Baroque with its oval nave surrounded by four chapels after Bernini; the Italian High Renaissance styled *Disputación* in *Barcelona*—a rectangular block with Doric porch and sculptured group above (1596–1617) by *Pedro Blay*—and *Jaén Cathedral*. This cathedral was built over a long period so that although the façade belongs to the Baroque style and period, the interior and the remainder are Renaissance. It is mainly the work of *Andrés Vandelvira* (1509–75), a pupil of Diego de Siloé, and he began work at Jaén in 1546 and continued until his death. It is built on hall church pattern, with slightly projecting transepts and a square east end, without ambulatory or radiating chapels. The interior has much in common with Granada Cathedral. There are similar nave piers of clustered Corinthian columns, standing on tall pedestals, with separate entablatures above which in turn support complex Gothic lierne vaults. The decoration of the cathedral is Renaissance and the aisle chapels are coffered and vaulted.

Gesù in Rome by Vignola. His chief work on this pattern is *São Vicente da Fora* in *Lisbon* (**737**). The interior is fundamentally similar to Il Gesù but the façade is more classical.

737 Church of S. Vicente da Fora, Lisbon, Filippo Terzi, 1582–1627

Northern Europe: The U.S.S.R.

Apart from some isolated instances, mainly in Moscow, the influence of the Italian Renaissance did not penetrate here; Byzantine trends were two strong. In the existing examples, Renaissance features are entirely decorative in character, acting as a covering upon a building, which was still Byzantine in structure and form. The emblems of classicism can be seen in the fenestration, the doorways and orders composed of pilasters supporting entablatures where neither the mouldings, proportions or capitals were of pure design. In this respect, Russian Renaissance

buildings are a parallel to Elizabethan ones in England or pattern book Flemish in Germany and Poland. But since in the Soviet Union the basis was Byzantine not Gothic, the variations differed.

The purest Renaissance building is in the *Moscow Kremlin*, the *Cathedral* of the *Archangel Michael* designed in 1505, not surprisingly by the Italian *Alevisio Novi*, who had worked for some years in Russia. He was asked to build an imposing church which would act as a resting place for the tsars and he was expected to follow the Vladimir type of structure, using also ideas from the existing Kremlin Cathedral of the Assumption (Volume 1, p. 140) which had also been designed by an Italian, Fioravanti. The interior of Novi's cathedral is on this theme, but on the outside he introduced, for the first time in Russia, Renaissance detail: orders, pilasters, Composite capitals, arches. This is entirely decorative and bears little relationship to the building form though the results are attractive. A particular feature of this external design is the shell decoration in the upper row of arches above the entablature. This addition is ornamental but meaningless structurally (**741**).

This cathedral and the other two described in Volume 1, (p. 140) are all in a central group inside the Kremlin walls. Also in the centre, nearby, is the *Faceted Palace* (Granovitaya Palata, *c.* 1490) which, like the Black Palace in L'vov and the examples in Italy and Spain (see p. 54), has its façades covered by diamond studding, broken only by decorated classical window openings flanked by Corinthian columns supporting entablatures. It was built by two Italians, *Marco Ruffo* and *Pietro Antonio Solario*. The ecclesiastical buildings are kept now as museums. The later Great Palace and other large buildings are used as government offices. There is only one modern building inside the walls, the Palace of Congresses (1961, Volume 4, p. 151). The *Tower* of *John the Great* (Ivan Veliki) is also inside the walls. This was a fine belfry, but was rebuilt after 1812 in a less vigorous and decorative version of the original structure. Fig **739** shows it as it is now. The photograph in PLATE 94 shows the belfry and the cathedral and palaces of the Kremlin viewed from the river Moskva, as they are today.

Surrounding the Kremlin are massive walls with towers and gatehouses set at intervals. These

Plate 91
Retablo 'Visitation of the Virgin'. Museum of Santa Cruz, Toledo, Spain. 16th century. Alonso Berruguete
Plate 92
Façade detail, Hospicio Real. Santiago de Compostela, Spain, 1501–11
Plate 93
Façade detail, Salamanca University, Spain, 1516–29

Plate 94

The Moscow Kremlin, U.S.S.R. Viewed from the banks of the River Moskva, showing the Cathedrals and Kremlin mural towers

RENAISSANCE IN MOSCOW, U.S.S.R.

date from different periods and several are of interest. The rebuilding of the walls from their original wood to red brick was begun in 1485 under Ruffo and Solario and completed in the early sixteenth century. Parts have been altered, but the general impression is still Italianate, reminding the viewer of those in Ferrara or Verona. The towers are a mixture of styles and dates, including Gothic, Byzantine, Renaissance and Baroque features. Among the most interesting are the *Spasskaya* (**738**), the *Nikolskaya*, the *Borovitskaya* and the *Troitskaya*.

The *Cathedral of the Archangel Michael* at the *Andronikrov Monastery* in *Moscow* illustrates a typical Russian adoption of Renaissance decorative forms on to a Byzantine church (**740**). Here, the corner columns and fenestration are classical, the remainder is traditionally Russian giving an uneasy appearance of fancy dress covering.

Scandinavia

There is little Renaissance architecture in Scandinavia, except in Denmark. In Norway, Finland and Sweden, this was a period of decline in architecture and in the arts in general. The Reformation led to the disbandment and demolition of monastic settlements. Not many new churches were built. Construction was primarily in defences and fortified houses, but few of these structures showed Renaissance features.

Denmark

The nearest part of Scandinavia to the rest of Europe, this country absorbed Renaissance ideas chiefly from Holland and also from Germany and England. Building was in the form of palaces and houses, still partly of a fortified nature but, with royal patronage, several large scale structures were erected. The work has mostly been extensively restored in the nineteenth or twentieth centuries but retains much of its original character.

The Renaissance style in Denmark closely resembles that of Holland and England. Much of it is in brick, with stone reserved for dressings and sculptured decoration. The gabling, chimney-stacks and doorways are very Dutch, the decoration and handling of the orders impure in the same sense and manner as English Elizabethan design.

King Frederick II was the moving spirit behind two of the great fortified palaces of the age. The earlier of these is *Kronborg Castle* at *Helsingør*, original of Shakespeare's Elsinore in 'Hamlet'. It was rebuilt from the early 1570s by Flemish masons in Mannerist style. The Renaissance character is seen in the horizontal emphasis of the elevations, though ornament and gabling are Flemish Mannerist. This large castle is built on a square plan on a headland overlooking the sea; the corners marked by tall, polygonal towers, it is surrounded by earth and brick ramparts. Inside, is an impressive, large, three-storeyed courtyard of grey sandstone with green copper, sloping roofs, interrupted by decoratively gabled dormers. The fenestration, ground storey orders and frontispiece doorways are like those of Elizabethan English great houses.

At *Hillerød*, inland between Copenhagen and Helsingør, Frederick II began his second great palace. He acquired the estate at Hillerød, on islands in the lake, in 1560 and replaced the existing manor house with a castle which he re-titled *Frederiksborg*. Christian IV, born there in 1577, demolished much of it and rebuilt once again, from 1602, on a grander scale. This palace remained the chief residence of the Danish kings until 1859, when tremendous damage was done to the interior by a great fire. It was carefully restored and rebuilt by Medahl (Volume 4, p. 65). Much of the exterior, however, belongs to the original Renaissance palace.

Frederiksborg is an impressive group of buildings, certainly the first Renaissance palace in Scandinavia. The palace is approached through a tall, spired gatehouse, which leads into the great outer court. In the centre of this is the *Neptune fountain*, a good copy of the original one by *Adrien de Vries* (1623), removed by the Swedes in 1659 and now at Drottningholm (p. 178). Behind the fountain is the bridge leading to the magnificent Renaissance screen, decorated with its Flemish Mannerist sculptured niches, set in a wall articulated with a Doric arcade. The two-storey gateway is ornamented by high relief sculptured panels and, above, a strapwork crested cartouche. The brick walls contrast attractively with the stonework ornament.

Behind this entrance screen rises the main structure of the palace, built round three sides of an inner court, reached by passing through the

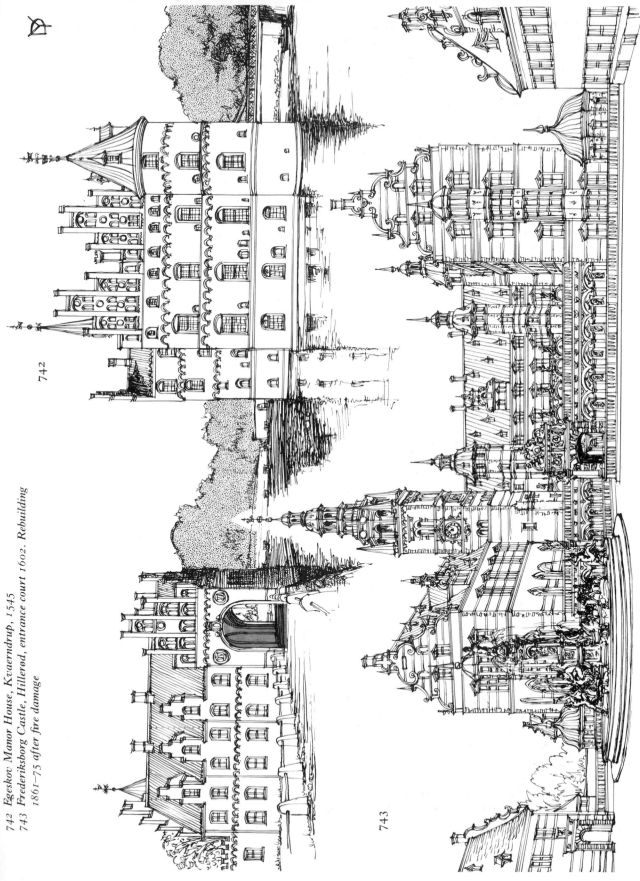

742

743

742 *Egeskov Manor House, Kvaerndrup, 1545*
743 *Frederiksborg Castle, Hillerod, entrance court 1602. Rebuilding 1861–75 after fire damage*

archway in the centre of the screen (**743**). Though laid out on the French *cour d'honneur* type of plan, this was the only concession to Renaissance symmetry. The buildings are romantically grouped round the courtyard, the elegant towers set asymmetrically, the gables, the turrets and dormers breaking the skyline like a Dutch or English great house of the period. The fenestration is classical, as is the two-storey entrance screen, but the use and handling of the ornamentation and orders are purely decorative rather than functional in the way that they would have been in Italy or France at that date. The restoration has been carefully done, closely following the available original drawings and, though a hardness of finish reminds one of the nineteenth century work here, the whole impression is of a remarkably coherent and homogeneous Danish Renaissance palace.

Christian IV was an influential architectural patron and was especially interested in town planning. Impressed by the ideal town planning schemes put forward by the Italian Renaissance architects, he envisaged a suitable layout for the centre of *Copenhagen*. Personally he drew up plans for an octagonal focal point with surrounding buildings. This scheme was not realised until the eighteenth century planning of the Amalienborg (p. 174), but the *palace* of *Rosenborg* was built from 1606 onwards and still stands much in its original form. It was designed as the summer palace and was built in brick and stone in similar style to Frederiksborg, but stands on a smaller ground plan, extending vertically rather than horizontally (**744**).

The most impressive Renaissance building in Copenhagen is the *Exchange*, constructed 1609–30 as a trading centre. It is an immensely long two-storeyed building with gabled ends and an unusual central tower with a spire made up of entwined dragons' tails (**746**). Although on Flemish Mannerist pattern, as shown in its row of tall, gabled dormers and sculptured caryatid decoration, the three-storeyed frontispieces on the two end elevations are of correct classical handling in the Doric Order.

A number of *manor* and *town houses* for the nobility and wealthier citizens were built in the sixteenth and early seventeenth centuries. Manor houses were still partially fortified, generally surrounded by a moat and approached via a drawbridge. Most of these were of brick and were still largely designed on Medieval pattern, though Renaissance features in gabling, fenestration and decoration were now being incorporated. The finest example is *Egeskov*, built 1545 near the village of Kvaerndrup, on the island of Funen, south of Odense. Magnificently sited in parkland on the edge of the lake, it is a structure based on the two-house principle, these houses adjoining one another and standing on a foundation of oak piles driven into the lake bed. The wall dividing the two houses is six feet thick and contains, in its thickness, stairways, small chambers and passageways. Egeskov has not been altered greatly over the centuries (**742**), only its gables and turrets were rebuilt in the nineteenth century and an iron suspension bridge built to replace the drawbridge approach. The gatehouse was altered in the same period.

A number of *town houses* survive from this period. A fine example is No. 9 Østeraagade in *Aalborg*, in the north of the Jutland peninsula. Built 1623–4 (**745**), this is a large, brick house with stone facings and decoration. It has a three-gabled facade to the street, an elegant oriel window and a finely sculptured doorway. In the High Street (Stengade) in *Helsingør* is a plainer example, at No. 76. Built in 1579, this has pedimented classical windows and a Mannerist gable. In *Aarhus*, the open air museum, 'Den Gamle By', contains many buildings reerected from the city and nearby towns and villages, preserved from different periods of architectural development. There are a number of examples—houses, shops, workshops and warehouses—from the sixteenth and seventeenth centuries, which are mainly of timber construction with brick or plaster infilling, like the English half-timber work. These are in traditional building style and are more Medieval in design than Renaissance. The windows are small and latticed, the roof pitch steep and the upper storeys overhang the lower. Only in the doorway surrounds and lintels is there a sign of impure classical decoration.

Norway

In this period, until the later seventeenth century, few buildings of note were erected in Norway and true Renaissance work is almost unknown. A

RENAISSANCE IN DENMARK

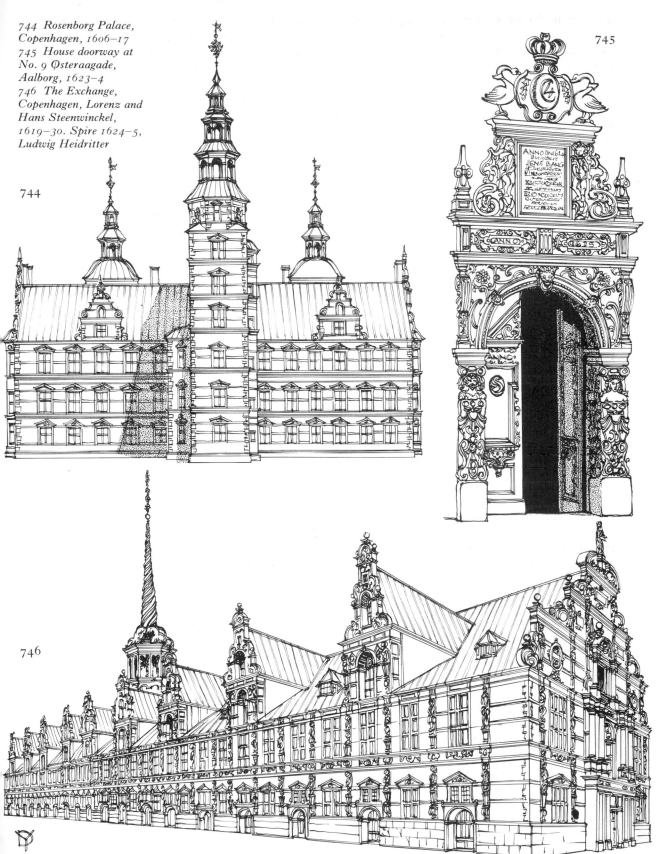

744 Rosenborg Palace,
Copenhagen, 1606–17
745 House doorway at
No. 9 Østeraagade,
Aalborg, 1623–4
746 The Exchange,
Copenhagen, Lorenz and
Hans Steenwinckel,
1619–30. Spire 1624–5,
Ludwig Heidritter

744

745

746

country still disturbed and unsettled, the chief buildings in permanent materials were castles and fortifications and these showed Renaissance features only in fenestration and ornament. Typical is the *Rosenkranz Tower* in the Bergenhus fortress in *Bergen*, built 1562–8. This was erected by Scottish craftsmen, as were a number of other such buildings at this time. The *Akershus Fortress* in *Oslo* had been established in 1270. Rebuilding and extension work continued intermittently through the centuries, particularly in the years 1588–1648, but little of it exists unaltered today.

Of the *manor houses* built at this time, few survive. One of these is the *Austråt Manor House* in the Trondheim Fjord, built 1654–6. The house was constructed round a quadrangle, of which the existing Medieval chapel was the focal centre. There is a stone entrance wall and gatehouse which leads into a square court lined by a wooden gallery supported on columns. On the first floor, carved and painted wooden figures hold up the roof; these are replacements of originals destroyed in the fire of 1916.

Several Norwegian towns possessed fine timber buildings dating from these years, but repeated fires have destroyed the majority of them. The chief building material was wood, even in towns, until the early years of the twentieth century, and towns such as Trondheim and Bergen have lost nearly all their beautiful structures dating from earlier than the later eighteenth century.

Finland

Almost no churches and few houses of note were built here in the sixteenth and seventeenth centuries. The architectural influence was Swedish and there is no Finnish Renaissance style.

Sweden

Remains here are fragmentary and chiefly in castle-palaces. The best and most complete example is *Vadstena Castle* (**747**), picturesquely situated on the eastern shore of the immense Lake Vättern. Begun in 1545, the castle has a medieval fortified exterior appearance with round corner towers and the walls lapped all round by water. Inside is the palace, which is Renaissance in its symmetry and fenestration. The interiors are richer and more decorative.

747

747 Vadstena Castle, Sweden, sixteenth century

2
The Changing Face of Classicism: 1580–1800

It is appropriate to discuss in one chapter the tremendous quantity of work created in Europe during these two centuries because, apart from isolated tendencies, the architecture is all classical in derivation. It is based upon the Roman then, later, Greek classic structure of orders, columns, capitals and pediments, interwoven skilfully with arched openings and vaults.

Though it is convenient to consider together such a long period of energetic endeavour, it should not be presumed that the architecture of this extensive area and time was all similar. The variations on the classical theme were widespread, depending upon national characteristics, religious beliefs, climate, available building materials and, paramount, the overall European development of thought and style. As with previous architectural forms, different countries entered new phases at differing times. Italy continued as the leader and creator of prototype designs until the early eighteenth century, by which time France took her place as arbiter of architectural fashion. Meanwhile, other areas were dominated by alternative sources. The German influence was widespread; the southern designs being popularised in Czechoslovakia, Switzerland, Austria and Hungary, while the northern approach had more in common with England, the Low Countries and Scandinavia.

These years were the most fruitful architecturally for nearly all countries, even those most distant from Italy and France, such as Russia and Scandinavia. Only eastern areas still under Turkish domination, such as Greece and southern Yugoslavia, were exceptions to the movement towards greater building activity in classical form.

The predominant styles were Baroque, Rococo and Neo-classicism. Of these, the most vivid and strongly marked was the Baroque. In past ages this type of work was thought of as a late Renaissance art form, and it is less than 100 years since it was recognised as a style in its own right.

The word, which it is believed to derive from the Portuguese *barroco* (Spanish *barrueco*), meaning an ill-formed or grotesque pearl, was first applied in a derogatory sense, just as 'Gothic' was first introduced (see Volume 2, p. 79). This was a reference to the strange curving, sometimes bulbous shapes to be seen in this type of architecture which, in the nineteenth century were thus deprecated.

Baroque art and architecture, like those of the Renaissance, originated in Italy so that, while other countries in Europe were beginning to adopt Renaissance forms, the Italians had moved on from these to Mannerism, then to full-blooded Baroque. The underlying force of the movement was, like that of the Renaissance, based upon a new process of thinking, this time not towards Humanism but from Humanism towards the Catholic Church. A deep feeling had arisen for a re-introduction of spiritual values; evidence of man's need for belief in something greater than himself. Among other Orders, the Jesuits were instrumental in re-establishing a Christian way of life more suited to the modern world than the outgrown Medieval concept. The Roman Catholic Church seized the opportunity and attracted people back to its fold with gaiety and pageantry in its buildings. Bernini, the greatest of Baroque artists, was a master of the dramatic form and lighting effects so typical of the Baroque interpretation of the current Christian approach.

From Italy the Baroque architectural forms spread throughout Europe, but it was suited chiefly to southern, Latin peoples of Roman Catholic faith. This was partly for its religious significance and partly because it is an extrovert, rich, colourful style. In the greyer north—in England, northern Germany, Scandinavia—it gained only a foothold; there, classical architecture remained cool and aloof, in straight lines and pure tones. Apart from Italy, therefore, we find Baroque architecture in its more vigorous and characteristic manner in southern Germany, Austria, Switzerland, Czechoslovakia, Hungary, Spain and Portugal. One of its predominant features is a free use of curves (within the classical framework of orders and ornament). These curves, often of whole walls and ceiling, move from convex to concave. It was Robert Adam in England who, describing Baroque design as a feeling for 'movement', quoted S. Peter's in Rome as the prime example. He refers to the balance and contrast of the convexity of Michelangelo's dome in relation to Bernini's concave piazza colonnade. Another important feature of Baroque architecture, especially the interior, is of dramatic lighting effects in painting, sculpture and architecture, since all three arts are always fused in the Baroque into a unified design. The favourite plan is oval as this lends itself to a maximum feeling for movement. Rich, sensuous vitality in colour, form and light is the keynote of all Baroque work in all media.

The Rococo theme was predominantly French in inspiration though it is to be found also in other countries, such as Austria and Scandinavia. This is again a theme of movement, but here more on a decorative, two-dimensional plane than the Baroque. The orders tend to be omitted or reduced in importance and Rococo decoration surrounds window frames, doorcases, mirrors and paintings as well as providing a framework to ceiling painting. The decorative forms are still curving and sinuous, but now become gayer, lighter, less sensuous and in low relief.

The northern European approach to classical architecture was predominantly neither Baroque nor Rococo. Countries such as England, Holland, northern Germany, Scandinavia tended to keep to Renaissance and Palladian themes, then later to neo-classicism. This was less colourful and, with its emphasis on orders, based more directly on Roman than on Greek traditions. The architecture of these countries is, in many instances, of high quality, dignified, well-designed and often impressive, but it was never as colourful, richly ornamented or breathtaking as that of the Latin South.

Italy

Early Baroque in Rome

In the last years of the sixteenth century several architects in Rome began to break away from the academic Mannerism which was dominating the architecture of the city. Chief of these was *Carlo Maderna* (1556–1629), who became architect to *S. Peter's* in 1603. He was commissioned to complete the basilica which had been in course of building since Bramante's original design (p. 9); little had been done since Michelangelo's death in 1564. It fell to Maderna to alter Michelangelo's centralised plan by lengthening the unfinished nave arm to the form of a Latin cross. Maderna was most reluctant to do this, but was overruled by the Pope who wanted the extra space thus provided. History repeated itself 50 years later at S. Paul's in London when Wren was unwillingly overruled for the same reasons. In both cases the clergy were responsible for putting expediency before aesthetics. In Rome, S. Peter's was lengthened by three bays. As a result, the view of the dome from the piazza is truncated and the basis of the design thus thwarted. Maderna did his best to minimise the aesthetic loss; he retained Michelangelo's articulation inside the nave and faithfully echoed vault and wall design. His façade is bold and well-planned and, again, the giant order and articulation are maintained (**749**).

With the Counter-Reformation came a new wave of church building in Rome. The Mother Church of the Jesuit Order, *Il Gesù*, was one of the first to be built (p. 17). Following this came *S. Susanna*, to which Maderna added the façade in 1595–1603. This was a true Baroque elevation and one which set the pattern for many others in years to come. Next door is *S. Maria della Vittoria* (1624–6) by *Giovanni Soria*. Maderna designed the interior here apart from Bernini's famous Cornaro Chapel sculpture of S. Teresa. Maderna also completed and enlarged *S. Andrea della Valle* in 1608. This is his best work, with a majestic dome over the crossing (**750**).

High Baroque in Rome

The two great architects here were Bernini and Borromini. Acutely contrasting both in personality and architectural approach, between them they set a standard impossible for their followers to excel. *Gianlorenzo Bernini* (1598–1680) was a genius whose qualities would have risen to the surface whenever he had lived. His particular abilities and personality were, however, made

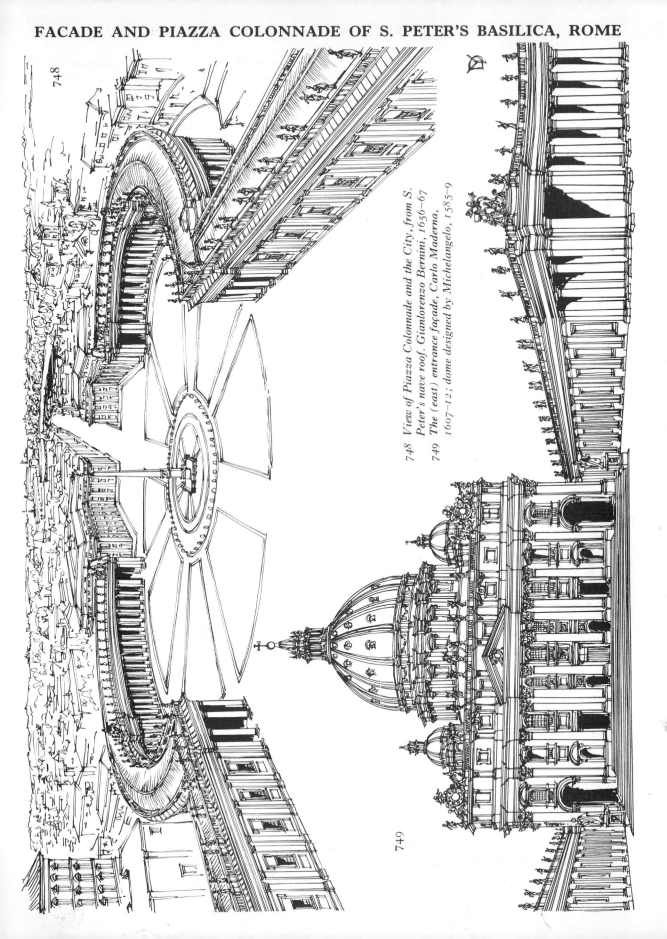

748 *View of Piazza Colonnade and the City, from S. Peter's nave roof. Gianlorenzo Bernini, 1656–67*

749 *The (east) entrance façade, Carlo Maderna, 1607–12; dome designed by Michelangelo, 1585–9*

751

752

750

750 *S. Andrea della Valle, Rome, Giacomo della Porta and Carlo Maderna, 1591–1623*
751 *Cupola interior, S. Lorenzo, Turin, Guarino Guarini, from 1666*
752 *North façade doorway, Lecce Cathedral, Guiseppe Zimbalo, 1659–70*

to measure for the period. He dominated his world for 50 years, towering far above all other artists of his time, creating achievement after achievement with consummate ease, concentration and energy. Only Michelangelo was ever respected and revered more by his contemporaries. Bernini was to the Baroque what Michelangelo had been to the Renaissance. The two giants had much in common. Both were strong personalities and of great religious conviction. Both lived long lives, master of their own artistic circle, to the end. Both were painters, architects and poets, but regarded sculpture as the most rewarding of the arts. They were both perfectionists, magnificent craftsmen, and would permit nothing to turn them away from the work in hand. In personality they were opposites. Bernini was a Neapolitan with all the charm and gaiety of his race. He was a happy husband and father and got on well with everyone; a contrast to the proud, introspective Michelangelo.

Bernini entered upon the challenge of the Counter-Reformation with zest. The drama and vividness of his work was essentially suited to this need. His sculpture especially portrayed an expression of instantaneous movement as in a snapshot, held it and perpetuated it as in life. He led a school of artists—architects, painters, sculptors—and kept Rome the centre of European art, cradle of the Baroque and inspiration of the Roman Catholic faith.

His architecture, like that of Michelangelo, was always sculptural in its handling of mass, but he displayed an exuberance and sensuality never to be seen in Michelangelo's work. Like his predecessor, his great work was at *S. Peter's*, where he became architect in 1629. His first work here was on the baldacchino and some sculptural groups, but his chief contribution was the designing of the piazza colonnade on front of the basilica. The problems of this layout were immense—aesthetic, practical, liturgical. It needed a man of Bernini's stature and artistic authority to solve them. He created a symbol of the Mother Church of Christendom embracing the world with his vast elliptical colonnades. The western ends adjoin the basilica façade with two long corridors. The piazza successfully provides space for the immense crowds who came to see and hear the Pope give his blessing to the city and the world from the façade loggia. Architecturally

the colonnades have made history. They are not arcades like most Ancient Roman examples; the continuous Ionic entablature rests directly upon the Doric/Tuscan columns which stand four deep, 60 feet high, surmounted by a procession of saints, extending outwards from the façade parapet of S. Peter's all round the piazza (**748** and **749**). All over Europe for 200 years these colonnades have been emulated, on large and small scale, in places as far apart as England and Russia. Bernini also adapted and re-designed the ceremonial entrance staircase, *the Scala Regia*; it is one of his masterpieces. It was so hemmed in by the existing walls as to appear a narrow dark well. The architect could not alter the physical situation but, by his wall articulation and adjustment of the stair flights, he contrived an impression of spaciousness. This was further enhanced by his Baroque treatment of the lighting and his elaborate coffered vault above. It is one of the great staircases of the world.

At the age of 60, Bernini built *S. Andrea al Quirinale* (**753**). This became a prototype for Baroque churches all over Europe. It is designed on centralised plan in oval form. The exterior is monumental with a tall curving porch, but the small, perfect interior is in contrast with its magnificent handling of lighting, colour and sculpture. The darkness below draws one's attention to the heavenly dome above with the figure of S. Andrew as centrepiece.

Bernini is also well known for his extensive work on *Roman palaces* and, in his capacity as sculptor and town planner, for his *fountains* in Rome. His monumental style is evident in the former but in his fountains, in particular, can be seen his breakaway from the Florentine Renaissance tradition into a powerful style, full of movement and vigour. The *Triton Fountain* (PLATE 95) in the Piazza Barberini shows this clearly, but his masterpiece is the layout in the *Piazza Navona* (PLATE 99). The unusual shape of this square is due to its following the exact pattern of the Roman Emperor Diocletian's stadium. The church of S. Agnese is built on one of the long sides and three fountains are equally spaced along the piazza's major axis. Bernini designed two of these, the Moro and the Fiumi. The latter, the fountain of the rivers, dates from 1648; it is the perfect centrepiece for the piazza. It sets off the church behind, showing it to advantage but not competing

Plate 95   The Triton fountain, Piazza Barberini, Rome. Gianlorenzo Bernini, 1642–3

BAROQUE CHURCHES IN ITALY

753

754

756

755

753 S. Andrea al Quirinale, Rome, Gianlorenzo Bernini, 1678
754 and 755 View and ground plan, S. Carlo alle Quattro Fontane, Rome, Francesco Borromini, 1638–40
756 S. Maria della Salute, Venice, Baldassare Longhena, 1631–87

for effect. The fountain represents the essence of Bernini's contribution to Baroque sculptural purpose in street architecture. It is a living, pulsating composition, the flowing water used as an integral part of the design to give vitality to the sculpture. The action is caught at an instant of time. It is not static but is about to continue the movement at any moment.

Francesco Borromini (1599–1667) was a contemporary of Bernini and a great contrast. He was a recluse, a neurotic, unhappy man who eventually took his own life. His work was quite different from that of the Neapolitan but, in his individual manner, also brilliantly original. He went much further than Bernini in challenging the concepts of classical architecture as they inherited them. Bernini was original in his handling of design, sculptural form, dramatic lighting and was a master of portraying the human spirit. He did not, however, contradict the basis of Renaissance thought; he adapted it to Baroque interpretation. Borromini went further. He cast aside the concept of classical architecture tied indissolubly to the proportions of the human figure as enunciated by Leonardo da Vinci. Borromini's concepts were of a classical architecture dependent on engineering thought rather than human sculpture and nearer to Medieval structure than Renaissance ideas. Despite these fundamental differences, Borromini's work is as indisputably Baroque as Bernini's. His contribution was almost entirely in ecclesiastical design, in an original form that had lasting and widespread influence.

S. Carlo alle Quattro Fontane (1638–40) was his first church. It caused an immediate sensation (**754** and **755**). It combines the fundamentals of several different types of design. On Greek cross plan, the walls are Baroque, in undulating form, and the oval dome is supported on pendentives. Borromini's structural unit basis is the triangle not the classical module pattern. The church is not large but, inside, appears of much greater volume than it actually is due to the sensation of movement from the alternately convex and concave wall surfaces. The lighting, in true Baroque manner, is controlled from one source, the dome, and accentuates the billowing quality of the wall design. The exterior façade was not built till nearly 30 years later and shows the architect's more mature approach. It is equally original and composed of undulating curves.

Borromini followed with his University Church, *S. Ivo alla Sapienza*, in 1642. This also is based on a triangular unit; an equally original structure, full of curves. In 1646 he was asked to restore the Cathedral of Rome, *S. John in Lateran*, an early Christian basilica, then in a poor state of repair. He was not permitted to rebuild, so he carried out the difficult task of making it structurally sound and re-clothing the interior in Baroque manner. He encased the columns in pairs and faced these piers with a giant order of pilasters extending the whole height of the cathedral. Between these he set arches containing large sculptured figures. He intended to vault the whole interior, but was not allowed to do this; the sixteenth century wooden ceiling was preserved, newly painted and gilded (**759**). Another of Borromini's triumphs is the fine Baroque exterior which he carried out on Rainaldi's church, *S. Agnese* in *Piazza Navona* (1652–6). This scheme was finished with an imposing dome flanked by twin Baroque towers. This became the basis for church façade design all over Europe.

Venice

The outstanding architect here was *Baldassare Longhena* (1598–1682), whose masterpiece is the church of *S. Maria della Salute*, built in thanksgiving for deliverance from the plague in the city in 1630 (**756**). Magnificently situated at the head of the Grand Canal, nearly opposite to S. Mark's Cathedral and the Doge's Palace, it is, apart from its picturesque exterior and position, one of the most interesting structures of the seventeenth century. The church is based on a mixture of themes; the centrally planned buildings of Ancient Rome like S. Costanza and the Byzantine pattern of S. Vitale. It is octagonal in plan with a surrounding ambulatory. The interior is plain in contrast to the flamboyant exterior, which has peculiarly Baroque giant scrolls which, supported on the ambulatory arches, provide abutment for the dome.

Northern Italy

Two gifted and contrasting architects in *Turin* created some magnificent architecture in these years. *Guarino Guarini* (1624–83) was the chief seventeenth century architect and had much in common with Borromini. He was also original and worked on Medieval and mathematical principles. He too used the triangle as his unit basis and clothed such structures in Baroque dress. His chief works in Turin were the *Sindone Chapel* in the *Cathedral* (1668), with its unusual cupola made up from 36 arches in triangular pendentive construction (**751**), the Baroque *Palazzo Carignano* with its undulating façade (**757**) and his *Church of S. Lorenzo* which was built to house the Holy Shroud. This chapel also has an unusual cupola. It is a complex Medieval structure, carried on pendentives set on the diagonal axes, which transform the octagon into a Greek cross at this level.

Turin continued to be a great architectural centre in the first half of the eighteenth century. Then *Filippo Juvara* (1678–1736) was the leader. He continued the development of the city where Guarini had finished and in his 20 years there achieved a prodigious quantity of work in churches, palaces and street layout. He varied his style according to the commission and four of his outstanding works illustrate this: the Church of S. Cristina, the Palazzo Madama, the Superga and Stupinigi. He added the façade to *S. Cristina* (1715–28)—a church which had been begun in 1639 as one of the twin churches in the Piazza San Carlo. This is Roman Baroque in style. His *Palazzo Madama* is a rich town palace with a superbly elegant staircase. The so-called hunting lodge at *Stupinigi*, outside the city, is an immense country palace with wide-spreading wings extending on each side of a monumental Baroque centrepiece. This contains the beautifully decorative curving, rococo hall.

Juvara was a Sicilian but much of his life was spent in Turin, from where he also travelled a great deal to build large-scale structures in other countries—Spain, for example (p. 115). His masterpiece is the immense royal burial church of Piedmont on the fringes of Turin. Entirely Baroque in concept, the *Basilica di Superga* represents the final great achievement of the Baroque era in Italy. It is fronted by a monumental Corinthian portico. The large central drum and dome, rising above the octagonal nave, are flanked by fine western towers. Here is Italy's last word on the centrally planned church theme

which had intrigued classical architects since the days of Brunelleschi.

Southern Italy

A different form of Baroque architecture flourished in the seventeenth and eighteenth centuries here and in Sicily. It reflected strongly the Spanish rule in the area, so the buildings are more richly ornamented than those of Roman or northern Italian Baroque origins. They have much in common with their equivalents in Andalusian and Central Spain (p. 114). The two outstanding architects of *Naples* were *Cosimo Fanzago* (1591–1678), whose work is mainly ecclesiastical, like his cloisters at *San Martino*, and *Luigi Vanvitelli* (1700–73), who is best known for the vast *royal palace* at *Caserta*. This immense building, 16 miles from Naples and still dominating the town of Caserta, was built as the summer residence for the Bourbon monarchy. Its extensive gardens echo Versailles and are immensely long, rising slowly for two miles from the palace in fountains, cascades and stairways to culminate in two fountains on a grand terrace below a steep cascade (PLATE 96). The water for these in this hot, dry region, comes via the aqueduct constructed by Vanvitelli from mountains 20 miles away. The palace is regular and dignified on the exterior. The interior is different; it is of Baroque splendour, especially in the state rooms and grand staircase, whose scenic quality is breathtaking.

Further south, to *Apulia*, the seventeenth century once again brought energetic building activity. Half forgotten since the great Norman empire of the twelfth century, these new forms were Baroque, but, as with the Norman work, different from interpretations elsewhere. This was due to the same racial mingling which had been effective 500 years before (Volume 2, p. 30). This time the foreign dominance was Spanish instead of Norman, and the Medieval and Byzantine Greek traditions mingled with Saracenic decoration, Spanish plateresque forms and southern Italian gaiety; all were fused into a strangely stable theme which imposed the rich decoration on the surface only of a Baroque classicism beneath.

The small town of *Lecce* was the centre of this type of building and still possesses many

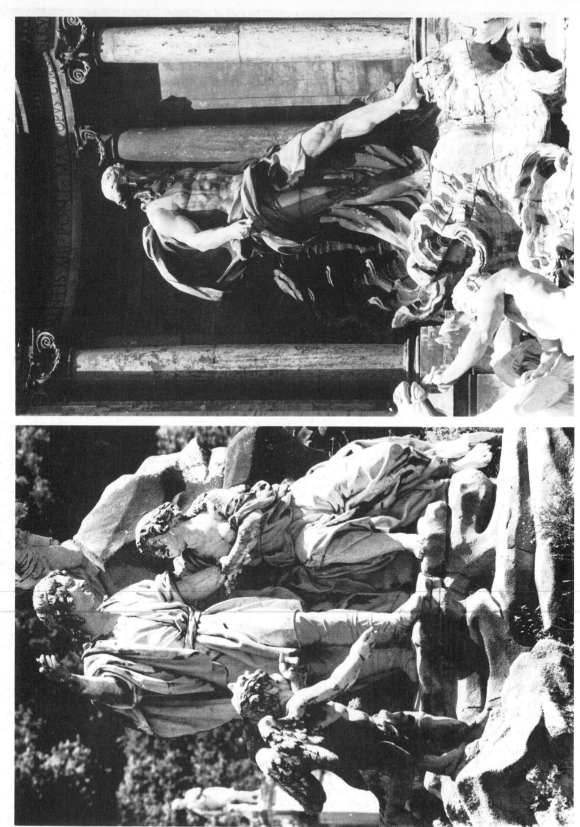

Plate 99
Fountain detail, Piazza Navona, Rome. 1653, Bernini

CLASSICAL ARCHITECTURE IN ITALY

758 The Spanish Steps, Rome, Francesco de Sanctis, 1723–5. Leading up to the Church of S.S. Trinità dei Monti from the Piazza di Spagna. Fountain 'The Barcaccia', Pietro Bernini, 1628

759 S. Giovanni in Laterano, Francesco Borromini, 1646–9

757 Palazzo Carignano, Turin, Guarino Guarini, 1680

examples built over a long period in the seventeenth and eighteenth centuries by many architects. Of particular note are the *Church of S. Croce*, the *Cathedral* façade and the adjacent *Seminario* (**752**).

Sicily

This area too possesses a rich Baroque heritage, much of it from the seventeenth century. It is different again from the Apulian work in that it is less riotously ornamented and is more a vigorous, Spanish-Sicilian form of northern Baroque. Buildings in *Palermo* such as the *Quattro Conti* and the *Arsenal* are typical; outstanding is the *Cathedral of Syracuse*. This will be remembered (Volume 1, p. 24) as unusual in incorporating a Greek temple in its nave, where the columns are still visible.

Town Planning by Streets and Grouped Buildings

Limited schemes by one or two individual architects had been essayed in the sixteenth century (p. 14). Larger scale plans were carried out in the seventeenth and eighteenth, but still by individual architects and clients. In *Rome*, the Piazza del Popolo, the Spanish Steps and the Trevi Fountain were such layouts. The *Piazza del Popolo* was the first Baroque scheme in Rome, a prototype of the later French development of the *rond-point* theme. The Porta del Popolo is one of Rome's entrance gateways and leads into a large piazza from which, opposite, three streets radiate to different parts of the city. There is an obelisk in the centre of the piazza and facing it are two island sites dividing the three roads. On these sites stand two Baroque churches— *S. Maria di Montesanto* and *S. Maria dei Miracoli*, built 1662–75 by *Carlo Rainaldi* and *Carlo Fontana*. They are not identical churches and the sites differ in size and shape, but they are sufficiently similar to complement one another and to act as focal centres for the view of the piazza from the Porta.

The *Spanish Steps* sweep in triple ascent, dividing as they go, up the steep hillside from the Piazza di Spagna to *Alessandro Specchi's* elegant church of *SS. Trinità dei Monti*. At Easter the Steps are one of the sights of Rome with colourful flowers banked up the sides of each staircase

(**758**). The *Trevi Fountain*, built 1735–72 by *Niccolò Salvi* is, apart from its romantic associations with coin-throwing, a remarkable composition and engineering feat. The classical palace façade in the form of a Roman triumphal arch acts as a backcloth to the sculptural drama in front (PLATE 97).

In the north, the idea of designing palaces in streets instead of individual buildings was developed in *Turin*, where Carlo Emmanuele I employed his architect *Carlo di Castellamente* to lay out the *Piazza San Carlo* and the beginnings of the *Via Roma* (1638). Work was continued throughout the seventeenth and eighteenth centuries under Guarini and Juvara. Similarly, in *Sicily*, *Giovanni Battista Vaccarini* replanned *Catania* after the earthquake of 1693, making it a Baroque city. The fine buildings of the Cathedral, the Palazzo Municipale and the Churches of S. Agata, S. Placido and S. Chiara were chief buildings in the scheme.

France

After Italy, France produced some of the finest architecture in Europe at this time, particularly in the seventeenth century, but only a little of it was in the Baroque style. This type of design was foreign to French artists, who preferred something less flamboyant, more correctly classical and with delicate decoration. This is not to say that there is no Baroque in France, only that it was not the fundamental style that it became in Italy.

The chief architect of the early seventeenth century was *Salomon de Brosse* (1571–1626). He designed, like Philibert de l'Orme, in bold, plastic manner, largely on Renaissance pattern. He was concerned with the architecture more than the decoration and his use of orders was correct and classical. He built three great châteaux and two palaces. Of the latter, the Parlement of Brittany at Rennes (near the Palais de Justice), which he built in 1618, remains fairly unaltered. Its simplicity and fine classical detail are notable. It has a rusticated lower storey and, above, are Doric columns and pilasters below a high gabled roof. His *châteaux* included that at Coulommiers (1613) (mainly demolished), Blérancourt (1619) and Luxembourg (1615). The *Palace of Luxembourg* in *Paris* built for Marie de' Medici was a

SEVENTEENTH CENTURY CHURCHES IN PARIS

760 *Church of Val de Grâce. Begun F. Mansart, completed Lemercier, 1645–65*
761 *Church of the Sorbonne, Lemercier, 1635*
762 *Church of S. Sulpice, begun Le Vau, 1655*
763 *Church of S. Gervais. Façade, de Brosse, 1616–21*

château, but has since been extended and turned into a large town house. At *Blérancourt* only a fragment exists in the entrance screen with gateway and bridge. These have been restored and maintained, fronting a museum, and clearly show the architect's style and intentions. The work is crisp, clear and well-proportioned; very classical and French.

In *Paris*, de Brosse also worked on two *churches*, the more important being *S. Gervais* where he added the façade in 1616–21 (**763**). This is a Renaissance rather than Baroque façade, far earlier in style than Maderna's S. Susanna in Rome of 1605. However, de Brosse was fronting a Gothic church and so needed a tall façade. He provided a three-storey structure with superimposed orders; a satisfactory answer to his problem.

The middle years of the seventeenth century saw the rise of a number of great French architects—Lemercier, F. Mansart, Le Vau, Perrault and J. H. Mansart. *Jacques Lemercier* (c. 1585–1654) became the chief architect to the Crown after de Brosse and worked largely for the King's chief Minister, Cardinal Richelieu, for whom he built a château (later much altered), the town centre which adjoins it and the Church of the Sorbonne in Paris. The *town* of *Richelieu* is still much as it was built, small, unpretentious, homogeneous. It is planned on grid-iron pattern, with two main streets at right angles to one another and with two squares at intersections. There are gateways at the four entrances to the town; these and the houses are all of stone or brick with plaster and have rectangular window openings and dormers in the gabled roofs. Time seems to have stood still since the seventeenth century in the peaceful Grande Rue of this little 'new town'.

The *Church* of the University of Paris, the *Sorbonne*, was commissioned by Richelieu and is Lemercier's best work (**761**). There are two fine façades to the street and to the university court. Both are of Roman design with two storeys of superimposed orders, pediment and side volutes linking the central portion to the aisle stages. The dome is impressive on the exterior, and also inside where there is an interior shell giving a different, more suitable silhouette within.

In 1646 Lemercier took over the completion of the *Church* of the *Val de Grâce* from Mansart, designing one of the finest domes of Paris (**760**). He also continued work on the Cour Carrée of the *Louvre*, repeating Lescot's wing on the north side.

François Mansart (1598–1666) was a more original architect than Lemercier and imparted to French architecture a national leadership which gave it a certain independence from Rome. Mansart had worked abroad and, in France, under de Brosse. His originality and qualities as an architect were offset by his personality, which was prickly and arrogant, losing him commissions such as the Val de Grâce Church, where he

764 *Château Vaux-le-Vicomte. Garden front, Louis Le Vau, 1657*

764

carried out much of the work but which was left to Lemercier to complete and take credit for.

Mansart designed several *châteaux* of which the one at *Balleroy* in Normandy is typical and exists today. Begun in 1626, it is a tall, well-planned, dignified country house built in local yellow stone with white ashlar facings and surmounted by high gabled roofs. It has a tall central pavilion with cupola and lower side blocks. At the *Château de Blois*, Mansart planned large-scale alterations and enlargements, but only part was built. The central block (1635–8) and quadrant colonnades are in Baroque style, towards which Mansart veered in his middle years. His best surviving work, and that which shows his mature ideas is the *Château de Maisons* (1642–50) (called Maisons-Lafitte since its purchase by Jacques Lafitte in 1818), near Paris. The surrounding gardens and estate are now curtailed by villa building, but the château itself stands altered only in part by nineteenth century development. Although not extensive it is impressive since it is one free-standing block, with short wings, built in stone with high slate roofs. It is the only one of his châteaux where the interior decorative schemes survive, and its hall and staircase are of great beauty. Both are vaulted, articulated with orders and decorated with carving and sculpture.

Mansart designed a number of *churches* of which the best is the *Val de Grâce* in *Paris*. This he carried out up to the first cornice line before Lemercier was commissioned to complete the work (though the whole plan was Mansart's). The interior is Baroque, and similar to Il Gesù in Rome; though structurally like the Italian church it lacks its warmth and colour. The vaults are panelled and decorated all over but not painted; high relief Baroque sculpture breaks the guilloche banding. There is a large, well-fenestrated dome and, below, a vast Bernini-style baldacchino.

French Baroque Architecture: Le Vau and J. H. Mansart

The second half of the seventeenth century was a great period for building and the visual arts in France. Louis XIV presided over an autocratic régime and thus dictated firmly the style that state artists should follow; if they did not do so

they did not receive further commissions. This type of rigid autocracy in the arts has, in many ages as, for example, in the Soviet Union today, had a restrictive, devitalising effect. This is because the state so often is dictating the course for political reasons and without insight and knowledge as a patron of the arts. Louis XIV's policy no doubt lost him the services of some gifted artists, but he was a great builder and an enlightened, cultured patron. The result, for France, was a time of spectacular success in such arts. Jean Baptiste Colbert was the King's chief advisor from the 1660s; he controlled artistic appointments as well as others and employed artists prepared to give their best for the greatness of France. He appointed *Charles Le Brun* to be in charge of the artistic activities of the Academies of France and Le Brun brought

765 *Church of S. Louis des Invalides, Paris, J. H. Mansart, 1679–1756*

together teams of artists: sculptors, painters, architects, craftsmen of all kinds.

In architecture, the official style was more Baroque than hitherto: Louis XIV liked its positive, theatrical quality. It developed in France on more restrained lines than in Italy, with less ornamental exuberance but the curving, plastic massing on buildings was seen more in the 40 years after 1660 than at any other time in French architectural history.

The two architects who adapted themselves best to this style were Le Vau and Mansart. *Louis Le Vau* (1612–70) was, in contrast to François Mansart, a pleasant, able, vigorous man who carried out successfully a large number of commissions in a style very near to Italian Baroque. Like Wren and Adam in England, he gathered a team of fine craftsmen around him, who decorated his buildings, which are chiefly large houses, with work of high quality. In Paris he built several hôtels such as those of the Île de S. Louis. The *Hôtel Lambert** was the best known of these; it still exists, but has been restored extensively and denuded of all exterior decoration.

France's most Baroque building is the *Institut de France*, built by Le Vau from 1661 as the Collège des Quatres Nations. This was the building, standing on the banks of the Seine, with its drum and dome rising above the central mass, which with its contrastingly concave colonnades so impressed the young Wren on his short visit to France. It is a classic Baroque layout, but with refined French style handling of orders and decoration. The sweep of these concave curves from the terminal pavilions to the domed centrepiece is viewed best from the Pont des Arts opposite (PLATE 100). The interior of the *Church of S. Sulpice* is also by Le Vau (1655); it is Italian in its decorative handling (**762**).

Louis Le Vau's most outstanding work is the *Château de Vaux-le-Vicomte*, begun in 1657 (**764**). This was commissioned by Nicolas Fouquet; and is the finest house of its day in France, forerunner of Louis XIV's Versailles. It is not an immense house; it is a free-standing block with tall, corner pavilions, built on a parapeted platform surrounded by a moat which encircles the house and inner court. The garden front has a convexly curved, pedimented centre-piece and dome to accommodate the cupola-

covered oval saloon inside. The gardens, laid out by *Le Nôtre*, are extensive, with fountains, grottoes, cascades, all foreshadowing Versailles. The interior decoration of the château is very fine, in stucco, sculpture and painting, mainly under the leadership of *Le Brun*. The saloon is the impressive room here; the lower part of the walls is articulated with Composite pilasters, with doorways and windows between in each bay. The doorways are on the entrance side leading from the hall and the windows face the garden. Above the entablature is a further stage of rectangular windows separated by caryatid sculptured figures and ornamented entablature above. Only the painted ceiling by Le Brun is not there, but his designs are shown on an easel in the saloon.

Fouquet, like Cardinal Wolsey at Hampton Court in England, paid the price for creating too magnificent a house while in the service of an autocratic, acquisitive monarch. He entertained the King and Queen and all the Court at Vaux-le-Vicomte in 1661 to show off his château with a suitable banquet, ballet and firework display. He was too successful. Within weeks he was arrested, imprisoned, his château and his team of artists taken over by royal decree.

J. H. Mansart was born Jules Hardouin (1646–1708), but later took the family name of his great-uncle François Mansart. His work soon showed him to be the successor to Le Vau rather than of his great-uncle and he became the most prolific, controversial and Baroque architect of France. Apart from his extensive contribution over long years at Versailles, his other works include the Church of Les Invalides, famous squares in Paris and the Château de Dampierre.

The great structure of *Les Invalides* had been built 1670–7 by *Libéral Bruant* to house disabled soldiers.* It is a severe but impressive layout planned in courts. Bruant built a chapel, but Louis XIV wanted a more impressive one; Mansart was commissioned to design it. The result, the *Church of S. Louis des Invalides*, is the most outstanding classical church of Paris, more Baroque than any other, especially in its stepped façade of grouped columns and its superb dome (**765**). It is designed on Greek cross plan, with circular chapels at the corners. The interior is very light and plain in contrast to the gilded richness of the dome and drum.

* This is attributed to Le Vau as stated on the façade plaque.

* The Royal Hospital, Chelsea was inspired by the idea of Les Invalides. It was built by Sir Christopher Wren 1682–92.

Plate 100
Institut de France (Collège des Quatres Nations), Paris, begun 1662, Le Vau *Paris, France*

Plates 101 and 102
Fountain, Place Stanislas, Nancy, France, 1760

Mansart rebuilt the *Château de Dampierre* in the early 1680s. He designed a large central rectangular block with recessed, pedimented front and advancing side pavilions. There is an extensive forecourt flanked by arcaded ranges. It is a pleasant, well-designed but not pretentious country house.

The Paris squares of the *Place Vendôme* and the *Place des Victoires* were laid out 1685–1700. The latter has been much altered, but the Place Vendôme still gives some idea of Mansart's Baroque street architecture. Its houses were built 1702–20.

The Palace of Versailles

Like most of the great royal palaces of Europe, Versailles was not the work of one architect or artist and, because of succeeding alterations, it is not the masterpiece it might have been. Many English visitors are disappointed in the palace itself. It is so famous yet it lacks vitality in its monotonous horizontal lines. What is superb are specific interiors, like the Hall of Mirrors, and the fountain layouts nearer the palace. The architectural importance of Versailles is that it is principally the *chef d'œuvre* of one king— Louis XIV—and that it became the prototype for subsequent palaces in all of Europe. Other countries did not copy Versailles but used it as a model: Spain, in Madrid and La Granja, Portugal, Queluz, Austria, Schönbrunn, Russia, the S. Petersburg Peterhof, etc. Only England has no Versailles.

Built over a long period from the early seventeenth century to the later eighteenth, Versailles is principally the work of three architects—*de Brosse, Le Vau* and *Jules Hardouin Mansart*. The palace, as a masterpiece, was probably created by Le Vau, but Mansart, on the King's insistence for greater accommodation space and impressiveness, made alterations and extensions which impaired the originality and character of Le Vau's palace. Mansart did not agree with what he had to do, but he was a court architect. *De Brosse* began Versailles for Louis XIII in 1624, *Le Vau* took over in 1661 under Louis XIV. In 1678, after Le Vau's death, *Mansart* was put in charge.

Today, the entrance front faces the vast Place d'Armes. From here, three roads radiate: the centre one, which leads direct from the King's bedroom, goes to Paris, 20 kilometres away. Turning one's back on the Place d'Armes, one enters the wrought iron gateway into the Cour d'Honneur, in the centre of which is the equestrian statue of Louis XIV. From here one comes to the Cour Royale and the Cour de Marbre; the state rooms are here. The Cour de Marbre is the oldest part of the present palace, parts of it surviving, though altered, from the Louis XIII building. It is now mainly the work of Le Vau, who extended the palace in a long rectangular block, adding on each side of the original court, leaving this still open on the main front but enclosed and with a terrace on the garden façade.

Mansart, when commanded to extend the accommodation and create a new impressive room, filled in Le Vau's terrace on the first floor, creating the Galerie des Glaces here and added further wings at each side, providing an immense 600 metre frontage on the garden side, monotonous in its repetition of Le Vau's articulation and unbroken horizontal skyline; there are no curves and no gabled roofs (**768**).

Apart from the fine buildings which Mansart constructed—the chapel, the stables, the orangery and, on the other side of the park, the Grand Trianon—he also designed some magnificent interiors, many decorated by Le Brun: the Hall of Mirrors and the chapel for instance. It is these and the extensive garden and parkland layout which have a breathtaking quality at Versailles. André Le Nôtre laid out these from 1665; there is a gradual descent from the garden elevation of the palace by means of terraces, sculptured cascades and fountains to the circular Apollo fountain at the end of the vista a kilometre away.

Mansart's Church of the Invalides and his *Royal Chapel* at *Versailles* are probably the most Baroque structures in France and the last before the eighteenth century developed along different lines. The chapel was begun in 1689 and completed in 1710. It is a tall, two-storeyed building, the lower floor for the courtiers and the public and the first floor, connecting with the King's apartments, for the royal family and guests. The exterior is richly articulated, and inside are painted ceilings and apse and colonnades of Corinthian columns, with an ambulatory all round at both levels. It illustrates the limits to

PALACES AND CHÂTEAUX IN FRANCE

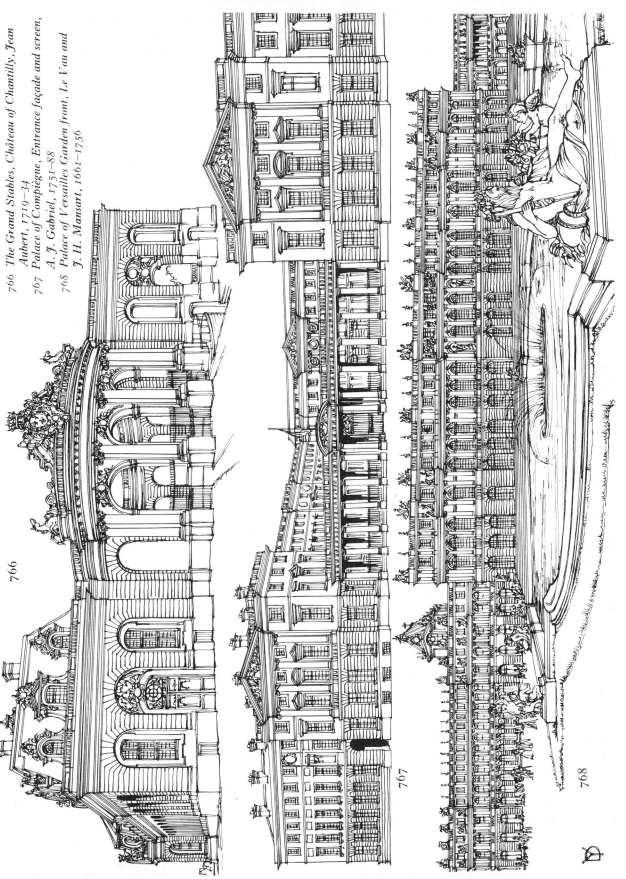

766 The Grand Stables, Château of Chantilly, Jean
     Aubert, 1719–34
767 Palace of Compiègne, Entrance façade and screen,
     A. J. Gabriel, 1751–88
768 Palace of Versailles Garden front, Le Vau and
     J. H. Mansart, 1661–1756

766

767

768

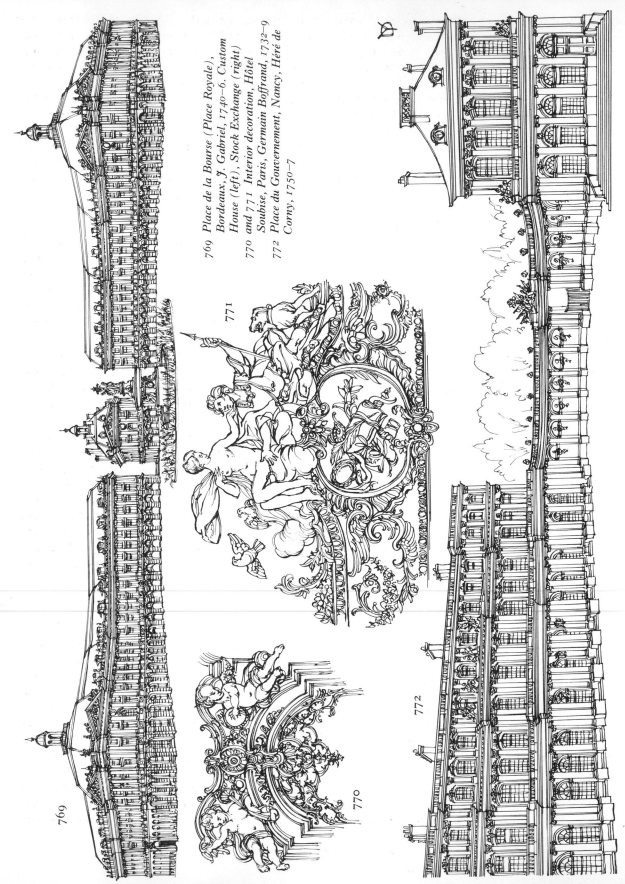

769 Place de la Bourse (Place Royale), Bordeaux, J. Gabriel, 1740–6. Custom House (left), Stock Exchange (right)
770 and 771 Interior decoration, Hôtel Soubise, Paris, Germain Boffrand, 1732–9
772 Place du Gouvernement, Nancy, Héré de Corny, 1750–7

which the French were prepared to go in their emulation of the Italian Baroque theme. There are few curves, entablatures and pediments are unbroken and rich colour is in the ceiling paintings only.

At this time also it was decided to complete the royal palace in Paris, the *Louvre*. Le Vau, who was building the Institut de France opposite, on the other side of the Seine, in the early 1660s, and who designed a bridge to connect the two buildings, was an obvious choice. He had already followed Lemercier in work on the east side of the Louvre in the 1650s. Colbert preferred to go elsewhere and at first asked François Mansart, then approached Italy. Bernini made several designs upon request, at first large-scale Baroque and later, in response to French preference, he designed an immense palace without curves. The plan was never fulfilled and Bernini did not trouble to hide his low opinion of French taste, architecture and craftmanship. Eventually the east façade of the Louvre was built 1667–70 as a three-man committee plan: *Le Vau, Le Brun* and *Charles Perrault*. There has always been discussion about who made the largest contribution. It is generally thought to have been Perrault—a writer, physician and amateur architect—and moreover, assistant to Colbert, perhaps the most important qualification of all.

Eighteenth Century French Classicism

Louis XIV died in 1715 after reigning for 72 years. His prolific, vigorous architect Jules Hardouin Mansart had died in 1708. A new style was ushered in, under Louis XV, which was in reaction from the majestic, imposing structures of the previous century. This style was Rococo and soon its popularity was spreading to other European countries, to Germany, Austria, Scandinavia, even to parts of Italy. The Italian dominance of the architectural and artistic world which had been unbroken since 1420 had passed and France became the leader of European fashion.

The style of Rococo is seen chiefly in the interiors and in decoration rather than structure. Exteriors were fairly plain, strictly classical and rather like work of the early seventeenth century. Inside, all was lightness, elegance and gaiety. Gone were the heavy gilding, the large painted schemes, the dark coloured marbling and the orders. Rococo

architecture tended to eschew the orders. The decoration which surrounded window and door openings and enclosed ceiling and wall panelling was in low relief and dainty with ribbons, scrolls, arabesques, wreaths of flowers, volutes, seaweed and shells replacing the Roman classical motifs. The term Rococo comes from the French *rocaille coquille*, the former appertaining to rocks or stones and the latter to shells. Colour schemes were also light, white being preferred for areas of wall with pastel shades and light gilding for decoration. Mirrors adorned the walls to increase the effect of light and to reflect the candelabra.

The chief architect of the years 1700–35 was *Robert de Cotte* (1656–1735) who built and decorated a number of Paris hôtels with his team of craftsmen. Another notable architect was *Jean Aubert* (*d.* 1741) who enlarged and redecorated the *Château de Chantilly* from 1719. He also built the fantastic stables there (**766**), the most impressive accommodation for horses in the world, and he redecorated in Rococo style Bullant's Petit Château adjoining the larger one (**678**). The main château was largely demolished in the Revolution and rebuilt in the later nineteenth century, but the stables remain.

Germain Boffrand (1667–1754) designed a number of hôtels and châteaux in these years. The latter include one at Lunéville and another at Craon. His best Rococo decoration is in the *Hôtel Soubise* in *Paris* (now the Archives Nationales). On the second floor, the Salon Ovale and the adjoining bedchamber were decorated by him in the years 1732–9. They are typical of high quality Rococo decoration and colouring (**770** and **771**).

Eighteenth Century Town Planning in France

In this century France took over the leadership from Italy in this field also. A number of schemes survive, still remarkably unspoilt and homogeneous. The most successful example is in the town centre at *Nancy*, which was mainly built in the years 1715–60. Boffrand had designed a royal palace when work was abandoned for political reasons. Later, in 1750, *Emmanuel Héré de Corny* carried out the grand scheme. He completed the palace (now the Palais Gouvernement) (**772**) and linked this by the tree-lined avenue, the *Place Carrière*, to the octagonal *Place Stanislas* (originally the Place Royale). A triumphal arch provides the entrance into the octagonal 'place' and on this side the buildings flanking it are only one storey high. At each lateral corner are beautiful sculptured fountains and iron gates (PLATE 101 and 102). The other three sides of the square are lined by taller buildings and opposite is the Hôtel de Ville. The whole scheme is in one style—rococo —one of the finest schemes of this type in Europe.

Others can still be seen in Lyons, Bordeaux, Rennes, Toulouse and Paris. The *Place Bellecour* (originally Louis le Grand) in Lyons was laid out by *Robert de Cotte* in 1713–38. It is an immense, tree-lined square which was unfortunately seriously damaged in the Revolution and was rebuilt in the early nineteenth century. The schemes in Rennes and Bordeaux are by the architect *Jacques-Jules Gabriel* (1667–1742) who was, after Robert de Cotte, chief assistant to Jules Hardouin Mansart. In Rennes, an extensive fire in 1720 made replanning necessary. Gabriel laid out the square round de Brosse's Palais de Justice and surrounded it with uniform classical buildings. Adjoining it, connected by an opening, he laid out another square containing the Hôtel de Ville and the theatre (1734–43).

Gabriel transformed the quayside area of the centre of *Bordeaux* in 1730–60 from a Medieval town to an eighteenth century classical one. This was his finest achievement, but the passage of years have not been kind to it. The *Place de la Bourse* (originally the Place Royale) is still there, with its fine buildings on an immense, shallow curve with a central fountain (**769**). Gabriel's nearby *Esplanade des Quinconces*, with its flanking Allées (originally the Place de Bourgogne), still possesses its entrance triumphal arch, but it is a sad, neglected place today; the former glories have long since departed.

The *Place Capitole* in *Toulouse* is an impressive, homogeneous square with a 400 feet long town hall along one whole side. This was the work of a local architect *Guillaume Camnas* in 1750–3. It has an imposing, boldly articulated Ionic façade.

The eighteenth century building in the Place de la Concorde in Paris is the work of *Ange-Ange-Jacques Gabriel* (1698–1782) who succeeded his father Jacques Jules Gabriel on the latter's death in 1742 as chief architect to Louis XV made his reputation in his designs for the *Petit Trianon* at *Versailles* (1762). The most outstanding French architect of the second half of the eighteenth century, Gabriel led the way in mid-century, together with architects like Jean Nicolas Servandoni (1695–1766) and Jacques Germain Soufflot (1714–80) away from rococo curves and to a return to symmetry, use of orders in a monumental manner and restraint in decoration. His Petit Trianon is a perfect, though small-scale example of this, while his *École Militaire* in the Champs de Mars in *Paris* (1751–68) is a larger, bolder one. These buildings have something in common with the contemporary English Palladians, but they are more vital, plastic and less stolidly monotonous.

It was decided in 1757 to develop a large square in *Paris* round the centrepiece of an equestrian statue of the King, to be called Place Louis XV (now *Place de la Concorde*). The square was to be laid out along the Seine with the Tuileries Gardens on its eastern side and the Champs Elysées on the west. The north/south axis would be formed by a new bridge on the south (not built till 1790, Pont de la Concorde) and a new road running northwards, the Rue Royale, which would terminate its vista with a church dedicated to S. Mary Magdalene (built in the early nineteenth century, the Madeleine). *Gabriel* built the two palaces in the square, flanking the southern end of the Rue Royale, 1761–70. They are twin palaces with Corinthian colonnades and pedimented end pavilions. The square itself was laid out to cover 810 by 565 square feet within the central space (though much larger to the building façades), and Louis XV's equestrian statue was placed in the centre. During the Revolution it was destroyed and the guillotine set up on the spot which today is marked by the obelisk.

Another fine work by Gabriel is the *Palace at Compiègne* which he rebuilt from the old château from 1751. This has similar qualities of monumentality and vitality to his Concorde palaces (**767**).

Eighteenth Century Churches

In France, as in England, this was not a great century for church building. The designs displayed the same tendencies as secular architecture; a return to symmetrical, monumental classicism. *Jean Servandoni* shows this quality in his façade for *S. Sulpice* in *Paris* (1733–45),

773

773 The Panthéon, Paris, J. G. Soufflot, 1757—90

while the *Madeleine Church* in *Besançon* (1766) is even more monumental. The outstanding church of the time is a pure example of neo-classicism: the *Panthéon* in *Paris*. It was begun in 1757, designed by *Jacques Germain Soufflot* and dedicated to the patron saint of Paris, S. Geneviève; the building became a Panthéon with the Revolution and great Frenchmen are buried here: Voltaire, Mirabeau, Rousseau, Victor Hugo and many more. It is a pure, cold, supremely classical building, based on its prototype and namesake in Rome but, being an eighteenth century structure, the dome is supported on a drum, which is carried on pendentives, in turn supported on the four crossing piers. The architect's idea was to provide a S. Peter's based on the Pantheon and to eclipse the other domes of Paris, notably that of Les Invalides. In fact,

Soufflot's dome is more like S. Paul's in London and, as a dome, much less fine than S. Peter's; it lacks the Baroque warmth of the original.

The exterior of the Panthéon is very plain. It is on Greek cross plan with four equal arms under a central dome. There is only one exterior feature, the great Corinthian portico. Apart from this, the one-storey exterior walls are plain, with only entablature and parapet.

The interior is in keeping, but a little less formal. There is still the same symmetry of an almost too perfect centrally planned church. All is light stone, apart from the wall paintings and sculptural groups. The wall paintings date from 1877 onwards. Some are very fine, particularly those by Puvis de Chavannes, representing the life of S. Geneviève. The Corinthian order is used throughout the building and a colonnade extends all round the church. Soufflot had intended columns to support the dome pendentives, but he died in 1780 before the church was finished and his successor, Rondelet, turned these into the present piers, which were a pioneering example in France of the use of concrete reinforced with metal. The central drum creates a light interior. The cupola is coffered and the lantern painted as are also the pendentives. Over each arm of the church are coffered saucer domes (773).

England

Although English architects built in classical form during this whole period from 1625 onwards, it never became the style at which the English excelled as they had in Gothic. In the Middle Ages England created buildings which compete on equal terms with the work of any country in Europe, even France. Many fine classical buildings were produced also, especially in country houses and terrace architecture, but few examples compare to the Italian Baroque or the best of the French contribution. Apart from the work of certain outstanding, original architects such as Wren, Vanbrugh and Adam, English productions tended to be stolid, well designed and built but lacking in originality and vigour. S. Paul's Cathedral in London, the only great English classical church, cannot compare to the Medieval ones at Canterbury or York or Salisbury. It remains derivate and non-indigenous.

The English continued to create their best classical work in domestic architecture. In the years 1650–70 a more purely classical style of house was evolved from the Flemish-gabled brick buildings of the previous 30 years. This new type is often incorrectly termed a 'Wren-style house'; incorrectly because the style was developed before Wren was practising as an architect and because he designed little domestic work. The architects building this type of house, which was really a version of Dutch Palladian, were *John Webb* (1611–74), *Sir Roger Pratt* (1620–84) and *Hugh May* (1622–84). Pratt's finest house was *Coleshill*, Berkshire (1650–2), sadly destroyed by fire in 1952. It was a simple, symmetrical, rectangular block with no orders on the façade. Above the entablature was a hipped roof and tall chimney stacks. Hugh May's *Eltham Lodge, Kent* (1663–4) still exists. This is a brick and stone house with an Ionic giant order in the central portico. The house is strictly symmetrical and with a horizontal emphasis like Coleshill. Such designs were still Renaissance in character and Eltham Lodge closely resembles the Mauritshuis in the Hague (**691**).

Sir Christopher Wren (1632–1723)

To say that Wren was England's leading architect is an understatement. No other architect has ever held such a supreme position in England, while his reputation has remained uniformly high ever since his death. He was fortunate in that when he was beginning to practise great opportunities opened up before him, largely due to the Great Fire of London. He obtained commissions for civic and eccleciastical building as a result and he was early able to establish his reputation for original design. Other architects of genius such as Inigo Jones and Robert Adam had the ill-fortune to miss such opportunities.

Wren's work dominated the architecture in England of the second half of the seventeenth century. He was the vital force in all the important schemes, directing, influencing and controlling the design and execution of large projects such as the rebuilding of London after the fire of 1666 and the layouts at Hampton Court and Greenwich. His entry into the architectural profession was, by today's standards, unconventional. He was a brilliant young man, interested in many subjects but chiefly scientific matters. He was one of the founder members of the Royal Society and was described by John Evelyn, a fellow member, as 'that miracle of a youth'. Not till after he was 30 years old did he begin to practise architecture and, only a year or two later, was appointed principal architect to rebuild the City of London after its devastation. He designed a new layout on classical lines which was approved by King and Parliament, but foundered on the commercial city interests, which refused to yield up part of their rights for the general good of the city of London. Only an autocratic King or State like Louis XIV could have enforced acceptance of the scheme and, as a result, Londoners lost the chance of having riverside quays and walks by the Thames, as the Seine has, and broad boulevards with architectural vistas such as Paris achieved under Napoleon III. In the seventeenth century, London's city was re-created on the Medieval plan of narrow streets with tall, restricted, buildings. After two World Wars, the City's intransigence continues and we now have skyscraper blocks on the same ill-designed Medieval sites.

Despite the abandonment of his plan, Wren's part in the rebuilding was a large one. He was responsible for 53 churches and a new S. Paul's Cathedral. The *city churches* are, even in a career so full of great schemes and original architecture, an outstanding part of it. They show clearly his fertility of imagination and his ability to solve the most difficult problems of site, limitation of space and variation of style. None of the churches is quite like any other, although they are nearly all classical. Some have towers, some tall steeples and, one or two, cupolas. They are of stone and/or brick. Some are large and richly decorated, others are small and simple. The sites vary enormously and few are level or possess any parallel sides of equal length. The quality differs also; more money was available in some cases and Wren was more closely associated with the supervision of some than others. The most outstanding are *S. Bride*, Fleet Street (1680–1701), *S. Mary-le-Bow* (1671–80), *S. Stephen Walbrook* (1675–87), *S. Martin Ludgate* (1685–95), *S. Andrew-by-the-Wardrobe, S. Lawrence Jewry* (1670–86), *Christ Church*, Newgate Street (1704) and *S. Magnus the Martyr*, London Bridge (1670–1705). Most of these churches were damaged, some seriously, in the Second World War, but all are now fully restored.

Wren gathered a team of craftsmen to work for him in the churches and in other commissions. Some of the glass, carving, ironwork and painting is superb. *Grinling Gibbons* is the best known name among the carvers; he acquired a reputation for his naturalistic free-carved groups of flowers, birds and fruit. *Jean Tijou* was a French ornamental ironworker whose gates and grilles in the churches, S. Paul's and Hampton Court Palace are in the highest standard of craftsmanship (**780**). *Sir James Thornhill* carried out many of the great ceiling paintings as, for example, at Greenwich, Hampton Court Palace and in the dome of S. Paul's.

Wren made several designs for *S. Paul's Cathedral*, one of which, based on Greek cross plan, would have been much more original and impressive than the present building. It was rejected by the Church Commissioners (as Michelangelo's Greek cross plan for S. Peter's had been by the Pope, p. 10), because more space was desired and this would be provided by a Latin cross plan (**775**). The clergy in England also wanted a tall steeple. Wren compromised with a lofty, imposing dome and, by means of an inner brick cone to support the lantern and an inner shell to give a suitable shape to the interior cupola, solved the problems as other architects had done before him.

S. Paul's is one of a limited number of seventeenth century buildings in England to have Baroque characteristics. Wren often designed partly in Baroque manner; he had been most impressed on his only visit abroad by his study of Le Vau's Château de Vaux-le-Vicomte and the Institut de France in Paris (p. 90). The Baroque characteristics can be seen in the west front of S. Paul's, particularly in its western towers and in their juxtaposition with the dome. Due to the length of the church and the uphill slope of the ground from west to east, it is difficult to get a good view of the dome and towers from the west. Post-war building on Ludgate Hill has worsened this situation but this is more than compensated for in the fine view now available from the south-east; a view created by war-time bombing and fortunately preserved (**776**). S. Paul's is a straightforward example of a classical church built on Latin cross plan with dome and drum over the crossing. It is cool, clear, well-designed and built but lacking that spark, vitality

774 *Chapel dome and colonnade, Royal Naval College, Greenwich*

775 and 776 *S. Paul's Cathedral, London. Ground plan and the view from the south-east, 1675–1710*

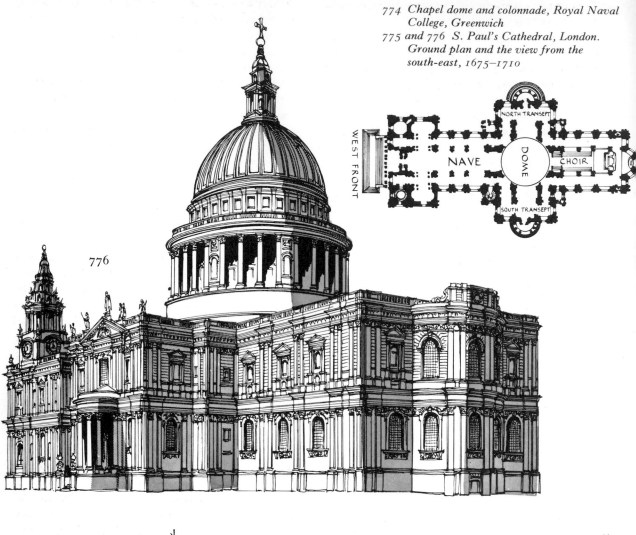

and warmth possessed by the great churches of the world in this style.

Much more of this quality is to be found in Wren's work at Hampton Court, Greenwich and the universities. *Hampton Court Palace* had been built in Tudor style for Henry VIII, but was in a neglected condition by the late seventeenth century. Wren was asked to enlarge the palace and he worked there from 1689–1701. He added new suites of fine rooms in buildings of brick and stone which, despite the very different styles, harmonise well with the Tudor brickwork. This is English classical domestic architecture at its best; a foreign style interpreted in indigenous materials by a great national architect, with no attempt to base the work on foreign models. Hampton Court Palace is unique; it could be seen in no other country but England.

The *Royal Hospital Greenwich* (now the Royal Naval College) was a larger project still. The Tudor Greenwich Palace was in decay. Inigo Jones' Queen's House remained and John Webb had begun a new palace but had only completed one block, the King Charles II building in 1669. The enterprise lapsed again. William and Mary decided to build here a naval counterpart to Chelsea Hospital (see Les Invalides, p. 90). Wren was put in charge of the project. He designed the whole scheme and carried out a fair part of it, though it was not finally completed till 1752. The layout is finest when viewed from the riverside as the visitor approaches the two main facing buildings with their colonnades and cupolas (which cover the hall and chapel respectively). At the end of the vista is Inigo Jones' Queen's House. The curving cupolas here contrast with the severe colonnades to illustrate Wren's version of Baroque (**774**).

Wren carried out a great deal of work at the two *universities*. At *Oxford* he designed the *Sheldonian Theatre* (1669) and, at *Cambridge*, *Pembroke College Chapel* (1663), *Emmanuel College* (1668) and, his best work here, the *library* at *Trinity College* (1676–84) (**783**).

Wren did not die until he was a very old man of 91, in 1723. Some years before this, styles in architecture had begun to change and new ideas were being put forward. The old master had lived too long. The work of the first quarter of the eighteenth century is more Baroque in general layout and massing of its architectural

forms than any seen in England before or since. Wren had used Baroque themes in the sense of 'movement', of curves, chiaroscuro and decoration. The architects of the early eighteenth century—*Vanbrugh, Hawksmoor, Archer*—were large-scale builders with a Baroque quality in their use of contrasting light and shade, mass against mass, though, in detail, the English version was unlike any other European Baroque; cube and rectangular blocks were more common than curves. Their contemporaries were divided, as have been their successors, in estimating their work. To study the creations of these architects is an experience which may excite and uplift or cause dismay and abhorrence; it cannot fail to make a strong impact.

Sir John Vanbrugh (1664–1726) had, like Archer and Hawksmoor, worked with Wren on a number of projects, at Greenwich, for example. When he designed his own great houses, he created grouped buildings of forceful, powerful masses, contrasting with one another, sometimes discordantly. This was quite different from his work under Wren. He was a master of handling masses of stone in a three-dimensional way, at creating exciting patterns in light and shade in settings of grandeur. His Flemish ancestry shows in his Baroque treatment of classical form, in the robustness of his porticoes, towers and wall articulation. His three famous houses are *Seaton Delaval* and *Castle Howard* in the north of England and *Blenheim Palace* near Oxford. All built in the early eighteenth century, they are large and imposing (**777**). Blenheim, for instance, has an entrance frontage of 856 feet, comprising an immense central block with portico and wings embracing a great court. These houses were the last of such gigantic residences, which became obsolete because of their size and cost.

Much of Archer's and Hawksmoor's work was ecclesiastical. *Thomas Archer*'s (1668–1743) Baroque style was reminiscent of Wren's, as at the *Church of S. Paul, Deptford* (1730), but *S. John's Church, Westminster* (1721–8) was much weightier; this, his best and most typical work, was gutted during the war, but has been rebuilt. His *Birmingham Cathedral* (1709–25) is especially Baroque in its tower and lantern. *Nicholas Hawksmoor*'s (1661–1736) designs, in church and university, were as controversial and forceful as Vanbrugh's. His best known churches are in the

777 *Entrance hall, Castle Howard, Yorkshire,*
    Vanbrugh, 1696–1712
778 *S. Mary-le-Strand, London, Gibbs, 1719*
779 *Ceiling, 20, Portman Square, London,*
    Adam, 1772–7
780 *Hampton Court Palace, iron screen, Jean*
    Tijou

781 *Queen's College, Oxford, Hawksmoor, 1709–59*
782 *Camden Crescent, Bath, Jelly, 1788*
783 *Trinity College Library, Cambridge, Wren, 1676–84*

781

782

783

East End of London and were damaged in the Second World War. *S. Mary Woolnoth* in the City survives to show his style clearly. He is also noted for his work at *All Souls' College, Oxford* (a Baroque Medievalism) and *Queen's College* nearby (**781**). Hawksmoor's architecture is highly original, especially his church steeples which are uncompromising and extremely bold.

Baroque architecture in England had been a foreign implant, duly anglicised. In the 1720s it died and was replaced by something much more English: *Palladianism*. The basis of this movement was also foreign—Andrea Palladio (p. 15) —but became, partly because it derived equally from the architecture of Inigo Jones (p. 34), particularly English. Palladian architecture in

784 The hall, Houghton Hall, Norfolk, Colen Campbell, c. 1730

784

England was the leading style from 1720–60; its chief patron, also an architect, was *Lord Burlington* and its leading architects *Colen Campbell* (*d.* 1729) and *William Kent* (1685–1748). The style developed into something neither Palladio nor Inigo Jones. It was more rigid and prescribed.

The outstanding contribution of the Palladian school was in country house building. The exterior of these houses was generally plain and monumental, almost severe. A porticoed central block would be connected to side pavilions by low galleries and colonnades. The whole scheme is fully symmetrical with careful attention to Roman classical proportion, orders and detail (as enunciated by Palladio). The houses appear to be four-square, solid and indisputably English. What makes them into masterpieces, on the exterior, is the siting and surroundings, for the parkland and gardens are in contrast and thus complementary to the architecture. The Palladian house was carefully set on rising ground, at the foot of a vista or by a stream or lake. The peculiarly English park was then laid out round it, with sweeping lawns, great spreading trees and natural landscape, decorated by classical temples and sculpture. Lancelot (Capability) Brown became famous as the chief exponent of this type of landscaping. He made lakes from streams and moved whole hillsides to where he needed them. This treatment is indigenous, very different from French or Italian gardens based on the geometrical formalities of Versailles. It was envied and copied later by other European nations, notably by Catherine the Great of Russia.

Typical of the large Palladian house are two examples in Norfolk: *Holkham Hall* designed by *William Kent* from 1734 and *Houghton Hall* by *Colen Campbell* (*c.* 1730) (**784**). The interiors are, in contrast to the plainness of the outside, masterpieces of Roman décor, or rather Roman orders and ornament adapted to the needs of English country house saloons, halls and dining rooms. The classical decoration is correct in proportion and handling; it is strong, three-dimensional and used in woodcarving as on doorcases and in stucco on ceilings and walls. There is nothing of the rococo delicacy in such interiors. Gilt and colours are used, though ceilings often have white grounds. Mahogany is employed for furniture and general woodwork and marble for chimney-pieces. At Holkham the hall and saloon are especially impressive. The Palladians also designed some houses more faithfully to Palladio's originals. Two examples are based on the Villa Capra (the Rotonda) near Vicenza (p. 17). *Lord Burlington*'s *Chiswick House* is one of these; a symmetrical block surmounted by a central cupola.

James Gibbs (1682–1754) was an architect whose work is neither fully Baroque nor Palladian; it is individually 'Gibbs', but with an affinity to Wren. This shows especially in his church steeples, though his years working in Rome are also reflected in these buildings. Churches like *S. Mary-le-Strand* (**778**) (1714–17) and *S. Martin-in-the-Fields* (1722), both in London, are among his best work; they had a great influence on other architects, especially in the U.S.A. Gibbs carried out much university work; his *Senate House* and his *Fellows' Building* at *King's College*, both at *Cambridge*, are fine examples of his meticulous classical detail and sure instinct for taste and proportion.

The Classical Revival: 1760–1800

It was in these years that Greek classical architecture was discovered and studied. Travellers, both professional architects and antiquarians as well as aristocratic young men on their 'Grand Tour', were setting out from all over Western Europe to see at first hand the masterpieces of the classical past. They now went further afield, not just to France and Italy as before but to Greece, Dalmatia, Egypt, Syria. Some returned travellers became ardent Greek enthusiasts, others retained a preference for Roman forms. In England, as in other countries, a 'battle of the styles' developed and some architects designed in only one or the other.

The two chief architects of these years were exactly contemporary, both Scottish, though in temperament and approach to architecture completely different from one another. *Sir William Chambers* (1723–96) was a close adherent to the Palladian tradition and designed most of his buildings in strictly Roman classical form. His work was of the highest standard, with fine proportion and an exacting excellence of detail and finish. He was the King's favourite architect and the Surveyor General, and thus in charge of all important building schemes. Among the public works of the time, Chambers was responsible for the new *Somerset House*, built on the site of the old palace. It was a difficult commission, being an unusual site: 800 feet on the river façade and only 135 feet on the north front in the Strand. There was then no embankment and the river elevation would be lapped by water, so Chambers built a masonry platform above tide level to support warehouses and offices and fronted it by a rusticated masonry arcade pierced by arches. The façade was divided into three blocks, with a central archway and two side watergates, so that the tide was controlled by the waters' entry into these archways. Contemporary drawings show that the building must have then been much more impressive as much of the height is now lost by the construction of

the modern roadway and embankment. This is still one of London's finest waterfront monuments, of Portland stone, built and finished in Roman classical design.

In contrast to Chambers the Roman traditionalist, *Robert Adam* (1728–92) was an innovator, a seeker after new ideas and designs. In the years 1760–90, he carried out a vast quantity of work mostly in domestic architecture and drew his inspiration from a wide variety of sources. Like Wren in his city church design, no two houses by Adam are alike. He drew from sources such as Roman Imperial palaces or baths, Greek temples of Athens or Asia Minor, villas from Herculaneum. Also like Wren, he used such sources and then stamped his own personal interpretation upon them. Unlike the Palladians, he followed no rigid rule system. He abhorred such practice,

785 The dining room, Syon House, Middlesex, Adam, 1761–70

785

considering it limiting to an artist's creative ability. He adapted the older classical forms and interpreted them, so that the result was always clearly and recognisably Adam but also, despite his amendments, had more of the spirit of the original than Palladian architecture ever approached of Palladio.

Some of Adam's finest houses show these qualities clearly. *Syon House*, near London (from 1762) and *Kedleston Hall*, Derbyshire (1758–68) illustrate his palatial Roman style. There is rich colour, fine coloured and white marbles, gilt decoration with stucco, and layouts influenced by the great Roman halls and baths. At Syon these can be seen in the Hall, the ante-room (PLATE 104) and the dining room (**785**), while at Kedleston the hall and saloon are monumental master-pieces. At *Osterley*, Middlesex and the library at *Kenwood* the decoration is more delicate with the motifs nearer Greek origins: slenderer columns and pilasters and ceilings in pastel shades and white with arabesques in stucco. In the 1770s Adam's decorative work became very low relief and finespun, almost filigree, a tendency of which his ceiling in the music room in the *Portman Square* house in London is a classic example (**779**).

Like Wren, Adam had some fine craftsmen working for him, including the painters *Angelica Kauffmann* and her husband *Antonio Zucchi*, the stuccoist *Joseph Rose* and the sculptor and carver *Joseph Wilton*. The ceiling paintings, stucco work, metalwork, carving and furniture in the Adam houses are, in many cases, works of art in their own right. Adam was a perfectionist; he de-manded and obtained high standards.

Terrace Architecture

As in France and Italy, a number of planning schemes were initiated, especially in the eight-eenth century. Since the days of Inigo Jones London had been laid out in squares, but the buildings differed from one another. From the eighteenth century, terraces, crescents and whole squares were designed as an architectural unit, with façades alike or in keeping with their neighbours. The earliest developments were in *Bath* where *John Wood*, and his son of the same name, built first *Queen Square* (1728–35), then the *Circus* (1754)—a complete circle of 33

identical houses with superimposed orders over three storeys—and, most impressive of all, the *Royal Crescent* (1765–75). This is an immense curving terrace of 30 houses separated by a giant Ionic order of 114 columns. It is built on a hillside overlooking the city. Other schemes were begun in *Bristol, Cheltenham* and *Brighton* (**782**).

One of the most magnificent and enterprising town planning schemes was the *Adelphi* fronting the river Thames in *London*, near Westminster. This was the work of *Robert Adam* and his brothers, and consisted of a row of houses in the form of Roman Imperial palace architecture high on a terrace platform above the river; the land had previously been a muddy backwater. Almost the whole scheme was demolished unnecessarily in 1937. Adam also designed two city squares in the last years of his life. He did not live to see them built, and both have been altered though some complete elevations remain largely as he designed them: *Fitzroy Square, London* (east and south side) and *Charlotte Square, Edinburgh* (north side).

The eighteenth century in England was a time of high architectural standards in building design and detail. Of the many good architects who created fine buildings in different versions of classicism, as well as a touch of sham Gothic or Indian or Chinese, were *Thomas Leverton, Henry Holland, George Dance II, Sir Robert Taylor* and *James Wyatt*.

The Iberian Peninsula: Spain

The Renaissance came late to Spain and lasted well into the seventeenth century. Most of the architecture between 1670 and 1780 is Baroque, then in the second half of the eighteenth century came some more formal neo-classicism. Spanish Baroque reflects, like Spanish Gothic, the mixed heritage of the peninsula. There are strong influences from Italian Baroque, more limited ones from France, and still the fundamental underlying Moorish and Mujédar art forms which appear in the new designs as much as they had in the Medieval. The warm-blooded vitality, the lack of control and restraint, the plastic approach which had been seen in late Gothic and Renaissance plateresque architecture found most complete expression in the Baroque style. It was made to measure for Spanish exuberance and

786

788

787

789

790

786 Plaza Mayor,
Salamanca. (Town Hall
centre), Alberto de
Churriguera, 1729–40
787 and 788 Details of
the Palace of the Marqués
de Dos Aguas, Valencia,
1740–4
789 Façade, the Cartuja
Church at Jerez de la
Frontera, 1667
790 Façade, the Univer-
sity, Valladolid. Begun
1715, Diego and Narciso
Tomé

fanaticism, spilling out in the Counter Reformation. Not all Spanish Baroque architecture is uncontrolled and frenzied; this type of work is often called Churrigueresque. Some Baroque work, especially in the seventeenth century and the later eighteenth is much more restrained and formal. In general, though, Spanish Baroque is original, emotional and free. It does not resemble French, English or German Baroque at all. It is fiercely individual and Latin.

In the second half of the seventeenth century the Spanish love of decoration began to assert itself in reaction from Herrera's plain Renaissance architecture and found expression in early Baroque experiments. Much of Spain at this time was economically unsettled and poorly developed, the east and north-east regions flourishing most because of close trade links with the Neapolitan kingdom in Italy. In this region is the *Church* of *S. Catalina* in *Valencia* with its hexagonal tower (1688–1705) and the *Cathedral of La Seo* in *Zaragoza*. This is a Medieval church, its interior mainly reconstructed in the sixteenth century in late Gothic and early Renaissance style, but the façade is Baroque with a tower of 1682–90 designed by the Italian *Giovanni Battista Contini*.

In the south the façade of *Granada Cathedral* was designed by *Alonso Cano* (1601–67) and built after his death. This is a massive west front, Baroque in its heaviness but without orders and with little decoration. The most beautiful example of Spanish early Baroque workmanship can be seen in the façade added to the Medieval *Church* of the *Carthusian Monastery* (Cartuja) at *Jerez de la Frontera* (**789**). Dating from 1667, by an unknown architect, the façade combines a classic Baroque structure on Italian lines with southern Spanish decorative forms.

The Eighteenth Century

The term *Churrigueresque* is taken from the family of four brothers and three sons of de Churriguera who worked largely in Castile in the late seventeenth and early eighteenth century. *José de Churriguera* (1650–1725), head of the family, was chiefly a carver who specialised in designing the ornate, complex retablos essential to all Spanish churches. He worked chiefly in Salamanca, as did several members of the family

(all carvers and architects), transforming colleges, churches and the New Cathedral with Baroque decoration inside and outside the buildings. There is irony in the fact that José's name became a synonym for all that is most extravagant in Spanish Baroque, for his own work, and that of several of his relatives, was restrained, even Herreran on occasions.

Alberto de Churriguera (1676–1750), a younger brother and the most talented member of the family, laid out the *Plaza Mayor* at *Salamanca* (**786**) with Andres García de Quiñones. This is a magnificent town planning scheme, a courtyard layout and, like that at Madrid (**730**) was closed to traffic by the four continuous sides of houses and arcades. Unlike Madrid, it is no longer traffic-free. Alberto also completed the façade of *Valladolid Cathedral* (1729) by adding the upper storey to the central portal. This is restrained, in keeping with yet a foil to Herrera's façade (p. 60), having plain pilasters and a pediment and side scrolls.

The Churrigueresque style, which was developed chiefly by other architects, is seen primarily in portal and frontispiece design on a building exterior or retablo within. It is characterised by barley sugar columns, broken and arched pediments and entablatures, pilasters with more than one capital and a quantity of ornament in the form of flowers, medallions, figures, fruit and drapery.

Working in central Spain were two of the chief exponents of the style: *Pedro de Ribera* (Rivera) (*c.* 1683–1742) and Narciso Tomé. De Ribera was the principal architect to Madrid, where most of his work was done, though, unfortunately, not a great deal has survived unaltered. Among his churches still exist *Nuestra Señora de Montserrat* (1720) and *S. José*. The façade of the former is impressive, built in brick with stone facings. There is a Baroque tower and steeple. Inside, the church is not finished and is fairly plain. His centrepiece to the *Hospicio San Fernando* (1722–9) is typical Churrigueresque. Built in three diminishing stages, it is a riot of exuberant decoration, ebbing and flowing, yet controlled (PLATE 106). His *Toledo Bridge* (1723–4) is monumental; it has a richly sculptured shrine on each side of the centre arch.

Narciso Tomé worked under José de Churriguera at Salamanca, then carried out the decoration of the *University façade* at *Valladolid* with

Plate 103
Carved wood altar
rail detail. Church of
S. Michael, Louvain,
Belgium, 1650–6
Plate 104
Wall panel, ante
room, Syon House,
England, from 1762,
Robert Adam.
Stuccowork Joseph
Rose

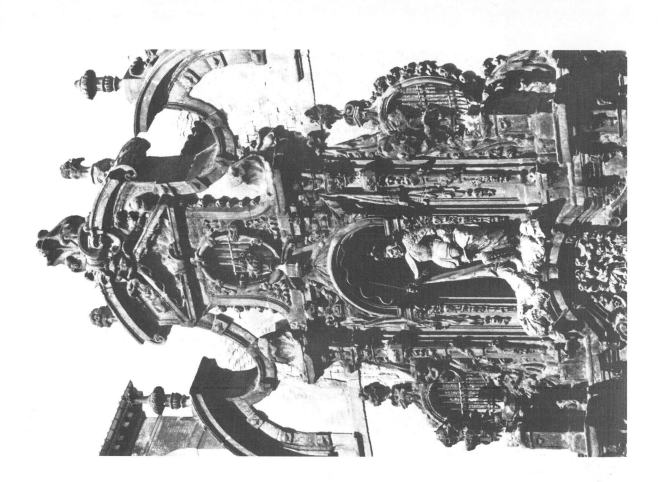

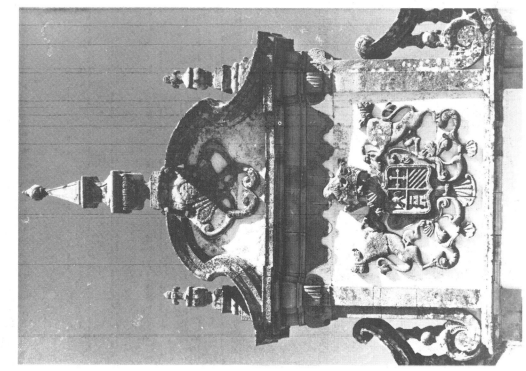

Plate 105
Gable detail, Palacio Mateus, Vila Real, Portugal. Early
18th century
Plate 106
Doorway detail, Hospicio de San Fernando, Madrid,
Spain. 1722, Pedro de Ribera

791 *The Cathedral from the south-west, Santiago de Compostela, Spain. Baroque towers and façade, Fernando Casas y Nuova, 1738–49*

BAROQUE CATHEDRALS IN SPAIN

792 *Façade, Valencia Cathedral, Rudolf and Vergara, 1703*

793 *Façade, Murcia Cathedral, Jaimé Bort y Meliá, 1740–54*

794 *El Pilar, Zaragoza (viewed from the river bridge to the north-east). From 1677, Francisco de Herrera; from 1750, Ventura Rodriguez*

792

793

794

his brother Diego (**790**). This has a tall frontis-piece decorated like a retablo. In 1721 Narciso Tomé was made the principal architect to *Toledo Cathedral* where he created the most fantastic monument to Churrigueresque art, the *Trasparente*, behind the high altar (1732). This is a masterpiece of sculpture and painting, the two blending together as a carefully contrived theatrical creation. Tomé produced his special lighting effects by cutting a circular hole in one bay of the Gothic quadripartite vault in the eastern ambulatory, raising the ceiling height to permit a large plain glass window through which the easterly sun shines. The window opening is then framed with Baroque sculpture and the whole area blends in paint and stucco. As the light shines through, the whole sculptural tableau of the *Trasparente* opposite comes to life; the brilliant sun on the upper part of cherubims, a lesser light on the Last Supper below, then it gradually diminishes as the eye descends past the golden rays radiating from the centre among the angels to the Virgin and Child at the bottom of the group. In a westerly light the whole tableau becomes dead and flat.

Contemporary with the Churrigueresque school in Castile was the Seville school led by the Figueroa family and, in the Granada area, the richly ornamental work of Hurtado Izquierdo. *Leonardo de Figueroa* (c. 1650–1730) worked in *Seville* with his two sons and nephew. They created a number of Baroque churches, very typical of the region and displaying the traditional Mujédar qualities of decoration. The area is stoneless, so brick was widely used, faced with brilliantly coloured ceramic tiling, especially on towers and cupolas. The *Church of S. Pablo* is like this, a Mujédar building rebuilt by Figueroa. The *Church of S. Luis* is more traditionally Italian Baroque, with its Greek cross plan and deep entrance narthex, but it has the Spanish Baroque decorative features of barley sugar columns, broken entablatures and rich decoration, as well as a brightly coloured tiled façade. Figueroa also built the *Seminary of S. Telmo* here which has an impressive frontispiece.

Francisco Hurtado Izquierdo (1669–1725) was the leading architect in the Granada area. Here, the strongest influence, even in the eighteenth century, was still Moorish. In the *Cartuja* at *Granada*, Izquierdo designed a *sacristy* (1713) based on the sumptuous richness of the Alhambra interiors, using the Arabic motifs and creating a masterpiece of flowing, vibrant richness in his all-over decoration. The walls are gleaming white marble, broken frequently with fantastically decorated pilasters and entablature. The ceiling is also riotously decorated and has a painted oval dome over the altar as well as painted pendentives. The materials used for ornamentation are all colourful and glowing: marbles, tortoiseshell, ivory, mother-of-pearl. It is extravagant, restless, beautiful and supreme Churrigueresque.

Izquierdo also designed the *Trasparente* for the Monastery Church of *El Paular* (near Madrid) in 1718. This is in the tiny Capilla de Tabernáculo behind the high altar retablo screen. It is Baroque run riot and of much coarser, poorer workmanship than the sacristy at Granada. However, it was built by Izquierdo's pupils and it is at the moment in poor condition.

There is a considerable quantity of Baroque work in the *cathedrals* of Spain especially those in the south and primarily in façades added to Medieval or Renaissance buildings. The most impressive large-scale example, the *Cathedral of Santiago de Compostela* in north-west Spain, is also the most successful blending of a Romanesque masterpiece with a Baroque one. The interior is still almost entirely Romanesque (**319**) as is the famous Portico de la Gloria. The cathedral has simply been clothed almost all over with a Baroque dress, rich and articulated; the combination of the two styles is outstanding. The façade, with its lofty, multi-stage frontispiece and flanking western towers was begun in 1738 by *Fernando Casas y Nuova* and it encloses the Portico de la Gloria, which is now a second entrance inside the Baroque one (**791**). Work had begun before this on the south transept and the north side was not completed till after 1770 and in more neo-classical form. The whole cathedral, exterior and interior, is built in the local grey granite, lichen-covered from the damp Atlantic atmosphere. This aids the harmonising of the two differing architectural styles, as does the unusual verticality of the Baroque façade.

Baroque fronts added to southern cathedrals include those at Jaén and Murcia. The *Jaén west front* is also of vertical design. Built 1667–88, it has twin western towers and a strongly articulated centrepiece. *Murcia Cathedral* façade was added 1740–54. This is much more Baroque and southern with a horizontal emphasis, a richly sculptured screen and central broad niche (**793**).

The façade of *Valencia Cathedral* was added in 1713 to front the Gothic building by *Conrad Rudolf*, the Austrian architect. The decoration here is Spanish but the architecture is much more in the style of Borromini. The design problem was difficult as the cathedral façade is squeezed in between the Miguelete tower and the chapter house. The façade had to be narrow and tall but the architect has created such a Baroque impression of movement with his undulating curved planes that it gives the feeling of being about to burst out of the restriction of the flanking buildings (**792**).

Cádiz is the only completely Baroque *Cathedral* in Spain. Built on the edge of the harbour which juts out into the south Atlantic, it was begun in 1722 but not completed till 1853. The architect was *Vincente Acero* who had earlier designed the façade at Guadix Cathedral. The cathedral at Cádiz is a remarkable structure, large, monumental and very Baroque, especially in the interior massing and blending of the curved planes. The Corinthian order is used with grouped columns and ornamented entablatures broken forward. An ambulatory extends all round the nave, transepts and choir, giving a wide façade, which is extended further by the towers flanking the aisles. There is a dome and drum over the crossing and the sanctuary has a rotunda and surrounding chapels.

Eighteenth Century Palaces

The handling of these buildings was, in general, more restrained than the churches. Partly this was due to foreign influence. The two royal palaces, in Madrid and La Granja, were designed by Italians and some of the interior decoration was also by foreign artists, Tiepolo, for example. In 1734 the old fortress type of *palace* in *Madrid* was destroyed by fire. The king commissioned *Filippo Juvara* (p. 81) to design a new one. Juvara's plan was for a large and complex structure, with several courts and long façades. By the time the king had accepted the plans, Juvara had died. The successor he had recommended was commissioned to build the palace.

This was *Giovanni Battista Sacchetti* from Turin who, on request, constructed a smaller palace but kept faithfully to Juvara's designs. The palace is still large. It is built round one great court (**795**) and has long façades reminiscent of Caserta. There is a horizontal emphasis in the balustrade, entablature and two storeys spanned by a giant order of Doric pilasters, interrupted by Ionic engaged columns on the main pavilions. The whole stands on a rusticated basement. There are several fine apartments inside the palace, especially the throne room with its Tiepolo ceiling representing the greatness of the Spanish monarchy, its gilt and red wall decoration and rococo furniture. There is also the interesting small porcelain room with its entire walls and ceiling covered in glazed ceramics in white and green with gilt decoration: *putti*, portraits, medallions. This rich ornamentation was made at the royal porcelain factory. The staircase is based on that at Caserta. The decorative scheme is on white marble and stucco with gilt and coloured marble enrichment; above is a painted ceiling. It is finely proportioned Baroque but less monumental than Caserta.

The mountain palace retreat of S. Ildefonso, called *La Granja*, was built 1721–3 to a traditional Spanish fortress design by *Teodore Ardemans*, of German origin. In 1735 the king decided to enlarge and rebuild parts of the palace and commissioned Juvara who, with Sacchetti, turned it into a Spanish Baroque version of Versailles. The garden front of the palace is essentially Italianate, all gleaming white and pale pink, with giant pilasters and Baroque sculptural decoration (**796**). The setting is magnificent, carefully chosen in a sheltered hollow high in the range of the Guadarrama mountains towards Segovia. The gardens are extensive, laid out by the Frenchman *Étienne Boutelon*, on classic Versailles pattern with geometrical design and avenues radiating from the palace in different directions, leading to cascades descending from the hills and sculptural groups and fountains at all vista points. Much of the sculpture is also French; the best is by *Réne Carlier* (PLATE 107). The garden front of the palace looks out on the most impressive vista, extending uphill via cascades, steps and fountains into the far distance.

is less impressive. Built by Herrera (p. 59), it

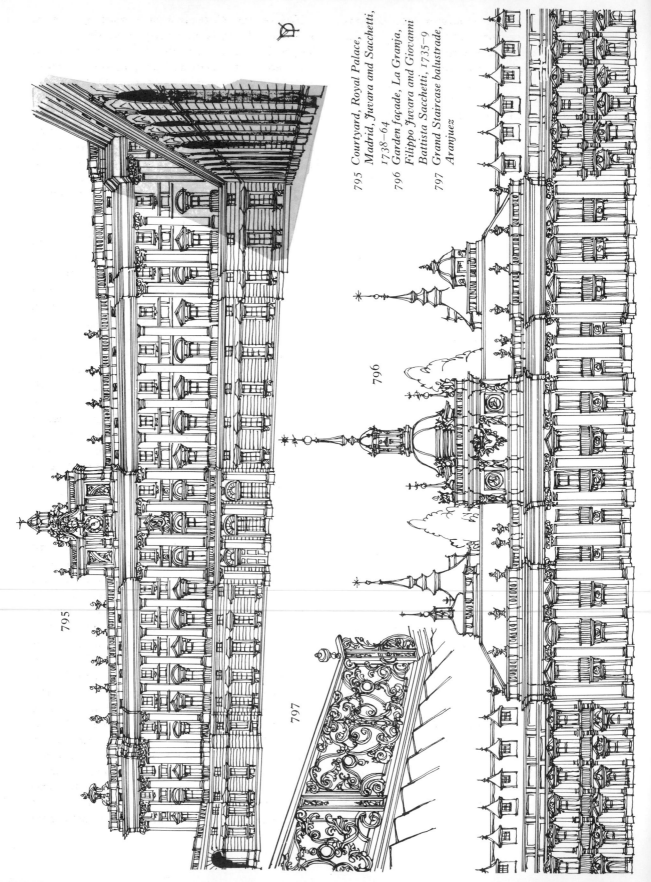

795 Courtyard, Royal Palace,
Madrid, Juvara and Sacchetti,
1738–64
796 Garden façade, La Granja,
Filippo Juvara and Giovanni
Battista Sacchetti, 1735–9
797 Grand Staircase balustrade,
Aranjuez

795

796

797

was enlarged and partly rebuilt in two periods in the eighteenth century: 1715–48 and in the 1770s. It now has a very large entrance court lined on three sides by classical ranges. Of the interior, the staircase is the finest part. The single central flight branches into two at the half-landing and these lead to the first floor. The steps are white marble and the balustrade decorative iron (**797**).

Among town palaces, the simple *Virreina Palace* in *Barcelona* (1722) was designed by *Manuel Arat*. The street façade is well pro-portioned and has ornament restricted to window frame cresting and balustrade vases. In complete contrast is the *Palace* of the *Marqués de Dos Aguas* in *Valencia*. This is a simple three-storey block building, but it is adorned in lively manner with rococo decoration round the windows and parapet. The painter *Hipólito Rovira y Brocandel* adorned the palace in 1740–4 with frescoes (which have now disappeared) over the walls and with the amazing entrance portal which was carved in white alabaster by *Ignacio Vergara*. This is carried out in a riotous use of rococo forms. The eye follows the nude figures on each side of the doorway, contorted and intertwined with pitchers, lions, palm trees and drapery up to the central figure of the Virgin and Child in a niche above, surrounded by further contortions and twirlings of figures, clouds, sun rays and plants (**787** and **788**).

Spanish Neo-classical Architecture

In the last decades of the eighteenth century there was a gradual abandonment of Baroque designs in favour of a return to a more severely pure classical structure with less decoration. One of the leaders of this movement was *Ventura Rodriguez* (1717–85). His earlier work, contributing with others on the Royal Palace in Madrid and in the design of his *Church of S. Marcos* in *Madrid* (1749–53) is partly Baroque. The church façade is severely plain, but has concavely curving side wings. Inside, it is Baroque. There is an oval dome over the crossing, painted and caissoned in panels, and an oval lantern above. The nave below is also oval and the church is aligned with the altar on the western side. It is a church closely dependent on Bernini's S. Andrea al Quirinale (p. 77).

The second *Cathedral* of *Zaragoza, Nuestra Señora del Pilar*, is an immense building. It was designed by Francisco de Herrera in 1677 and intended to be Baroque throughout. *Ventura Rodriguez* took over the work at the cathedral from 1753–66 and clothed the interior in more neo-classical form. It is dark inside as there are no windows in the aisle walls, only circular ones in the nave wall above the entablature which light the painted saucer domes but little else. There are also windows in the lantern of the dome over the crossing, but these too are few and small. The whole interior is treated with Corinthian piers and pilasters. The exterior is more satis-factory and is most impressive, especially when viewed from the bridge over the Ebro (**794**). There are four great corner towers with Baroque steeples and eight domes with lanterns. It is a Baroque design tempered with the neo-classical.

More purely and severely classical are the façades of Vich and Lugo Cathedrals. *José Morato* added a plain, neo-classical façade to *Vich Cathedral* in 1780–1803. This has only one decorative feature: the two-stage entrance portal. The Doric order is used throughout. The façade at *Lugo* was built 1769–84 by *Julian Sánchez Bort*. It is larger and less severe, with the Composite Order used across the main front. There is a central pediment and lofty towers which were completed in 1830.

Portugal

Portuguese architecture followed a similar pattern to Spanish in these years. There was not a great deal of building in the seventeenth century and most of that which survives dates from the later decades. At this time the Portuguese were experi-menting with the Baroque style which they developed fully by 1740. The buildings were simple in structure but, like the Spanish, richly decorated. The work is also free and exuberant but lighter and gayer than Spanish counterparts. The façade of *Alcobaça Abbey Church* dates from these years (**797**), as does the redecora-tion of the Gothic Church of *São Francisco* in *Oporto*. On the exterior a double-stage entrance portal has been added, with barley sugar columns, while the rather later interior is a riot of Baroque decoration—almost every inch is covered in gilded enrichment. The high altar is unbelievably

798 *Basilica da Estrêla, Lisbon, designed Mateus Vincente, 1779–90*

799 *Alcobaça Abbey Church. Baroque façade, later seventeenth century*

800 *Carmelite Churches side by side in Oporto. (Left), Carmelite Church, 1619–28; (right) Terceiros do Carmo, 1756–68*

over-ornamented. Some of the village and small town churches are more successful, having an equally high level of decoration but used with greater restraint. Examples include the *Church of S. Vincente* at *Braga* (1691) and *S. Pedro* in *Amarante*. The triple-stage portal added to another Amarante church, *S. Gonçalo*, dates from this time also (**803**).

The twin *Carmelite churches* in *Oporto* (**800**) illustrate well the differences between the seventeenth and eighteenth century Portuguese work. The Baroque is fully advanced by the mid-eighteenth century with resultant richly ornamented exterior. The whole side of this church is covered in blue and white ceramic tiles. Such murals are seen all over Portugal especially in seventeenth and eighteenth century buildings. Another example is on the interior walls of the *Convent Church* of *Madre de Deus* in *Lisbon*. The décor of the interior of this church is by *João Frederico Ludovice* (1670–1752), a German architect (Johann Friedrich Ludwig) and illustrates the earlier Baroque style. This church dates from 1711 and is of high quality in workmanship and design. The ceiling is barrel vaulted and covered with painted panels in gilt frames. There is a triumphal arch approach to the high altar, very ornate in gilt decoration on white marble. Ludovice also decorated the *Chapel* of *S. John the Baptist* in the *Church* of *S. Roque* in *Lisbon* (1742–8). Much of the workmanship was done in Italy. The Corinthian Order is used and above is a central mosaic and caisson vault decorated with white marble *putti* and angels. The ornamentation of the small chapel is incredibly rich, all in precious materials: lapis lazuli, marbles, mosaic.

A genuine structural Baroque, as distinct from the decorative version which had been used in Portugal to date, was introduced by the Italian architect *Niccolò Nasoni* when he designed *Nossa Senhora de Assumpçao* (1732–50). This is an unusual building; it is situated on top of a hill near the centre of *Oporto*. Traffic now moves along a main road passing on either side of the church, which occupies almost an island site. The plan is long and narrow, with the tower (Torre dos Clérigos) at the far end and the oval nave at the other. The exterior (apart from the decorative tower) is simple. The entrance portico is more richly Baroque and the interior is en-tirely oval, after Bernini. The church is entered through a vestibule which one approaches by climbing up further steps to the higher nave floor. The small choir leads off the oval nave and contains a heavily ornamented altar. The walls and vault are well-proportioned and controlled. There are Corinthian pilasters all round the walls and a panelled, oval dome above. There is no drum but oval windows in the lower cupola.

Two interesting later, fully Baroque churches, are those of *Nossa Senhora de la Encarnaçao* at *Milagres*, on a hill top six kilometres away above the town of *Leiria* and *Senhor dos Passos* in *Guimaraes*. The Milagres church has a wide, twin-towered façade with imposing curved gabled centrepiece. The façade is two-storeyed with Baroque windows above and simple arched openings below, providing a wide entrance gallery at the top of the approach steps. The Guimaraes church is quite different. It is tall and narrow with lofty steeples on either side of the convex front. It is approached by a monumental staircase. The churches are nearly contemporary, both having been completed in the 1790s.

Characteristic of Portugal are the *pilgrimage churches*. The famous examples at Lamego and Braga are dramatic. The theatrical quality of Baroque architecture is extended to landscaping. In each case the church is built on a hill top and is approached up the steep hillside by a terraced stone staircase, decorated all the way by finials and figure sculpture. The Pilgrimage Church of *Nossa Senhora dos Remédios*, designed by *Nasoni*, is the simpler of the two but is still a dramatic composition. Long flights of steps lead up from the town of Lamego by stages and platforms to the twin towered Baroque façade at the top. The upper part of the scheme is shown in Fig. **802**. Inside, the church is less impressive. In Baroque style, it is not large. It has a shallow curved ceiling decorated with rococo panels; the walls are articulated in the Composite Order with enriched entablatures. The altarpiece is gilded and ornate.

Bom Jésus do Monte is on a larger scale. The church has a magnificent situation on a hill top five kilometres away from the town of *Braga*. The hillside is wooded; the stone staircase ascends the escarpment through a gap in the trees. It is not as long a stairway as that at Lamego, but is more richly sculptured. The

BAROQUE IN PORTUGAL

801

802

803

801 *Palacio Mateus, Vila Real,
1710–20*
802 *Pilgrimage Church of Nossa
Senhora dos Remédios, Lamego,
Nasoni, 1761*
803 *Portal, Church of S. Gonçalo,
Amarante*

804 *Pilgrimage Church of Bom Jésus do Monte, near Braga, Portugal, Cruz Amarante, 1723*

804

Plate 107
Garden fountain.
Royal Palace of
La Granja, Spain,
1722–39

Plate 108
Gateway sculpture, Palace of Queluz, Portugal,
1758
Plate 109
Pilgrimage Church of Bom Jesus do Monte,
Braga, Portugal, begun 1723

Plate 110
Staircase Hall, Schloss Brühl, Germany. 1744–65, Neumann

church itself (**804**) has a more monumental façade and is a larger building. The best sculptured figures are on the terrace (PLATE 109). Inside, the church is plain and light, on traditional Latin cruciform plan. The workmanship is somewhat provincial. As at Lamego, it is the dramatic exterior and setting which are remarkable.

Eighteenth Century Palaces

The two principal palaces of Portugal are at Mafra and Queluz. The *monastery—palace* at *Mafra* is an immense undertaking reminiscent, in its complexity and size, of the Escorial in Spain. *João Frederico Ludovice* had come to Lisbon from Rome in 1701. After designing the Madre de Deus convent church in Lisbon (p. 119), he was commissioned in 1711, by the king, to build the great convent-palace at Mafra. This is a mature Baroque structure, monumental and powerful; it dominates the vast square in front of the principal elevation, indeed, the whole town. The church façade is in the centre of this elevation (**805**), standing four-square with its Baroque twin towers, central pediment and crossing dome visible behind. The interior is brightly illuminated, well-proportioned Roman Baroque. It is entirely homogeneous, built in white and pinkish marble and with a patterned marble floor. The plan is Latin cruciform, with barrel vaulted arms and an apsidal east end. The Composite Order is used throughout the main church. The crossing dome is supported on pendentives. The drum is articulated with Corinthian columns and pilasters and the dome is coffered and painted.

Queluz is in complete contrast. This is the Portuguese La Granja, a summer palace for Lisbon, in gay insouciant pastel-coloured rococo. The palace itself is, however, no Versailles or La Granja. Designed by *Mateus Vincente de Oliviera*, it is smaller and less imposing. It has great charm and grace as well as an inconsequential, provincial air. Like La Granja, the garden façade, in particular, is white and pink in dainty rococo decorative form (**806**). The gardens are also French in design. They were laid out by the Frenchman *J. B. Robillion* in small-scale formal manner. There are fountains and lakes and some good, lead sculpture (PLATE 108).

A smaller, elegant, very Portuguese Baroque palace is that at *Vila Real*. The *Palacio Mateus* stands in attractive gardens fronted by a large lake. The façade has long, low wings and a central block which is approached by a small courtyard and a double entrance stairway (**801** and PLATE 105). The palace is, even more than Queluz, a little provincial, its sculptural decoration a little larger than life, but it possesses charm and compatibility.

The Germanic Influence in Central and Eastern Europe: Germany

Baroque design was the paramount artistic expression over an extensive area of central and eastern Europe, but it did not fully develop under German architects till about 1700 and its use is predominant in the regions of Roman Catholic influence. The style transcended national frontiers so we find typical German Baroque workmanship in southern Europe, in Austria, in Switzerland, in Czechoslovakia, southern Poland and in Hungary. In the more northerly regions in Germany and Poland, the freer, rumbustious Baroque forms are more rarely to be found and, as in northern France, England or Holland, architecture is of a more severe, sparingly decorated, classical type.

The Baroque architecture which flourished with such vitality in Bavaria, for instance, carries the theme of pulsating life and movement further than either the Italian or Spanish versions had done. Italian Baroque, despite the undulations of alternately convex and concave curved planes, always gives precedence to the classical structure in orders, capitals, vaults, etc. The Spanish tends to obscure these by over-ornamentation and lack of coherence. The German achievement was to carry the Baroque principle of movement to the ultimate degree. Thus, though some churches are heavily ornamented, others are restrained in the use and area of decoration. It is not in the quantity of enrichment but in the flowing, undulating, always sinuously curving architectural forms that the summit of Baroque expression is obtained. Walls, vaults, capitals and piers, windows and doorways all contribute to this restless, surging movement and the delicate, pastel coloured, rococo ornament

EIGHTEENTH CENTURY PALACES IN PORTUGAL

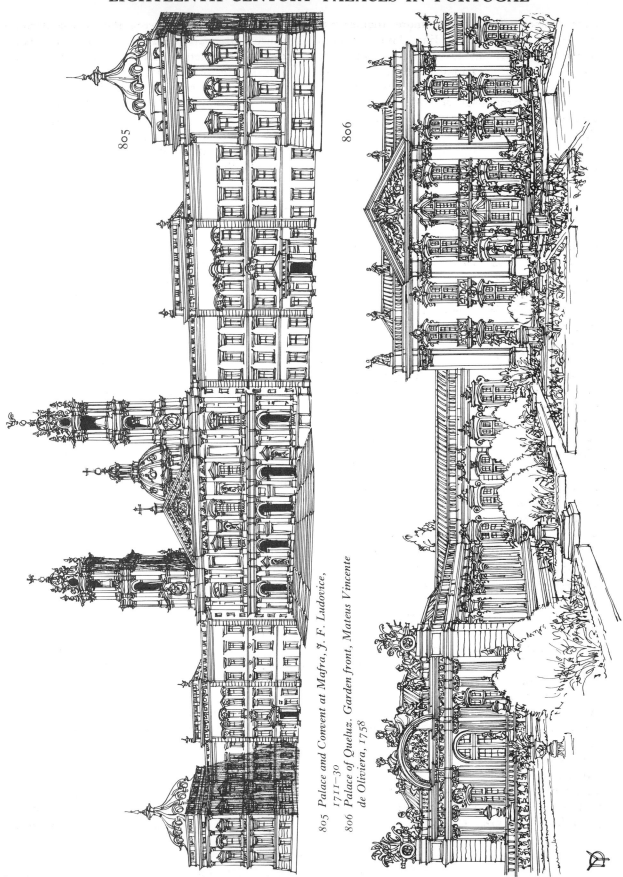

805 *Palace and Convent at Mafra, J. F. Ludovice, 1711–30*
806 *Palace of Queluz. Garden front, Mateus Vincente de Oliviera, 1758*

completes the scheme. Church interiors illustrate the way in which craftsmanship in painting, sculpture and architecture, all of the highest quality, merge into one scheme of illusion and grandeur, so that it is often difficult to discern what is painted to represent three-dimensional form and what is three-dimensional reality. Motifs are taken from nature, from plant and animal life, but the treatment is not naturalistic. The leaf, tendril or stem is used as a design form. Though German rococo decoration is much more sensuous than the more delicate, subtle French prototype, both forms are sophisticated, not merely reproductions of nature's design.

In the seventeenth century building was either still Renaissance or Mannerist, like Holl's work in Augsburg (p. 40), or was carried out or influenced by Italian architects who designed in Roman Baroque. It was nearly 1700 by the time that German architects were ready to create their own Baroque buildings. *The Fountain Court* of the *Munich Residenz* is a good example of German work of the early seventeenth century. In simple classical style, it was laid out in 1612–18. The Thirty Years' War then followed (1618–48) and effectively frustrated building enterprises. In the second half of the century, under architects of Italian origin such as Barelli, Zuccali and Viscardi, construction of important buildings began again and, this time, in Italian Baroque form.

The *Cathedral* at *Passau* is a typical example. The interior was rebuilt from 1668 by *Carlo Lurago* (c. 1618–84). The basilican church has aisle chapels to the nave but none to the choir. The decorative scheme is all in white, with rich contrasting colour in the ceiling panels and pendentive spandrels. This is an early instance of the introduction of these transverse ceiling saucer domes which became such a feature of German Baroque churches in the eighteenth century. In Lurago's cathedral, the decoration is rich and Baroque; the quality of Carlone's stucco work is beautiful and both form and colour are expertly handled. But this is still Italian Baroque; the classical structure is paramount over the spatial movement.

Even more Roman Baroque is the *Theatinerkirche* in *Munich*, although it was not finally completed until the mid-eighteenth century (**810**). It was designed by *Agostino Barelli* on the lines of S. Andrea della Valle in Rome (**750**). It was built 1663–71 and decorated by *Enrico Zuccali* (1642–1724) from then until 1715. The interior is especially Italian Baroque; it is all white, with colour and gilt only in the altars. The church is correctly classical, on cruciform plan and with chapels in the thicknesses of the walls. A bold, enriched Composite Order is used. Above the entablature is a deep, sculptured frieze and windows. The barrel vaulted ceiling is sparingly decorated. The crossing dome stands on a sculptured drum, completing a finely proportioned, beautifully decorated interior.

Between about 1685 and 1710, *Enrico Zuccali* and *Giovanni Viscardi* (1647–1713) dominated the architecture of southern Germany. They designed in Italian Baroque style but gradually this became freer and less classical and thus more Bavarian. These two architects helped to set the pattern for the mature Austrian and Bavarian Baroque of Fischer von Erlach and Balthasar Neumann. From 1684, Zuccali enlarged and redecorated the *Palace of Schleissheim*, just north of Munich. Much of this has been rebuilt, but the three-storey central block (completed by Effner in 1726) with its giant Composite Order, remains. Inside is a magnificent staircase with centre flight which doubles back on each side. The stucco ornamentation here and in the saloon was carried out by *Joseph Zimmerman* from 1720. This rococo work is of very high quality. In 1702 Zuccali was commissioned to reconstruct the Medieval *Abbey Church* of Ettal near Oberammergau. This is essentially Roman Baroque in its pure classical lines and in its undulating façade (**811**). The dome and the interior décor are the work of *Joseph Schmuzer*, after 1745, but the treatment is similar throughout. The church has an oval nave covered by the immense dome; the chancel, leading off it, is a smaller oval.

Both Zuccali and Viscardi worked on the enlargement of *Schloss Nymphenburg* just outside Munich. Zuccali had designed the work and Viscardi was put in charge of carrying it out in 1702. He extended the façade by galleries and pavilions and began work on the saloon.

Southern Germany in the Early Eighteenth Century

While these Italian architects were developing

BAROQUE IN GERMANY

807 Pilgrimage Church of Steinhausen, Domenikus Zimmermann, 1728–32

808 The Zwinger, Dresden, Daniel Pöppelmann, 1711–20

809 Zwiefalten Abbey Church, J. M. Fischer, 1740–65

810 The Theatinerkirche, Munich. Begun Barelli and Zuccali 1663. Completed Cuvilliés, 1767

807

809

808

810

their style of work, the Vorarlberg school of artists were also building and decorating, but in indigenous form. They worked mainly in families, of which the Thumb and Beer families built monastic churches in Germany as well as in Austria and Switzerland. The *Abbey Church* at *Kempten* is an early example. Designed by *Michael Beer* (d. 1666) and built 1652–60, it is large and monumental. It has a twin-towered, flat façade and a wide, low central dome. Inside, the four-bay nave has pilastered walls with flattened round arches between piers. There are chapels in the wall thickness. It is a simple, classical building, decorated sparingly. The *Abbey Church* of *Ober Marchtal*, on the Danube west of Ulm, followed. It was built 1686–1701 by *Michael Thumb* (d. 1690) and *Franz Beer* (1659–1726). The development into Baroque was here taken further, with the octagonal façade towers surmounted by cupolas and lanterns and, inside, the fine stucco decorated, panelled vault and carved pulpit.

The mature style of the Vorarlberg school can be seen in their masterpieces, the *Abbey Church* of *Weingarten*, begun 1715, and the *Abbey Church* at *Birnau* (1746–58). Many architects and artists worked at Weingarten. In connection with the architecture both *Franz Beer* and *Johann Jakob Herkommer* (1648–1717) had a share in the design and later Donato Frisoni and Joseph Schmuzer. It is an immense church, nearly 400 feet long, and rises above the town with an imposing façade of tall twin towers and, between, an undulating concavely and convexly curved front. It is built on a plinth and is articulated with the giant Corinthian Order. The inside is based, like many of the Vorarlberg type churches, on Il Gesu, but here the structure has developed further towards the later German Baroque pattern of free-standing piers. At Weingarten the piers project inwards from the wall, with their multi-pilasters and separate entablatures to support the barrel vault ribs of the nave. Galleries then connect the piers. The central vault is immensely wide, with arched ceilings—painted masterpieces by *Cosmas Damian Asam*. There are also painted saucer domes and a giant cupola and drum over the crossing.

The façade of the *Abbey Church* of *Birnau*, facing the shores of Lake Constance, is almost plain and only the tower displays Baroque

qualities. Thus far the church is typical Vorarlberg work and in contrast to the imposing façade of Weingarten. Inside is a different world. Here, the Vorarlberg masters created a mature Baroque on Bavarian pattern. The architect and mason in charge was *Peter Thumb* (1681–1766), son of Michael who had worked at Ober Marchtal. His interior at Birnau is a classic of its type. There is light and movement, spatial form in magnificently controlled curves. The broad flattened ceiling panels representing the Ascension are ideal for displaying the paintings of *Gottfried Götz* and the stucco framing, capitals and galleries of *Joseph Anton Feuchtmayer* are a wonderful foil. The interior is broad and open. There are no columns, aisles or screens to obscure the view. It is a fine vehicle for the high quality of craftsmanship with which it is decorated (PLATE 117).

Northern and Eastern Germany—Early Eighteenth Century

Two important centres in this area were *Berlin* and *Dresden*. Some outstanding artists were working in both cities; men who, like those of Renaissance Italy, often excelled in the handling of more than one medium. Andreas Schlüter in Berlin was sculptor and architect, as was also Marcus Dietze in Dresden. German architecture, and the world suffered a tragic loss in the almost total destruction of the eighteenth century work in both cities in the Second World War.

Little is known of the early life of *Andreas Schlüter*, who became one of Germany's greatest artists. It is thought that he was born about 1662 in Danzig (Gdansk). He came to *Berlin* from Warsaw in 1694 and quickly established a reputation. His most important architectural works were the *Arsenal* and the *Royal Palace*. The former, built 1695–1717, was damaged in the War, but is now restored. The Palace (1698–1707) was an even greater masterpiece. Designed in a bold, sculptural, Roman Baroque style, it was a fine design, superbly executed. It suffered only slight damage from bombing in 1945 but, in 1950, was razed to the ground by order of the Russians to create the Red Square (now called Marx Engels Platz) of East Berlin.

Schlüter's sculpture was equally of Roman Baroque quality. Again, little survives, but his magnificent equestrian statue of the Elector

BAROQUE CHURCHES IN GERMANY

811 *Ettal Monastery. Designed by Enrico Zuccali; dome by Schmuzer, 1710–52*

812 *Aldersbach Abbey Church, Asam brothers, 1718–29*

813 *Façade, Church of S. John Nepomuk, Munich, Asam brothers, 1733–46*

EIGHTEENTH CENTURY PALACES IN GERMANY

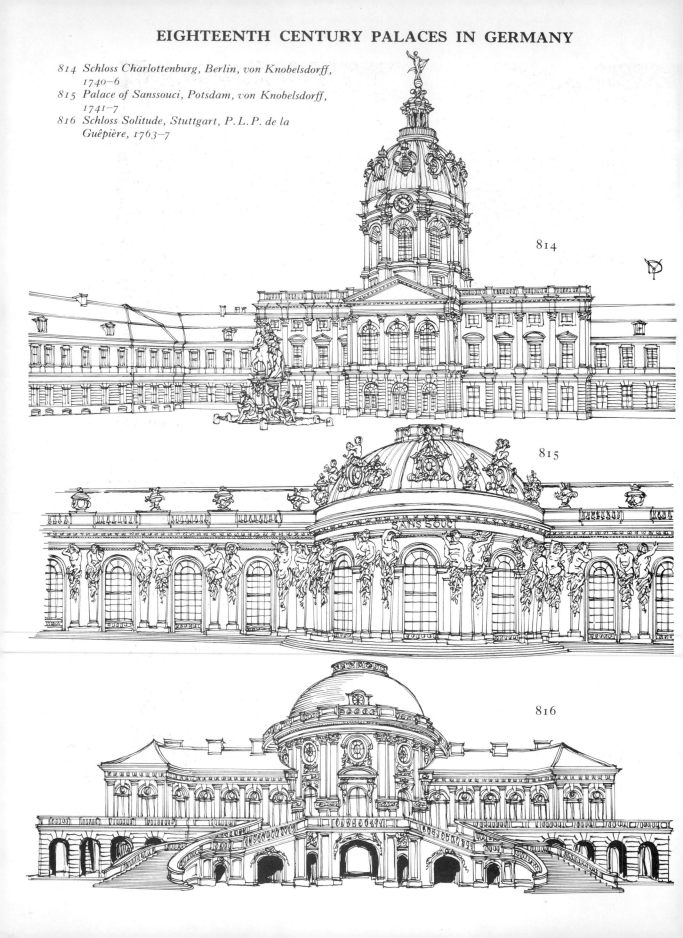

814

815

816

Plate 112 Baroque altar, Osterhofen Abbey Church, Germany, 1726–40, Asam brothers

Plate 111 Interior rococo decoration. Palace of Sanssouci, Potsdam, Germany, 1745–7, Von Knobelsdorff

Frederick Wilhelm I of Brandenburg was removed from its position near the Palace and now stands in the forecourt of Schloss Charlottenburg (**814**). Based on the Roman model of Marcus Aurelius in the Capitol in Rome, the statue is typical of Schlüter's vigorous, powerful style.

The chief work in *Dresden* was the rebuilding of the old part of the town after a serious fire in 1685. Disconcertingly called the Neustadt, it was laid out on classical pattern. Work began in the late seventeenth century under *Marcus Conrad Dietze* (d. 1704) and continued under *Daniel Pöppelmann* (1662–1736) and other architects until 1750, creating the Saxon Baroque style in buildings such as the Zwinger, the several palaces, the Frauenkirche and the Hofkirche. Almost all of this was lost in the Allied bombing raid in 1945, though much has now been rebuilt. Pöppelmann was the architect who set the pattern for Saxon Baroque. He took over the redevelopment of the Royal Palace in the Dresden Neustadt on Dietze's death in 1704. The *Zwinger** was the main part of this built. A court was constructed within the fortress walls of a Medieval bastion. The arcades and pavilions built by Pöppelmann were used as an orangery and accommodation for watching performances of festivals and tournaments which were held here. The famous wall pavilion (now reconstructed) from the Zwinger is shown in Fig. **808**. *Balthasar Permöser's* sculpture is an integral part of the design, acting as a foil to Pöppelmann's architecture. The building now houses a Dresden art collection.

In the north, the *Church of S. Michael* at *Hamburg* (now fully restored) is a good example of the tendency of this area towards Roman Baroque forms. It is a brick church, built 1751–61, by *Sonnini* and *Prey*, and has a lofty classical steeple. Inside, the décor of this oval planned building is in white and gold. The Composite Order, though in Baroque style, is dominant, the barrel vaults panelled and simple. In a monumental interior, the Baroque emphasis is displayed in the gallery curving sinuously round much of the church. At one end of the long dimension of the oval is the high altar, at the other the organ.

Central Germany—Eighteenth Century

The area around Bamberg, Nuremberg and

Würzburg was a centre for outstanding Baroque art and architecture. The earlier work was created by the Dientzenhofer family and the later by Balthasar Neumann. There seemed to be as many members of the Dientzenhofer family working in the arts as there were de Churrigueras in Spain. In Germany three brothers were engaged in Baroque work: Georg, Leonhard and Johann. Another branch of the family created some outstanding buildings in Prague (p. 157).

Georg designed the façade of *S. Martin's Church* in *Bamberg* (1681–91)—a monumental structure —and the *pilgrimage church* at *Waldsassen* (1685–9). *Leonhard* built the *Abbey of S. Michael* at *Bamberg* (1696–1702) and worked on the rebuilding of the *Schöntal Monastery* (1700–17). The most talented of the brothers was *Johann* (1663–1726). He rebuilt the *Cathedral* at *Fulda* (1704–12). This is very Roman, reminiscent of S. John in Lateran; it is an immense, monumental church with a twin towered façade and large dome over the crossing. His best works are the *Abbey Church* at *Banz* (1710–18), north of Bamberg and *Schloss Weissenstein* at *Pommersfelden* (1711–18). The church at Banz, which is situated on a hill near the edge of the River Main, has a bold German Baroque interior. A sensation of lively movement is produced by the ceiling of interlacing framed oval panels, causing constant conflict of curving planes. These vaults are all painted in symbolic manner with scenes from the New Testament. The architectural form of this church is broad and open, giving full rein to the decorative sculpture and painting; a mature example despite its early date.

In the *Schloss* at *Pommersfelden*, Dientzenhofer has created a monumental summer palace. On 'H' plan, it has boldly projecting wings and a plastic central portico with coupled Corinthian columns and pilasters and surmounted by a sculptured pediment. In front is an immense entrance court with, opposite to the façade, the curving sweep of the stable block. There are some fine interiors. Notable is the almost cube, three-storey, *staircase hall*. The first floor is articulated by coupled Corinthian columns while the second floor has caryatid figure supports. The beautiful coved ceiling is painted all over in allegorical manner, showing Apollo the sun god with the continents. The staircase ascends on both sides of the hall, its branches meeting at

* *The word means a bailey or outer courtyard.*

first floor level. Each newel is ornamented by vases and *putti* like Hildebrandt's Schloss Mirabell in Salzburg (**830**). Other notable interiors include the *Hall of Shells*, its whole surface covered with shells and stones and glinting touches of mica, and the *Festsaal*, the Marble Hall, which is a lofty imposing room.

Balthasar Neumann (1687–1753) was the leading genius of this period of German Baroque, taking an equivalent place to Fischer von Erlach in Austria. He was born in Eger in Hungary and was for many years an engineer in the Austrian Army. Like Sir Christopher Wren in England, his early training and thought were on scientific and engineering matters and, also like Wren, when he turned to architecture the aesthetic quality of his work was enhanced by his deep appreciation of things structural and scientific.

After some years in Paris and Vienna, he settled in *Würzburg* and here made his reputation in town planning in streets and houses, and also in the building of his chief work: the *Residenz*. His contribution covers several decades (in collaboration with von Hildebrandt) on buildings grouped round a *cour d'honneur* and a number of inner courtyards. Work was begun in 1719 and continued till his death in 1753. The elevations are all in Baroque style and the garden façades are particularly fine.

The Residenz had some magnificent interiors, but the disastrous air raid of 1945 caused great damage, especially to the Imperial apartments and the Hofkirche. Mercifully the great interiors of the staircase hall, the Kaisersaal and the Weisser Saal were more fortunate and today are once more in beautiful condition. These apartments are the result of the combined artistry of the architect, *Balthasar Neumann*, the stuccoist *Antonio Bossi* and the painter *Giovanni Battista Tiepolo* who came from Italy in 1750 to work for three years on these immense frescoes. The *staircase hall* is superb (**819**). The staircase ascends in a simple flight to the half landing, where it branches into two to climb to the galleried upper landing. The vaulted ceiling is immense, nearly 100 feet by 60 feet, and is unsupported. The architect Hildebrandt did not believe that it would survive, but not only did it pass the test of time but withstood the 1945 air raid also. Tiepolo here covered the vast surface with his allegorical painting of Apollo as patron

of the arts, the personified seasons and the continents.

The *Kaisersaal*, on the first floor, is a large rectangular apartment with its corners cut off, the lower walls articulated by the Corinthian Order in column form with windows and doorways between; there are sculptured niches at each end. The coved ceiling, decorated by Bossi's stuccowork and Tiepolo's paintings, of which there is a central large oval panel with further paintings on the coved section, is pierced by oval windows. The *Weisser Saal*, next door, is, in contrast, all in white stucco and more Rococo than Baroque in treatment. The *Hofkirche*, the court chapel of the Residenz, was seriously damaged in the 1945 air raid but is now beautifully restored. It is a small but perfect interior, richly but not over-ostentatiously decorated and totally homogeneous. Designs for it were altered several times, but the present structure is predominantly Neumann's with decoration to Hildebrandt's design. The colours are strong and rich with an extensive use of gilt. The Composite Order is employed on the lower storey, mainly in column form, while above, in the gallery, is a rich profusion of gilded stucco and white sculpture with the painted cupola over all: a truly magnificent interior.

Apart from his extensive contribution at Würzburg, Neumann carried out a great deal of exceptional work in civic construction, palaces and churches. He collaborated with Hildebrandt at *Schloss Werneck* (1734–45) and at *Bruchsal* designed the wonderful staircase to the *palace* (1731–2), which was decorated by Feuchtmayer's rococo stuccowork. The palace itself is now largely restored, but the staircase was almost a total loss after war damage. *Schloss Werneck* is now in use as a hospital, though the park, on Capability Brown lines with a lake, is open to the public. The garden façade is fine, with a typical Neumann central curving mass, restrained yet powerful.

Schloss Brühl, in the Rhineland south of Cologne, was more fortunate. Neumann built the staircase here also (now fully restored), which is an impressive Baroque design in marble, wrought iron and stucco. The central flight is flanked by life-size sculptured figure groups; it culminates, at the half-landing, in a monumental centrepiece. The staircase then

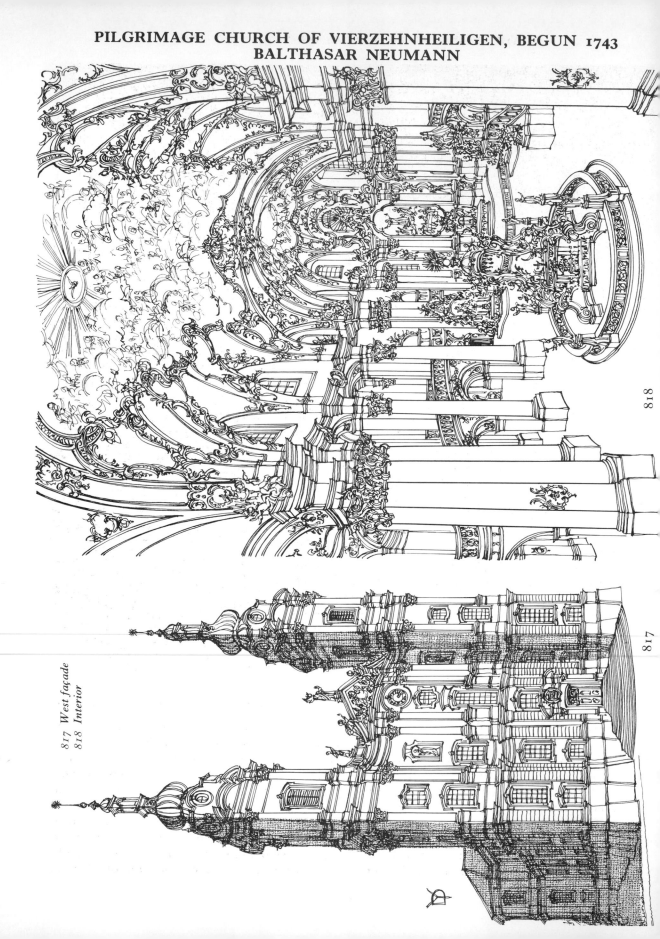

818

817

817 West façade
818 Interior

819 The Staircase. Würzburg Residenz, 1734–53. Architect, Balthasar Neumann ; painter, Giovanni Battista Tiepolo

divides and doubles back to the galleried landing above, also in rich marble, ironwork and with beautiful sculptured figure-supports to the central, painted ceiling oval. The ceiling is illusory in that it is flat but appears, by its painted quality, to be concave (PLATE 110).

Neumann built several churches and chapels. His two supreme achievements are the pilgrimage church at Vierzehnheiligen and the abbey church at Neresheim ; both of these are among the out-

standing examples of German Baroque. The *church* at *Vierzehnheiligen*, built 1743–72, faces Banz, which is on the other side of the river Main. It occupies a magnificent site on the crown of the hill. Its tall, striking exterior (**817**) has twin façade towers and a convexly and concavely curved centrepiece between. The church plan is basilican, on Latin cross, and has a drumless dome over the crossing. The interior is superb, a classic masterpiece of the best of German

Baroque workmanship in its architectural form, its stucco, iron and sculptured decoration. It is completely homogeneous, the ornament forming an integral part of the design and not, as in some examples, excessive (**818**). The scheme is in white, with the piers and columns painted to represent light coloured marble in mauve, cream and grey-green; bases and capitals are gilded. The ceiling is painted in curving panels which have scrolled, gilt borders. Colour is used sparingly throughout the church and to great effect. In form, the interior is in three ovals, the central nave being the largest oval. Curving galleries extend round the walls. It is very much a pilgrimage church, the magnificent 'fourteen saints altar' standing in the centre of the nave; this, the Mercy Altar (PLATE 113), was designed by *J. M. Küchel* and carried out, as was much of the stucco and sculpture in the church, by *J. M. Feuchtmayer* and *J. G. Übelherr*. All the craftsmanship is of superb quality (PLATE 116).

Neresheim Abbey Church is further south. It was one of the last works of the master, built 1747–92 and verges on the neo-classical. Nonetheless, the interior is still in the trend of spatial movement, based on ovals and curves, concave merging into convex. It is decorated in white except for the shallow saucer domes which cover all the open spaces and which are painted with Biblical scenes. A Composite Order is used throughout, with separate entablatures and the columns standing on plinths. There is an oval centre and semi-circular chancel as well as a corresponding semi-circle on the entrance side. The whole, as so often with Neumann's churches, is based on the oval structure, one curving form intersecting with another. This is a late Baroque version which displays the master's harmonious handling of these forms, acquired after a lifetime's experience.

Southern German High Baroque—Eighteenth Century

Several talented artists and architects were working here contemporaneously with Neumann. The most outstanding of these were the Asam brothers, the Zimmermann brothers and J. M. Fischer. Between them they built or rebuilt a number of abbey churches in the area of southern Germany, from lands just north of Lake Con-

stance in the west to just south of Regensburg in the east. Over the years 1715–60, under the guidance and skill of such artists, southern German Baroque reached the ultimate stage in its development. The exteriors of these churches were fairly simple, apart from the decorative steeples, concavely and convexly curving walls and ornamented portals. Inside, they were vehicles for rococo sculpture, stucco, paintings and carvings of the highest quality. The general architectural design was broad, superbly lit, designated by sweeping curves in vault and wall. No free-standing piers interrupted the view of the complex but unified composition. The enriched entablature and piers continued in the wall décor round the whole church, with designated space for the rich altars, culminating in the high altarpiece which swept up to the vault with its vibrant sculptural figures. The ceiling, designed in circular and oval patterns, was painted and stucco decorated all over. A magic world of perfection in human, animal and plant form is depicted in these gloriously alive, beautifully coloured and decorated interiors.

The *Asam brothers* were acknowledged masters at creating this supernatural world, *Cosmas Damian Asam* (1696–1739) was primarily a painter, his brother *Egid Quirin* (1697–1750) a sculptor and stuccoist, but both practised architecture. Sometimes they decorated churches for other architects as at *Osterhofen*, which was designed by *J. M. Fischer* 1726–40; on other occasions they carried out all functions themselves.

They worked at *Weltenburg* on the Danube near Regensburg from 1717, and at *Rohr* (PLATE 77) nearby (1717–25). They continued at *Aldersbach* from 1718 and created their most mature work, *S. John Nepomuk* in *Munich* (often called the Asamkirche) from 1733–46. The example illustrated in Fig. **812**, Aldersbach, is typical of all these in the harmony of the artistic parts: architecture, painting, sculpture. The architecture is basically simple; the stucco is rococo and decorated in white and pale, dull pinks with touches of gilt on the altars, which are very richly ornamented. The ceiling and altar panels (toned in the drawing) are all painted in full, rich colour, giving glowing life to the whole interior. Weltenburg and Aldersbach are the largest of these interiors, but the Asamkirche in Munich is the

Plate 113
'Erasmus'. The Mercy Altar. Church of Vierzehnheiligen, Germany. 1763, Küchel, Feuchtmayer and Übelherr

Plate 114
Church of S. Nicholas in the Lesser Town, Prague, Czechoslovakia. 1703–53, C. and K. I. Dientzenhofer

Plate 115
Putti
Exterior entrance staircase, Church of S. George,
L'vov, U.S.S.R. 1738–58
Plate 116
Angel at the Francis altar. Church of
Vierzehnheiligen, Germany, 1763
Plate 117
Birnau Convent Church, Germany. 1746–50,

Feuchtmayer
Plate 118
Staircase. Schloss Mirabell, Salzburg, Austria.
1726, von Hildebrandt

most fantastic. It is a small church with a narrow façade decorated with Baroque sculpture (**813**). The interior is the essence of Baroque—all curves in planes and masses—there is no rigid classical grammar here. The church is divided into two tiers with galleries all round, curving alternately convex and concave. There are no aisles, no transepts, only one sumptuous room. The ceiling is painted in one large panel. The decoration is a riot of gilt and colour in barley sugar columns, sculpture and painted panels. The centrepiece over the altar is the *pièce de résistance*, as it is in all Asam churches. The sculptural figure group above floats away upwards without visible means of support. Their 'Ascension of the Virgin' at Rohr is the most incredible of these altarpieces. Here, the life-size figures below are struck in attitudes of astonishment and awe as the Virgin is borne aloft by angels. This central group seems to float ethereally despite the solidity of the sculptural material (PLATE 98).

Domenikus Zimmermann was chiefly a stonemason and his brother *Johann Baptist* a stuccoist and painter. Together, as with the Asam brothers, they decorated and also built a number of beautiful Baroque churches. The *pilgrimage church* of *Steinhausen* stands in open country north of Lake Constance (**807**). This is a simple but very Baroque church on both exterior and interior. It is oval in form with ten square piers supporting the oval dome, creating an ambulatory all round the church. The interior is decorated in white, pale pink and pale green with touches of gold. It is very light and restrained. The magnificent painted ceiling and altarpieces act as focal centres of colour.

Zimmermann's *Pilgrimage Church* of *Wies*, near Steingaden, south of Munich (1745–54) is very similar, but is larger and richer in decoration. There is the same oval nave but an added chancel. The exterior is very plain, in tremendous contrast to the interior.

Johann Michael Fischer (*b.* 1692) was one of the last of the great Baroque church builders of southern Germany. He designed the *Abbey Church at Osterhofen* (PLATE 112), that at *Zweifalten* (1740–65) (**809**) and that at *Rott-am-Inn* (1759–63): all are very fine Baroque churches, developed to the ultimate style of this type of decorative architecture. Fischer's masterpiece is the immense

Abbey Church of *Ottobeuren* in Bavaria, north of Kempten. Begun in 1737, this is the largest in scale and most lavish of all the Baroque monasteries in this region. The church dominates the small town with its tall twin towers and convexly curving façade between. It is an imposing, cruciform church with shallow domes over all the bays and the crossing. The interior is extremely rich, all in white, blue-grey and gilt. This is more architectural and monumental than the Asam churches; there is something of Roman Baroque here, but the altar sculpture, saucer dome paintings and carved pulpits almost, though do not quite, dominate the architecture. It is a magnificent, coherent swansong of Bavarian Baroque; a fine scheme of light and shade, white with colour, richness, but not cloying ornateness.

The Later Eighteenth Century

From 1740 onwards the influence of French rococo then, later, neo-classical forms began to supersede the German Baroque. A number of French architects were employed especially on royal and aristocratic palace structures. *François de Cuvilliés* (1695–1768) was court architect in Munich for many years where he worked in rococo style at the *Residenz* and the *Amalienburg* (Nymphenburg) in the 1730s and completed the *Theatinerkirche* (**810**). A beautiful example of his later work is in the *Residenz Theater*, which is in rococo style of 1751–3. The work of another Frenchman, *Pierre-Louis-Philippe de la Guêpière* can be seen at the country palace near Stuttgart, *Schloss Solitude* (**816**), a Baroque theme with central oval room but rococo in treatment.

In northern Germany, the greater part of the building work of the eighteenth century was destroyed by the bombing of the Second World War and, later, the advance of the Russian and Western armies. This applies especially to work in Berlin, Dresden, Leipzig, Kassel, Hamburg and Bremen. Only the buildings which survive in good or well-restored condition are discussed here.

The chief architect designing in rococo or neo-classical style in Prussia was not a Frenchman. He was *Georg Wenzeslaus von Knobelsdorff* (1699–1754), a Prussian aristocrat. He designed and carried out a number of town planning schemes and civic buildings for *Berlin*, especially in the area of the Unter den Linden (almost totally destroyed and now in East Berlin). His *Schloss Charlottenburg* in the western part of the city was damaged, but is now well restored (**814**). This is a large palace with extensive Versailles-type gardens. The equestrian statue of the Great Elector stands in front of the palace in the *Cour d'Honneur*.

Von Knobelsdorff then carried out extensive building at *Potsdam* in East Germany. He rebuilt the town palace (the *Stadtschloss*) in 1744 on monumental scale and an elegant palace nearby in rococo style, the smaller *Palace of Sanssouci*. The centre of the town of Potsdam was largely destroyed in the war and the Stadtschloss was a total loss. Sanssouci, fortunately, in its parkland, was untouched. The garden front (**815**) is approached up many flights of steps while the famous vines grow under glass on the terraces on either side. The palace façade is in white and yellow, with stone caryatid sculpture and detail. Inside, the finest rooms are the entrance hall, the music room and the oval saloon under the central cupola. The rooms are all in white with gold rococo decoration, and the Corinthian Order is used throughout (PLATE 111).

Johann Boumann, a Dutchman, continued von Knobelsdorff's work in Potsdam. He built the *Old Town Hall* (1753), which was damaged but is now restored and used as a Museum of Culture, and in the park near Sanssouci, another large palace, the *Neues Palast* (1763–6). This also survives intact.

Along the Baltic coast of northern Germany, the old Hanseatic pattern of Medieval building with narrow house fronts and hall churches survived, though Baroque clothing encompassed the structures. Dutch architectural styles, especially from Amsterdam, were the prime influence here. Lübeck, Bremen and Hamburg had some fine examples of such work, but much of it was lost in the Second World War.

Switzerland

Medieval architecture lingered on in Switzerland, especially in ecclesiastical work. By the middle of the seventeenth century Jesuit influence began to be felt. The *Jesuit Church* at *Lucerne* (1666–73) is in restrained Baroque style (**822**). The interior is a simple barrel-vaulted hall: no aisles, no crossing, dome or transepts. There are four chapels along each side of the church. The whole interior is in white and gold with painted panels; it is very light due to large windows in the vault. The *Jesuit Cathedral* at *Solothurn* has an impressive Italianate Baroque exterior, raised on a high podium with entrance steps (**821**). The light interior is well balanced and proportioned, simple and not over-decorated. The choir and transepts are apsidal-ended, with half domes over them. There is a dome and drum over the crossing. The influence here is partly Italian, partly the Vorarlberg school. It is also strongly influenced by the type of cathedral as at Passau (**820**).

The Vorarlberg school of artists became paramount in the late seventeenth century. Influenced by Bavarian Baroque, the families of *Thumb, Beer* and *Moosbrugger* expanded their influence and art. At the *Abbey Church* of *Disentis, Caspar Moosbrugger* produced a typically Bavarian Baroque interior (**824**) in the great monastery, finely sited lonely and high in the mountains at the head of the Lukmanier Pass which descends into Italy. At *Kreuzlingen* too, a quite different area near Konstanz, the simple exterior contains a rich Baroque interior (**825**).

The two outstanding eighteenth century achievements were at *Einsiedeln* and *S. Gallen*. The *Benedictine Abbey* and Pilgrimage Church at *Einsiedeln* near Lake Zurich was rebuilt 1719–50 by *Caspar Moosbrugger*. The exterior is large, imposing but basically simple (**826**). Inside is fantastic Baroque, comparable to Vierzehnheiligen in its quality of spacious architecture and decoration in white, mushroom, red, grey, green and gilt. The domical vaults are magnificently painted and these, with the rococo stucco work are, characteristically, by the Asam brothers who have given of their best in this superb Swiss Baroque interior.

The *Abbey Church* of *S. Gallen*, only a few miles away to the north-east, has a classic, imposing Baroque exterior (**827**). This is a highly important work by the *Thumb* and *Beer* families in the Vorarlberg tradition. The Abbey library is a beautiful rococo room with painted ceiling and carved bookcases.

BAROQUE ARCHITECTURE IN SWITZERLAND

820   821

822   823

*820 Interior and 821 façade of
Solothurn Jesuit Cathedral
1680–8, Probably under the direction of Hans Georg Kuen*

*822 Jesuit Church, Lucerne, Vogler,
1666–73*

*823 Eighteenth century houses,
Altstätten*

BAROQUE ABBEY CHURCHES IN SWITZERLAND

824 Disentis Abbey Church interior,
      Moosbrugger, c. 1685
825 Chancel screen, Kreuzlingen
      Convent Church
826 Convent Church at Einsiedeln,
      Moosbrugger, 1710–50

825

824

826

the oval pattern followed; the *Church of the Servites* in *Vienna* (1651–77), for instance.

While the Austrian school of Baroque was slow to develop, the gap was filled by Italian influence. Most of the major buildings between 1640 and 1680 are by Italian architects. The most famous early church is the *Cathedral of Salzburg*, which was finally carried out to designs by *Santino Solari* and was consecrated in 1628. It is a cruciform cathedral on Latin cross plan, with apsidal ended transepts and choir and a dome upon an octagonal drum over the crossing. The façade is Roman Baroque with twin towers and superimposed orders in three stages. In front of the cathedral are the fine Baroque statues of S. Peter and S. Paul by *Mandl* (1697–8). Inside, the plan is much like Il Gesù in Rome, but the church is narrower and taller. It is a light interior, well designed and proportioned and very much on Roman Baroque lines.

The Carlone family carried out a number of

827 *Abbey Church at St. Gallen, Switzerland, Thumb and Beer, 1752–66*

827

Austria

As in Germany, the Thirty Years' War curtailed building activity till the second half of the seventeenth century. An indigenous Baroque slowly began to materialise in the Tyrol where the Gumpp family were court architects at Innsbruck. Several designs were based on centrally planned buildings and on the oval form (the Graz Mausoleum had been an early example of this). In 1647 *Christoph Gumpp* built the *Mariahilfkirche* in *Innsbruck*, which is a domed, circular structure with well-handled interior spatial forms. Other Baroque churches based on

projects; *Carlo Antonio Carlone* was the most talented. His work was fully Baroque, often Italianate, but the ornamentation had an Austrian flavour of richness and gaiety. Among his works are the *Abbey Church* of *S. Florian* (1686–1708), *Garsten Abbey Church* (**829**) (1677–85), the *Jesuit Church* of the *Nine Angelic Choirs* in *Vienna* (1662) and the *Esterházy Palace* at *Eisenstadt* on the Hungarian border (1663–72). The church interiors are especially Baroque, very richly decorated but always, in Italian manner, the classical architecture dominates the ornament, as at Passau Cathedral.

Johann Bernhard Fischer von Erlach (1656–1723)

Fischer von Erlach was the Bernini or Wren of Austria. Until he began to practise, Austrian Baroque was derived second-hand from foreign sources by largely foreign architects. He was born in Graz, the son of a sculptor. He left the town at the age of 22 and went to study for himself in Italy. He spent 12 years there, mainly in Rome and Naples. He returned to Austria and established himself in Vienna. Like Bernini and Borromini he had learned that full Baroque architecture is a successful merger between the three chief visual arts: architecture, sculpture, painting. Like his predecessors he established an architectural style which utilised all three as one unit, creating beauty and force in his handling of light and spatial effect. Like Neumann in Germany he carried the art of Baroque further than the Italians had done, producing powerful three-dimensional exteriors and interiors which were of exceptional dynamic beauty. He realised the exciting possibilities in the use of ceiling paintings in ovals and circles, framed by stucco sculpture which, in their curving planes, with the merging of the three arts, created a grand illusion of open sky effect.

Fischer von Erlach settled in Vienna by 1690, but carried out a great deal of work in *Salzburg* in this decade. His two famous *churches* here are the *Dreifaltigskeitskirche* (the Holy Trinity, 1694) and the *Kollegienkirche* for the Benedictine University (1696–1707). The exterior of the Dreifaltigskeitskirche is like that of S. Agnese in Piazza Navona in Rome (p. 80), with a large dome and drum flanked by two Baroque towers connected by a curving façade. This is a wider, lower front than the Roman example. The inside is more like Bernini's S. Andrea al Quirinale. A vestibule opens into a longitudinal oval church with recesses for altars in the centre and at the two sides. Corinthian pilasters continue round the walls and above is the drum and oval cupola with a painted ceiling.

The *Kollegienkirche* façade (east) is similar, but is taller and the central part is convex instead of concave. The site is more restricted so the building has to extend upwards not sideways. Inside, the cruciform church has no aisles or columns; tall Corinthian pilasters line the walls. The church is

barrel vaulted above the entablature. The altar is richly Baroque in its sculpture, culminating in billowing clouds.

Fischer von Erlach's church masterpiece is the *Karlskirche* in *Vienna* (**828**) (1716). Here he had the opportunity, on an open site, to put into practice his mature Baroque style. The church was dedicated to S. Charles Borromeo as a thank-offering for deliverance from plague. The columns in front of the façade were designed by the architect with the minarets of eastern mosques in mind. They are based, decoratively, upon the Trajan Column in Rome and the spiral reliefs depict scenes from S. Charles' life. The exterior is fully Baroque in its curving façade, temple portico and vast drum and dome. Inside, the great oval space, articulated with Composite pilasters supporting an oval entablature, are surmounted by the drum and oval, painted dome with lantern above. The oval nave is recessed with three altars and one entrance; above this is the organ gallery. There is a great sense of dignity and harmony in the interior. The colouring is Roman, a little sombre, gilt and painted marbling, with none of the light rococo treatment of Bavarian Baroque. This is Austrian Baroque monumentality.

Fischer von Erlach became the official architect to the Imperial Court at Vienna. His two chief works in this connection were the *Palace of Schönbrunn* and the *Hofburg*. He made impressive, large-scale Baroque plans, but both structures were greatly altered from his original designs. At the *Palace of Schönbrunn* (the summer palace on the outskirts of the city) he was asked to modify his first great design on grounds of economy. In 1696 he made a second plan which was smaller and simpler. This was built, but was much altered by his son Josef Emmanuel and again in the eighteenth and nineteenth centuries. Schönbrunn is the Versailles of Austria, but the garden façade, as it stands today, is monotonous; a long, flat elevation only slightly broken by the central block. The gardens are still fine and include raised terraces and fountains. The immense entrance *cour d'honneur* and front are much more characteristic of Fischer von Erlach's work.

The *Vienna Hofburg* (the royal palace) has been added to and altered many times between the building of the *Leopold Range* (1661–8) by

BAROQUE IN AUSTRIA

828 *Karlskirche, Vienna, Johann Fischer von Erlach, 1716*
829 *Pulpit, Garsten Abbey Church, Carlo Carlone, 1677–85*
830 *Schloss Mirabell, Salzburg. Staircase, Lucas von Hildebrandt, 1726*
831 *Façade, Mariakilfkircke, Graz, Josef Hueber, 1742–5*

832 *National (formerly Imperial) Library, begun 1722, Johann Fischer von Erlach*
833 *Hofburg. Imperial Chancellery Wing, Josef Emmanuel Fischer von Erlach, 1729*
834 *Entrance front, Upper Belvedere of the Garden Palace of Prince Eugene, Lucas von Hildebrandt, 1721*

Philiberto Luchese and the later nineteenth century additions under the Emperor Franz Josef. The Leopold Range is simple, Renaissance to Mannerism, pleasant and dignified. Johann Fischer von Erlach designed far reaching plans for the Hofburg's extension, but he died before very much could be carried out. The *Imperial Library* (**832**) was begun in 1722 to his designs and, though largely built by his son Josef Emmanual, it is still the father's design. Here is shown his later phase of work, an abandoning of Baroque ground in favour of the rising tide of neo-classicism. It is still monumental but the projection of blocks and mouldings is less than before and decoration is restrained. The library was completed in 1735. The *Imperial Chancellery Wing* was entirely the work of *J. E. Fischer von Erlach*. Though it lacks the rich originality of his father's work, it is a competent, well-balanced design, with detail and decoration of high quality. It carries further the development towards neo-classicism (**833**).

After Fischer von Erlach came several outstanding Austrian architects. The most talented were *Johann Lucas von Hildebrandt* (1668–1745) and *Jacob Prandtauer* (1660–1726). Von Hildebrandt was born in Genoa and was half Italian. He studied in Rome for a number of years and his work always reflects this Italian background together with a preference for the light, French type of decorative design. He and Fischer von Erlach together embrace the whole spectrum of Austrian Baroque; one complements the other.

Von Hildebrandt began practice in *Vienna* in 1696. He designed the *Piaristenkirche* there (1698). This has a lofty, twin-towered Baroque façade with convexly curving two-stage frontispiece. The interior is much like his *S. Peter's Church* in the city (1702–33). There is the same central plan based on the oval motif, with painted saucer dome, without drum, overhead. Both interiors have beautifully handled spatial forms in curving planes.

Von Hildebrandt built and altered a number of *palaces*. The largest and most important of these commissions was the garden palace for *Prinz Eugen* in *Vienna*. There are two palaces here. The earlier one—the *Lower Belvedere*—was built at the foot of a slope in 1714–15. This is a modest, simple design. The Prince then commissioned a

more elaborate palace and von Hildebrandt built the *Upper Belvedere* on the crown of the slope, which is connected to the lower one by paths, steps, cascades and fountains. There is a considerable distance and difference in height of ground between the two structures. The Upper Belvedere is the magnificent palace; it is an elegant building with decorative pavilions and accomplished massing of the component parts of the elevation. On the entrance side of the Upper Belvedere is a large lake in which the palace is reflected (**834**).

Among von Hildebrandt's other palaces are the *Schwarzenberg Palace* (1697), near the Belvedere and now a hotel, and the *Daun-Kinsky Palace* (1713–16), also in Vienna. At *Salzburg*, he made a number of alterations and additions to the *Schloss Mirabell*, where his staircase is particularly successful (**830** and PLATE 118).

He carried out little ecclesiastical work, but one good example is his enlargement and re-modelling at *Göttweig Abbey* (1719), which has, like a number of Austrian abbeys, a dramatic position high on a bluff above the river Danube, with a magnificent view of the plains below. The abbey buildings are set round an open court with the church as part of the group (**837**). The church interior is impressive; it is richly decorated with stucco ornamentation, ceiling paintings and painted marbling: a rich Baroque décor, part Austrian and part Italian; it bears little resemblance to the Bavarian Baroque of Ottobeuren or the Asamkirche. This is an ornate, late interpretation of Passau or S. Florian, with barrel vaulted ceiling.

Jacob Prandtauer came from the Tyrol. Like Fischer von Erlach, he was a sculptor and architect. Nearly all his work was in the great Austrian *abbeys*, generally enlarging or modernising existing structures. These are nearly all large-scale plans, of which the chief examples are at *Melk* and *S. Florian*.

He began work at *Melk* in 1702, extensively reconstructing the abbey from its Medieval origins. He separated the church from the surrounding conventual buildings so that its Baroque façade, with twin towers and central dome, serve as a landmark, perched on the escarpment at a bend of the river Danube (**835**). Melk and Göttweig share first place for dramatic siting along this river valley.

BAROQUE ABBEYS IN AUSTRIA

835 *Melk Benedictine Abbey, Jakob Prandtauer, 1702–36*
836 *Zwettl Abbey Church, Matthias Steinl*

837 *Göttweig Abbey. Enlarged from 1719 by Lucas von Hildebrandt*

At *S. Florian* he continued the work begun by Carlo Carlone (p. 143). Prandtauer's contribution is primarily the staircase block (1706–14) and the Marble Hall (1718–24). Both exteriors have Baroque pilastered fronts with rococo decoration. The monastery forms a large square court inside with the staircase block on the entrance façade and a fountain in front. The staircase is in two sets of flights, separating at the bottom and

838

838 University Church, Pest (Budapest), Hungary, Andreas Mayerhoffer, 1730–42

returning at the top. Square Doric pilasters are used and life-size sculptured figures are set in niches round the hall. The Marble Hall has a fine interior. Coupled Composite columns on plinths frame the windows along the two long sides; there is a coved, painted ceiling above.

A number of Baroque architects were working in Austria in the eighteenth century. *Joseph Munggenast* worked especially at Altenburg and Dürnstein; both are between Linz and Vienna. The *Abbey Church of Altenburg*'s interior is very Baroque, with an oval nave surrounded by Composite pilasters, the rectangular chancel barrel vaulted and entrance vestibule oval. There is a fine harmony of painting, stucco and carving. Over the nave oval is a beautiful painted cupola with small cupola and drum in the centre. The Library here is also remarkable. The room is large and rectangular, but it is covered by painted saucer domes and stucco decorated vaulting. Around the room is the Composite Order, its entablature returned over each column. It is a harmonious, colourful interior, the architecture by Munggenast and the decoration mainly by Sud-Tyrol artists.

Dürnstein Priory on the Danube was rebuilt 1716–33. Munggenast worked here, largely as a stonemason. Prandtauer also made designs and *Matthias Steinl* too contributed much to the architecture and sculpture. Steinl and Munggenast also worked at *Zwettl Abbey*. The church here has a tall Baroque façade decorated by sculptured figures, notably a group of S. Michael and the Devil (**836**). None of the original Romanesque interior remains; all is designed on Gothic hall church pattern, restored by Munggenast.

Buildings in Baroque style were being constructed or altered in a number of Austrian towns. In *Graz* there is *Joseph Hueber*'s *Mariahilfkirche* (**831**). In *Innsbruck* there are several and here the Gumpp family was active. A good example is *Georg Anton Gumpp*'s *Landhaus* (1725–8), which has a rich, dynamic façade. *S. Jakob's Church* (1717), by the Bavarian architect *Johann Jakob Herkommer* (p. 128), is dramatic and very much on the southern German pattern, as in its boldly concave, twin-towered façade. This is an unsophisticated version, but the interior is of high quality (**852**). The cruciform church is aisle-less, with apsidal terminations to the transepts, but the choir is square-ended on the interior. Three shallow domes cover the nave, while over the choir is a dome with lantern above and drum beneath. Herkommer had designed this beautiful church in 1712, but died soon after its commencement. The work was completed to the designs of the architect and the magnificent interior decoration is mainly by the *Asam brothers*, the beautifully painted ceilings by *Cosmas Damian* and the stucco work by *Egid Quirin* (p. 136).

The *Heblinghaus* nearby, a Gothic building, was redecorated in Rococo manner in 1775. It is a rich, plastic example (**849**).

Hungary

Because of the turmoil caused by war, and the Turkish occupation which continued till nearly the end of the seventeenth century, little classical architecture was produced in Hungary till the early eighteenth century. From this time reconstruction of the country began and some early classical buildings were produced in the capital. *Buda* was being extended and rebuilt when it suffered a serious fire in 1723. Few great buildings survived unharmed. One of these was the charming *town hall* (1692) with its corner oriel window and tiny lantern. The *Royal Palace* was built and extended by 1770, but, unfortunately little of it now survives. *Pest*, on the other side of the river Danube, was then expanded. The Roman Catholic Church was supporting an extensive programme of church building and a number of these structures were Baroque. The influence was Italian, for some time, under architects such as Martinelli, but soon the Austrian Baroque style percolated through. The *University Church* in *Pest* (1730–42) by the Austrian architect *Andreas Mayerhoffer* is the outstanding example of this type of work in Hungary. There is a fine Baroque exterior (**838**). The interior is simple architecturally, but it is richly decorated. The ceiling is painted all over, partly in panels and partly to represent architectural features in the vaulting. There is a triumphal arch entry to the chancel, which is apsidal ended. The church is rectangular, without aisles but with chapels in the nave walls. The pulpit and high altar are highly ornate but the standard of craftsmanship is high. Mayerhoffer also designed the *palace* at *Gödöllö* (1744–50) in rococo style.

Other good examples of Baroque churches can be seen in *Esztergom, Györ* and *Eger*. The *Jesuit Church* of *S. Ignatius* in *Esztergom* has a typical Baroque façade (**839**). Several Baroque buildings survive in Györ. The *Carmelite Church* (**840**) is a good example and there are a number of *houses* in Köztársaság Square. These, like those in *Eger* in Kossuth Lajos Street, are typical of Hungarian Baroque domestic architecture. They are unpretentious, low buildings with simple classical façades with or without orders. They have fine wrought-iron balconies and window grilles.

Eger, in the north-east part of the country, is still very much the unspoilt Baroque town created by *Jakob Fellner* and *Matthias Gerl*. Both architects adapted the Austrian pattern of Baroque to Hungarian needs and taste. Gerl's outstanding work here is the *Minorite Church* in the Market Square (now the Attila Jozsef College), which has a classic twin-towered façade and convexly curving front (**841**). Both Fellner and Gerl designed some of the houses just mentioned and Fellner was responsible for the *High School* (formerly the Ecclesiastical College) (**843**). He also designed the *episcopal palace* at *Veszprém* (**842**), which is an imposing building on top of the hill in the old town, next to the cathedral.

The best of the *palaces* remaining in Hungary is the large-scale layout at *Fertöd*, the *Eszterházy palace* (**844**). Fertöd is a small place between Sopron and Györ, till recent times called Esterháza. The palace was built by *Erhard Martinelli* from 1720 and was then extended by *Miklos Jacoby* (1762–6) and, again, later still. It has a magnificent horseshoe courtyard and entrance front, guarded by beautiful iron gates. In front of the central block is a double, curving staircase of stone and ironwork (**845**). The sweeping wings of the palace lead round to pavilions and then low stable blocks. The decoration of the façade is in low relief with simple decoration, mainly of rococo type. The palace contains 126 rooms, all rococo ornamented. It belonged to the Eszterházy family but is now an agricultural research centre, though open to visitors.

Yugoslavia and Rumania

The northern part of *Yugoslavia* remained under

BAROQUE CHURCHES IN HUNGARY

839 *Jesuit Church of S. Ignatius, Esztergom*
840 *Carmelite Church, Györ, 1725*
841 *Minorite Church (now the Attila József College) Eger, Matthias Gerl, 1758–73*

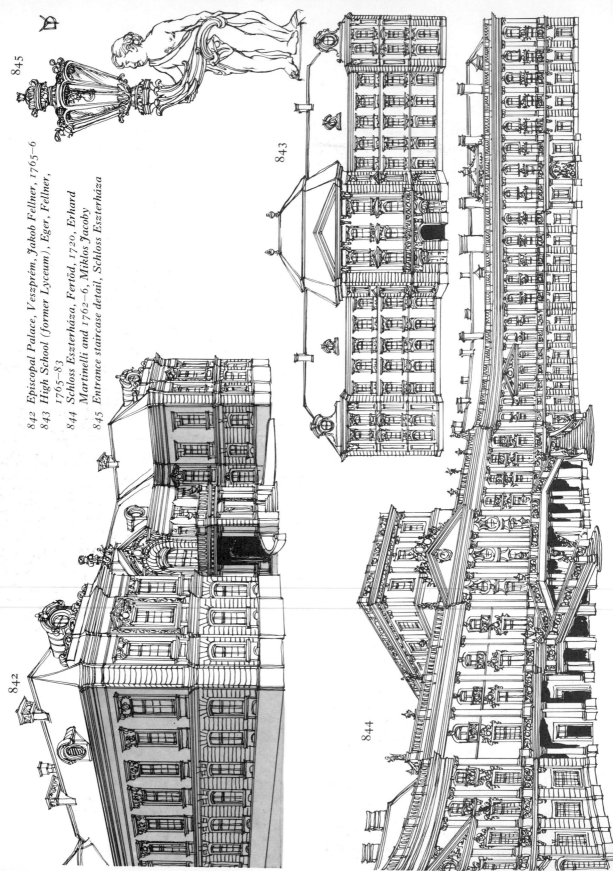

845

843

842

844

842 Episcopal Palace, Veszprém, Jakob Fellner, 1765–6
843 High School (former Lyceum), Eger, Fellner,
1765–83
844 Schloss Eszterháza, Fertöd, 1720, Erhard
Martinelli and 1762–6, Miklos Jacoby
845 Entrance staircase detail, Schloss Eszterháza

846 *Church of S. Biagio (S. Blaise). Rebuilt 1706–15*
847 *The Cathedral, east façade, 1671–1713*
848 *The Jesuit Church, 1699–1725*

Austro-Hungarian influence, the coastal region under Venetian. Inland and further south towards Greece the Turkish monopoly continued. The buildings illustrated on p. 153 of *Dubrovnik* from the seventeenth and eighteenth centuries show, therefore, the Italian style of building. All are ecclesiastical structures.

Rumania also has very few classical buildings dating from the seventeenth and eighteenth centuries. The majority of work is either Byzantine in approach or, as is shown in the Village Museum in Bucharest, of peasant, timber craftsmanship (Volume 2, p. 190). The *palace*, or villa, at *Mogosoaia* on the outskirts of Bucharest, is one classical structure from the eighteenth century. It is a modest, simple building, set in grounds laid out with a large lake.

Czechoslovakia

Baroque architecture was adopted enthusiastically in Czechoslovakia. It was influenced from several sources. The earlier work, in the seventeenth century, was primarily Italian: at one time at least 25 Italian architects were building palaces, churches and houses for the wealthy lay and ecclesiastical aristocracy. There was then a short period of limited French influence but, more strongly towards the later seventeenth and early eighteenth centuries, ideas came from Vienna and Bavaria, chiefly stemming from Fischer von Erlach, Hildebrandt and the Dientzenhofer family. There exists, therefore, a fine Baroque heritage in Czechoslovakia, in the remote country and mountain areas as well as in the towns, especially Prague.

The *Valdštějn Palace* had been begun in *Prague* in 1621 by *Andrea Spezza*. The loggia was in Renaissance style (p. 46) (**713**), but the façade and courtyard are boldly Baroque. Here was the beginning of the Italian influence, with the Czech characteristics only visible in smaller features such as the dormer windows. The courtyard is on the classic Roman Baroque pattern, with three orders superimposed, one above the other, articulating the three-storeyed ranges.

Italian Mannerism also came to Prague and was soon adapted to Czech design. It can be seen at the university, but more particularly in the extensive façade of the *Černin Palace* on castle hill (**856**). This was designed by *Francesco*

Caratti who created the façade, 465 feet long in 29 bays, its giant, three-quarter columns with their richly carved Mannerist capitals, standing on a rusticated base of diamond pattern. Inside he designed an immense saloon over two storeys high.

The Italian influence was strong in Baroque church design. A classic late example is the *Piarist Church of S. John* at *Kroměříž* (**855**). On oval plan, it has a large oval dome, painted all over inside. There is no drum and circular windows pierce the lower part to provide adequate daylight. The oval nave has no aisles or transepts. There is a high altar at one long end of the oval and the entrance is opposite, at the other. The workmanship in marble, painting and gilded stucco is of a high standard and the concept is after Bernini at his most monumental.

Buildings in *Tábor* also show the Italian Baroque style, though on more provincial lines. The later seventeenth century *Convent Church* by *Antonio da Alfieri* is one example, while the *Convent Church* at *Klokoty*, outside the town on the opposite hillside, was built by architects of the school of *Giovanni Battista Santini*. The exterior is fine and occupies a magnificent site.

A French influence was provided by *Jean Baptiste Mathey*, who worked in *Prague* from 1675–94. His palaces are, in contrast to Caratti's Černin Palace, more subtle and less plastic, designed with low projection and pilasters rather than columns. He built some churches, such as the *Abbey Church* of *S. Josef* on the Malá Strana, which is on elliptical plan.

In the early eighteenth century *Johann Bernhard Fischer von Erlach* was working in *Prague*. He designed the *Clam-Gallas Palace*, which is typical of his work, bold and sculptural, especially in the famous doorways, the sculptured figures of which are by *Braun* (**854**).

The *Castle of Vranov* is romantically sited on a shelf of the steep mountainside above the gorge of the river Dyje (**850**). It was rebuilt in 1678–95 when the great oval saloon was designed by *Fischer von Erlach*. This is the chief room of the Baroque castle. The large oval cupola is painted all over, as is much of the wall area between the oval and rectangular windows, the coupled Corinthian pilasters and the sculptured niches. The sculpture is by the Viennese *Tobias Krackner* and the paintings by *Hans Michael Rotmayer*. It

BAROQUE IN AUSTRIA AND CZECHOSLOVAKIA

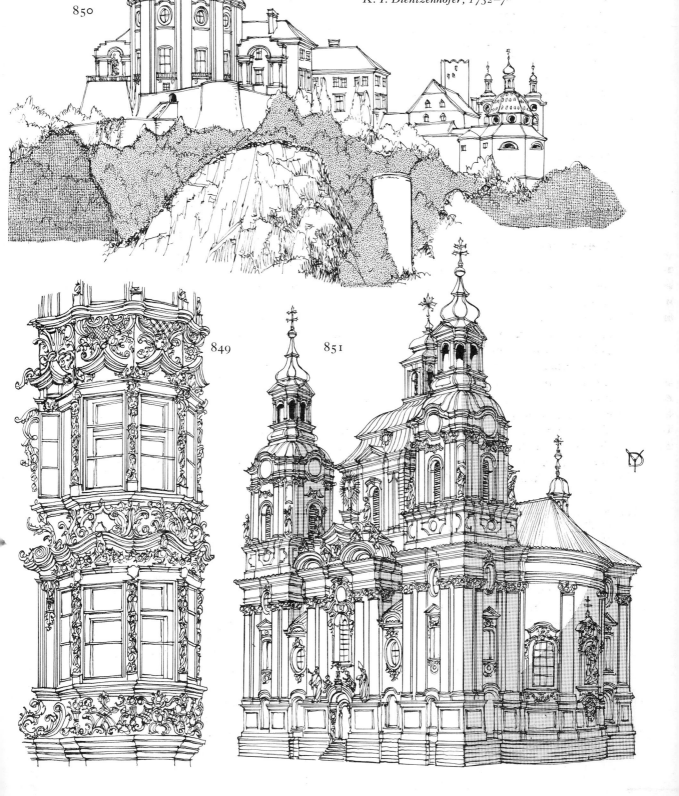

849 *Oriel Window, Heblinghaus, Innsbruck, 1775*
850 *Castle Vranov on the Dyje, Czechoslovakia. Rebuilt 1678–95. Oval Saloon, Fischer von Erlach*
851 *Church of S. Nicholas in the Old Town, Prague, K. I. Dientzenhofer, 1732–7*

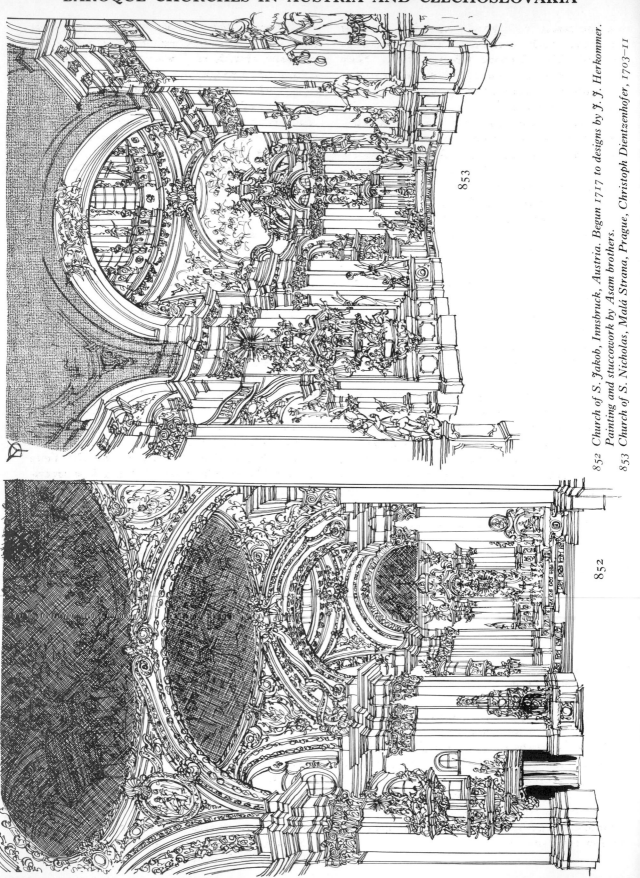

852 Church of S. Jakob, Innsbruck, Austria. Begun 1717 to designs by J. J. Herkommer. Painting and stuccowork by Asam brothers.

853 Church of S. Nicholas, Malá Strana, Prague, Christoph Dientzenhofer, 1703–11

is a fine saloon with good proportions, but the decorative work is not of the best Viennese standard. The Baroque Chapel of the Holy Trinity adjoins the saloon. Both it and the rest of the castle were completed by A. E. Martinelli between 1723 and 1732.

Hildebrandt also came from Vienna in the last years of the seventeenth century and worked on church design in Czechoslovakia. By the early years of the eighteenth century, the Austro-Bavarian influence on Czech Baroque architecture was asserting itself over the Italian. The change-over was completed with the establishment of some of the Dientzenhofers in Prague.

This remarkable Bavarian family were responsible for many fine Baroque buildings in Germany (p. 132). A branch of the family came to Prague in 1678 and set up practice there. The most outstanding of this generation of *Dientzenhofers* in Czechoslovakia was *Christoph* (1655–1722), who worked there most of his life. His best building is the *Church of S. Nicholas* in the Malá Strana at the foot of castle hill. This Jesuit church adjoining the monastery was begun in 1703. It is a very Baroque design, showing the influence of Guarini. The interior especially, with its curving balconies at gallery level and concave niches has a quality of perpetual movement, the walls undulating sinuously, articulated boldly in the Composite order. The large dome over the crossing is supported on a drum articulated with coupled Corinthian columns; between are windows and sculptured figures. The cupola interior is painted all over, as is also its lantern. The choir and transept apses are covered by semi-domes, while the nave is shallowly barrel vaulted and painted like Il Gesù in the Baroque movement manner. Though on Italian lines of structure and design, this is a Czech/Bavarian church in decoration and treatment. The pulpit and altars are typical, as are also the large figure statues ornamenting each pier (PLATE 114). The whole décor is in painted and gilded stucco, imitating white and coloured marble. It is rich but not over ornate: a superb, unified interior (853). The exterior is simpler, also Baroque with its undulating convex/concave façade and great dome and lantern but restrained in the ornamentation of its plastic monumentality. The Ionic order has a plain frieze, and decoration is confined to a few large sculptured figures and window tympana.

Christoph Dientzenhofer carried out a great deal of other work in Czechoslovakia, such as the monastic church at *Břevnov*. Other architects continued through the first 50 years of the eighteenth century designing in Baroque manner. The work of the Czech architect *Johann Santin-Aichel* is typical, as can be seen in such examples as his remodelling of the Cistercian *Abbey Church* at *Sedlec* and the Benedictine *Abbey Church* at *Kladruby*. The *Church of S. Saviour* in *Prague* and the remodelled interior of *S. Michael* at *Olomouc* are further instances of the wide spread of the Baroque style in Czechoslovakia.

The outstanding architect of this last phase of the Baroque in mid-century here was *Kilian Ignatius Dientzenhofer* (1690–1751), son of Christoph. He completed the Church of S. Nicholas in 1727, finishing the choir, dome and tower. He built many churches, using strongly Baroque, plastic forms and designing on octagonal, oval and circular ground plan. By mid-century, when the European tendency was towards classicism and away from Baroque, he still continued in his bold chiaroscuro designs. His churches in smaller towns and villages have mainly survived but, sadly, some of those in Prague are in poor condition. His Benedictine *Abbey Church of S. Nicholas* in the *Old Town* in Old Town Hall Square* has a fine monumental exterior (851), with a straight front but full of movement in its plasticity and ornament. Inside, the building is less successful. Kilian's Church of *S. John on the Rock*, in the city (begun 1730), has a fine position on the edge of a hillside. The building is in poor condition on the exterior and is ruined inside but, even in this state, the magnificence of the monumental design is clearly visible. A branching double staircase leads from the pavement steeply up to the façade doorways. The elevation itself is curved, articulated in massive Doric Order, with tall twin towers set inwards at an angle to the central portico.

Poland

Just as the Italian influence had brought the Renaissance architectural forms early to Poland, the same source was responsible for the introduction of Baroque architecture in the late sixteenth century. By this time Renaissance design had been assimilated and was in extensive use;

* *Not to be confused with his father's Church of S. Nicholas on the Malá Strana.*

BAROQUE ARCHITECTURE IN CZECHOSLOVAKIA

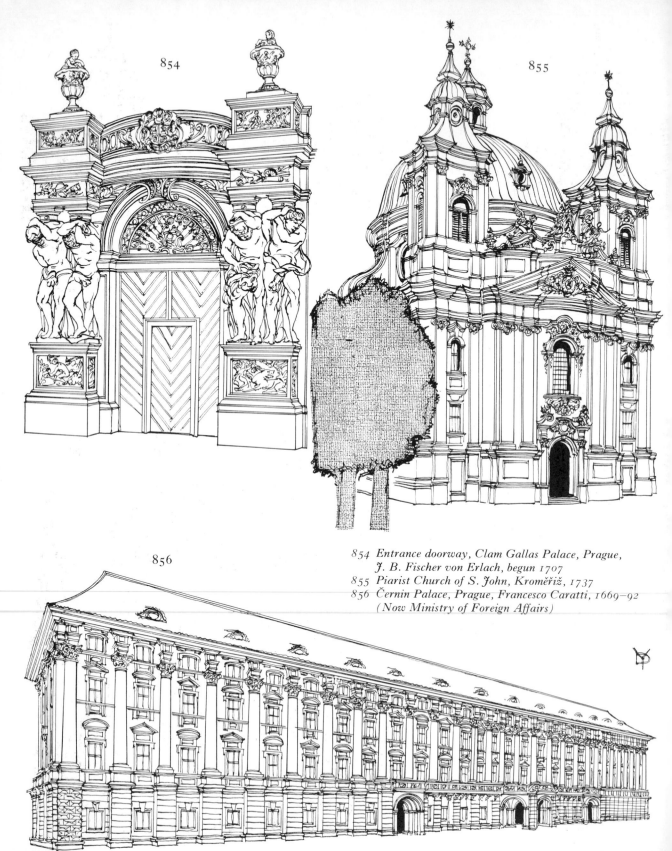

854 *Entrance doorway, Clam Gallas Palace, Prague,*
J. B. Fischer von Erlach, begun 1707
855 *Piarist Church of S. John, Kroměřiž, 1737*
856 *Černin Palace, Prague, Francesco Caratti, 1669–92*
(Now Ministry of Foreign Affairs)

BAROQUE ARCHITECTURE IN POLAND

857 *Wilanow Palace, near Warsaw. Begun Agostino Locci after 1677 ; completed by Spazzio and Fontana 1725–33*

858 *Jesuit Church of S. S. Peter and Paul, Cracow, Giovanni Trevano, 1596–1619*

859 *High altar, Abbey Church of Trzebnica near Wroclaw, Gottleib Daene, 1780–5*

designers were ready for an early introduction of the new theme. The Roman Catholic Church brought about the creation of the first buildings, which were erected for the Jesuit and Cistercian Orders. The Jesuits had established themselves in *Cracow*, where at first they used the existing churches, then decided to build to their own designs, using their own architects of Italian origin. The *Church of SS. Peter and Paul* was one of the first of these and it is closely modelled on Il Gesù in Rome. The façade (**858**) is clearly based on Vignola's prototype, though his side scrolls are replaced by concave sweeps. The interior is Roman Baroque on the classic pattern. The Corinthian order, in coupled pilasters, is used all round the church as well as on the crossing piers. The dome stands on a drum and is capped by its lantern. Nave and transepts are barrel vaulted in monumental style and, in the apse, the conch is decorated all over with relief sculpture.

A later Jesuit example is the *Church of S. Matthew* (1689) at *Wroclaw*. Later called the University Church, it is constructed within the university group of buildings. The exterior was badly damaged in the Second World War but the classic façade remains with Corinthian pilasters and concave sides to the upper gable. The interior is very fine and typical ornate Baroque of the late seventeenth century. The walls are articulated in the Composite order and there is a gallery round the sides of the church. Richly ornamented altars occupy each bay, while the monumental, Composite order high altar extends over the whole of the east end of the building. The barrel-vaulted ceilings are painted all over in one immense scheme. There is a quantity of good quality sculpture and gilded decoration. *Wroclaw University* is itself an outstanding Jesuit Baroque achievement. Begun in 1728, the river façade (**862**), designed by *Domenico Martinelli*, presents an elegant scheme, seen from the University Bridge over the Oder.

Elsewhere in Poland, Baroque church design developed in the seventeenth century on varied lines. Some examples had the southern German type of façade, with tall, twin towers and curving, undulating centrepieces. Others, especially the early buildings, still used Renaissance strapwork of Flemish type or Italian Renaissance orders.

In the later years of the seventeenth century,

Baroque church design illustrated the Polish love of rich ornamentation. The *Church of S. Anthony* at *Poznan* is an example. The façade is based on that of Il Gesù. The interior is aisled, an altar set at each Doric pier, and there are clerestory windows above. The barrel-vaulted ceiling is painted all over. An incredibly ornate, gilded high altar, with barley sugar columns, occupies the whole of the end wall of the church. The best example of these years is the *Church of S. Anne* in *Cracow*, built to the designs of the Dutch born *Tylman van Gameren* and supervised by *Francesco Solari*. Much of the sculpture on the façade and inside is by *Baldassare Fontana*. The façade is three-storeyed. Ionic pilasters are used on the ground level, concave scrolls set the sides of the storey above, while at the top is a plain gable. The exterior is monumental and on classic pattern, and its simplicity contrasts with the richly ornamented interior (**861**). This is on Roman Baroque lines with Composite pilasters (**861**) and aisles containing chapels. The barrel vaults are sculptured and painted. The cruciform church has similarities to S. Andrea della Valle in Rome (**750**), but the dome over the crossing is smaller and the standard of craftsmanship inferior to the Roman church.

Eighteenth century Baroque church design in Poland is generally on monumental lines and often large-scale and bold. In 1716, *Fischer von Erlach* introduced Viennese Baroque in his *Electoral Chapel* added to the east end of the *Cathedral of Wroclaw*. Designed in his classic style it has an oval dome, contrasting with the circular cupola of the Renaissance chapel next to it. In *L'vov*, now in the U.S.S.R., the *Dominican Church* is a bold design (**860**) on elliptical plan. This is surmounted by a large oval dome on its drum, both carried on eight piers. It is a mixture of styles, part Italian and part Bavarian; a fine, monumental, vigorous Baroque. On different lines is the Greek Catholic *Cathedral of S. George* in the same city (**863**). It has a fine position on the crest of a hill and is approached up a flight of steps with sculptured *putti* finials (PLATE 115). Also something of an architectural blend, it is a centrally planned church but cruciform. A tall, four-sided drum, capped by a low dome, rises over the crossing, while the four subsidiary domes are concealed by the attic mouldings. A magnificent Baroque façade, sur-

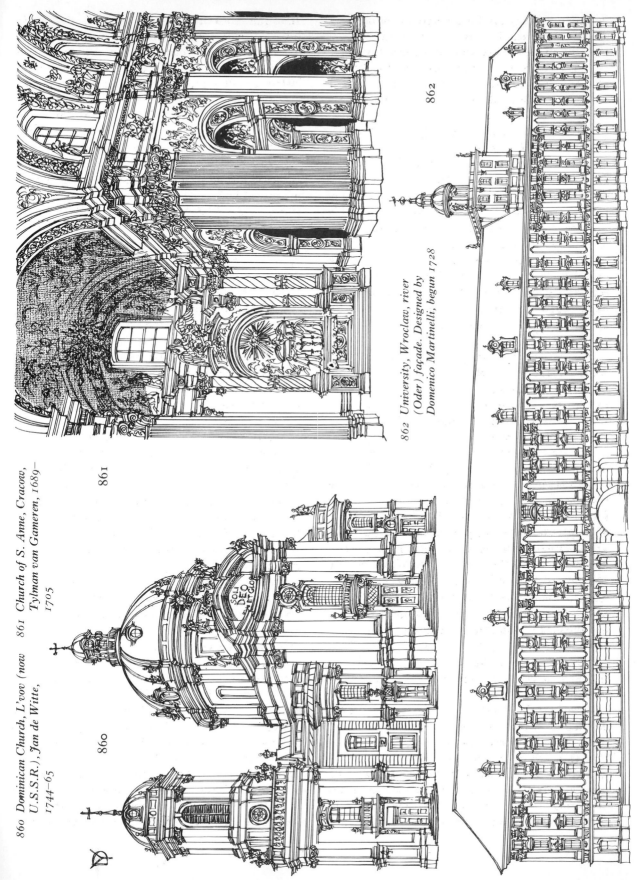

862

862 *University, Wrocław, river
(Oder) façade. Designed by
Domenico Martinelli, begun 1728*

861

861 *Church of S. Anne, Cracow,
Tylman van Gameren, 1689–
1705*

860

860 *Dominican Church, L'vov (now
U.S.S.R.), Jan de Witte,
1744–65*

*863 Cathedral of S. George, L'vov, U.S.S.R.,
Bernardo Meretyn, 1738–58 (completed 1776)*

863

mounted by a sculptured, equestrian group of S. George, fronts the building. It is an interesting blend of Italian and eastern European architectural traditions. A late example of a richly decorated Baroque interior is the *Abbey Church* at *Trzebnica* on the outskirts of Wroclaw. The building itself is all white inside and of monumental design, but the numerous altars, some of immense size and complexity, give an impression of gilded and sculptured richness to the whole interior (**859**).

A large proportion of the seventeenth and eighteenth century building of palaces and large houses was devastated during the Second World War but much rebuilding has been carried out. This is particularly so in Wroclaw and Warsaw. Typical was the *Krasinski Palace* in *Warsaw* (1676–97), built by *Tylman van Gameren*, with decoration by *Andreas Schlüter* (demolished 1944 but now rebuilt). In the later eighteenth century a number of rococo palaces were also built in Warsaw, but little survived the war.

The *Palace of Wilanow*, however, eight miles south of Warsaw, escaped severe damage. It was the royal palace of King John III Sobieski, who bought the village of Wilanow in 1677 and commissioned a country house near the capital. It began as a moderate sized house (its name derived from Villa Nova), designed by *Agostino Locci*, a Pole of Italian origin, and built 1677–96. The chief sculptor was *Andreas Schlüter* from Gdansk (p. 128), who carried out much of the rich, sculptural decoration and, possibly, influenced the architectural design. The building was enlarged between 1725 and 1733, by the Italian architects *Spazzio* and *Fontana*. Wings were extended and Baroque towers were added, while the entrance façade was considerably altered later in the century. The garden elevation (**857**), however, has retained much of its original appearance. The interior was seriously damaged in the War, but it has been largely restored and the palace is now part of the National Museum of Warsaw.

Northern Europe:
The U.S.S.R.

It is impossible to apply the same type of architectural labels and time scale to European Russia as to other countries of the Continent. Northern nations like Poland and even Sweden and Denmark had kept fairly strong links with western culture over the centuries, largely through the Roman Catholic and Protestant Churches; Russia remained aloof. The majority of outstanding buildings up till 1700 have, therefore, been discussed in Volume 1, Chapter 3 because, despite a sixteenth and seventeenth century date, they are of Russian Byzantine design. Some buildings, while reflecting the national style generally encouraged by the Tsars and Russian Church, began to include Medieval and Renaissance features, usually in fenestration and doorways. Those have been included in Volume 2 Chapters 1 and 2.

A number of interesting buildings, especially churches, have survived from the seventeenth century, still displaying this fundamentally Byzantine and national approach. The *Church of the Georgian Virgin* in *Moscow* (1634–54), for example, has much in common with the Putinki Church in the city (**246**). There is the same rich colouring and surface decoration, the rows of *kokoshniki* surmounted by grouped onion domes on tall drums. The windows and doorways show some classical influence, but the entrance porch is essentially Russian. The *Church of the Nativity* in *Gorky* (1699) is similar.

In the early seventeenth century the city of *Yaroslavl*, north of Moscow, became prosperous and a number of churches were built. Though plainer than the Moscow ones, they show the same construction and design as, for instance, the *Church of S. Elijah*. At *Rostov*, just south of Yaroslavl, the extensive Kremlin layout was built in the seventeenth century (Volume 2, p. 192 and Fig. **562**). This is a fortified monastic town with a great barbican Medieval type gatehouse, into which the church is incorporated; a not unusual procedure in Russia, which can be seen in the *Pechersk Monastery* at *Kiev* (**865** and **866**), though this is a more Baroque than Medieval example.

In the later seventeenth century the national Byzantine style was still in use, though classical features were now more obvious. The *Archangel Cathedral* group at *Gorky* illustrates this tendency as does also the *Cathedral of the Assumption* (1693–9) in the *Riazan Kremlin* built by *Bukhvostov*. This Cathedral is still in the form of a tall block surmounted by grouped domes on tall drums, but the entrance doorway and window design combine classical detail with eastern cresting. The belfry of the Kremlin Cathedral group is purely classical as it was built later, in 1789–1840 (**869**).

The uniting of the Ukraine with Greater Russia in the late seventeenth century brought a timid westernisation of both clergy and culture. Baroque architectural ideas began to seep through from Austria, Hungary and Czechoslovakia. In *Moscow* this progress was slow and the Byzantine theme remained paramount for a long time, as is shown by the *Church of the Twelve Apostles* in the *Kremlin*. This has the five Russian domes on the cubical block structure like the early Kremlin cathedrals here (Volume 1, p. 140). The eighteenth century belfry in *Chernigov* in the Ukraine is much more classical, as is the Kiev example (**866**). There is one crowning dome, in both cases, but the columns and fenestration are entirely western.

Peter the Great: the Early Eighteenth Century

The eighteenth century in Russia saw a complete reversal of the earlier policies of the Tsars and the Church towards closing all frontiers against foreigners. As today in Intourist hotels, travellers from abroad had been kept separate from the native population by segregation in a different part of the city. Fear of infection from more liberal political and ecclesiastical views was then, as now, fundamental to Russian philosophy. The autocratic rule during the eighteenth century by three great Tsars (or Tsarinas), Peter, Elizabeth, Catherine, broken only by the short, unstable reigns of the ineffectual male line that descended from Peter, altered the whole picture. Russia became part of Europe again as she had been in the early days of Kiev's greatness.

Peter I returned to Russia after his first visit to western Europe in 1697. He planned to pursue vigorously a policy of trade and interchange of ideas and cultures with the west, which he saw as an advantage for Russia. He deemed it foolish for his country to be cut off from the development, social, political and artistic, which had been emerging in western Europe during the previous two centuries.

In architecture, his most important contribution was the foundation of *S. Petersburg* (now Leningrad). The site where this great city stands today was, in 1703 when Peter decided to build his capital there, as inhospitable and unpropitious as could be imagined. Situated at a latitude of 60°, the climate was bitterly cold in a long, dark winter, damp and misty in a short cold spring and autumn, and enjoying only a brief summer. The islands in the mouth of the River Neva, where S. Petersburg was founded, were of marshy ground; the water was shallow and unsuitable for large ships. The site was cut off from the rest of civilised Russia by extensive, dense forestation.

In spite of much criticism Peter carried on. He ordered works to begin on a fortress and sea-port based on the islands and necessary living structures were erected. He wanted a fireproof stone and brick city, but the area had only wood, so many of the early structures had to be in this material. He brought an enormous labour force from all over Russia, of whom thousands died from cold, hunger and exhaustion. He ordered a cessation of all building in stone and brick elsewhere in Russia in order to conserve sufficient supplies for his city. He ordered aristocratic, merchant and government official families to leave their homes and estates and come to live in the capital. Being an autocrat, with the power of the State behind him, and being Peter the Great, he succeeded. When he died in 1725, the foundation of a Baroque town was established. By the end of the century, S. Petersburg was one of the great classical cities of the world, a water city like Amsterdam or Stockholm though not, as is sometimes claimed, in the least like Venice.

All the great monarchs of the eighteenth century in Russia employed predominantly architects of foreign origin. This was because they were importing a foreign architectural style and needed to train their native artists in an unfamiliar manner. This influx from western Europe—chiefly Italy, France and Germany—not only of architects, but of their staffs of artisans in painting, sculpture, glazing, wood and stone carving, ironwork and stucco brought tremendous vitality to Russian art, but it also tended to curtail the national culture and crafts. These became unfashionable and many skills were lost, especially in timber and ceramic work.

Partly because much of the building was in wood and partly due to the shift from the original building on the islands in the Neva to the mainland, much of the architecture of the time of Peter the Great has been replaced or altered. But the planning of the city remains. This was carefully worked out from the beginning. The city centre was established on and near the waterline of the Neva, mainly on the north-facing bank. Here was a great central square with long, wide boulevards radiating southwards from it. The large islands opposite to the north bank continued to be used for important structures.

The first important architect whom Peter employed at S. Petersburg was *Domenico Tressini* (1670–1734) from Italian Switzerland. Tressini (in Russia: Andrei Petrovich Trezin) built the great *Peter and Paul Fortress* on the large island opposite to the Winter Palace. With foundations of earth and wood, on pentagonal plan, he used brick facings. Inside, in the great court, he built the *Cathedral of SS. Peter and Paul*; the burial church of the tsars. The present structure was restored in the later eighteenth century, to the original design, after earlier storm damage and neglect (**871**). From contemporary engravings it can be seen that it lacks some of the Baroque boldness due to its rebuilding in an age of neoclassicism.

Tressini carried out a great deal of other work —government buildings, hospitals, barracks, fortifications—but most of this has disappeared or been severely altered. He designed an ambitious plan for the Alexander Nevsky Monastery in 1715, for example but nothing of his work remains in the existing structure.

After Tressini came a stream of foreign architects of greater or lesser note. They include *Andreas Schlüter* from Berlin (p. 128), *Gottfried Schädel* and *Theodor Schwertfeger*. Much of their work has been lost or altered. A similar fate befell the contribution by the French architect *Jean Baptiste Alexandre Le Blond* (1679–1719). He was tempted to S. Petersburg in 1716 from Paris by an offer of a large salary but, like Schlüter, died after a few years. His chief work was Peter's great summer palace on the Gulf of Finland, nearly 25 kilometres west of S. Petersburg. This had been projected by Tressini 1711–14. It was begun according to Le Blond's designs in 1716, on restrained, French-classical pattern, with a two-storey central block with low,

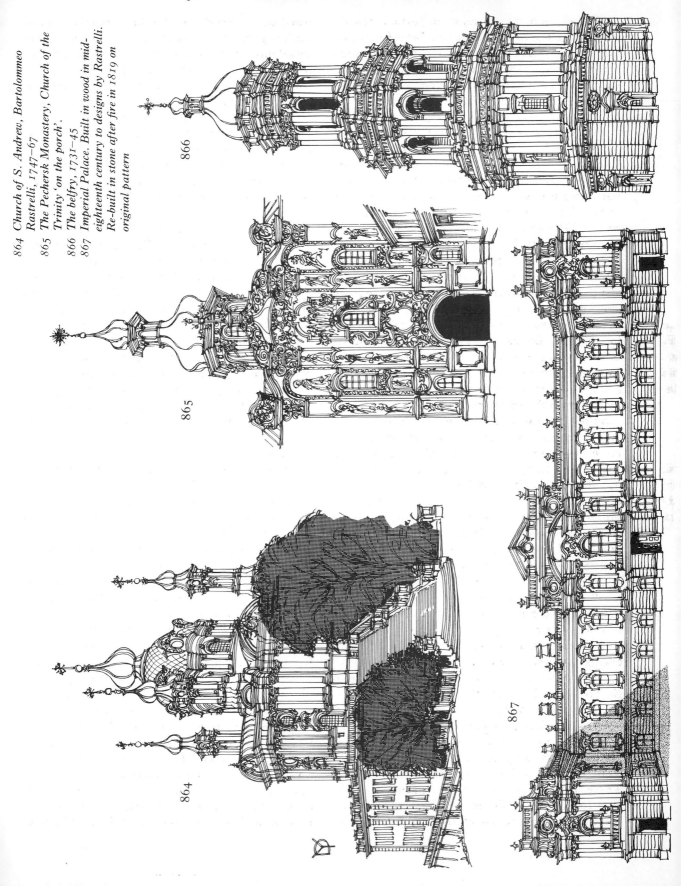

864 Church of S. Andrew, Bartolommeo
Rastrelli, 1747–67
865 The Pechersk Monastery, Church of the
Trinity 'on the porch'.
866 The belfry, 1731–45
867 Imperial Palace. Built in wood in mid-
eighteenth century to designs by Rastrelli.
Re-built in stone after fire in 1819 on
original pattern

866

865

864

867

Plate *119*   The Winter Palace, S. Petersburg, 1754–6, Bartolommeo Francesco Rastrelli

Plate *120*   Town Hall balcony, rococo design, Bamberg, Germany, 1732–7

straight-wings terminating in pavilions. *Petrodvorets* (Peter's Palace), originally called by the German name of Peterhof, became the site for rebuilding and extension throughout the eighteenth and nineteenth centuries and a number of different palaces were built for the tsars and members of the aristocracy along this stretch of the Gulf of Finland (pp. 169, 172).

The Empress Elizabeth—Mid-Eighteenth Century

Elizabeth Petrovna (1709–1762) was Peter's younger daughter. In 1741 she succeeded in overthrowing the unsatisfactory government of the Regency and reigned for 20 years, displaying many of the characteristics of strength, wisdom and tact of her father. Architecturally, this period saw the establishment of Russian Baroque under the leadership of *Bartolommeo Francesco Rastrelli* (1700–71), who was born of an Italian family but who had come to Russia as a very young man with Le Blond. The son of a sculptor, Rastrelli soon showed his outstanding talent. He settled well in his adopted country as Bartholomei Bartholomeevich Rastrelli and was allowed to work and study for some years in Paris, Austria, Germany and Italy.

Rastrelli's opportunity came under Elizabeth. From 1741 to 1762 he designed all the important buildings in Russia, especially in S. Petersburg. His contribution was even more enduring than his own buildings, which in themselves established Russian Baroque architecture as of international standard. The younger school of Russian architects were trained in his ways and learnt their profession from him. A fully national school was established once more which kept pace with the stylistic changes in Europe but retained, like France, Germany or England, its national interpretation of them.

Rastrelli's buildings, churches and palaces, were always powerfully, three-dimensionally Baroque in form, with decoration which tended more to rococo as time passed. They were Russian in the greatness of their sheer size and in the use of colour on the exterior as well as inside. Some of his palaces have disappeared or have been much altered, but a great deal remains. The work in S. Petersburg was nearly all damaged in the Second World War, but much of it has been restored. It is doubtful that the modern standard of craftsmanship in stucco decoration, painting and sculpture is anywhere near as good as it was on Rastrelli's original buildings, but the general impression is fine; it is only on closer inspection that the poverty of the finish and form becomes clearly apparent. Two particular examples of this decline are the Winter Palace and Petrodvorets.*

Of the many *palaces* which Rastrelli built for the aristocracy in *S. Petersburg* two examples especially survive: the *Vorontsov* (1743–5) and the *Stroganov* (1750–4). The latter (**872**) is typical of his work in its bold Baroque projection of the giant order together with rococo fenestration and ornament.

He built two imposing ecclesiastical schemes: the *Smolny Convent* in *S. Petersburg* and *S. Andrew's Church* in *Kiev*. The Smolny Convent is an immense layout with the great Cathedral of the Resurrection in the centre. This is a landmark over much of the city (**876**). The convent was started by Elizabeth for orphan girls. Rastrelli laid out conventual buildings on a Greek cross plan, with the cathedral in the centre. This, in particular, shows his restoration to Russia of its national Byzantine monastic church plan married to Baroque powerfulness and rococo decoration—a masterly combination. For colour and size its equal could be found in no other country in Europe. The interior was completed long after Rastrelli's death in cool, neo-classical form. It is now in poor condition and requires further restoration. The *Church of S. Andrew* in *Kiev* has a fine hill-top situation and is approached by long flights of steps. Once again Rastrelli's talent for combining a magnificent Baroque silhouette of a church on cruciform plan with the Russian traditional grouping and design of domes and tall drums is clearly shown (**864**).

Rastrelli's outstanding achievement is in his three great royal palaces for Elizabeth: the *Winter Palace* in *S. Petersburg*, *Petrodvorets* and *Tsarkoe Selo* on the Gulf of Finland. The Winter Palace along the edge of the south bank of the river Neva was the last and most successful of these (**874** and **875** and PLATE 119). It has an immensely long façade to the river on the north side and to the vast palace square on the south, scene of the massacre of 1905. Rastrelli controls this length, retains the interest by his bold treatment while the white and green rococo gleams in

---

* It is interesting to see in East Berlin that the rebuilding and restoration of old buildings in the devastated city, though slow in completion, are of a very high standard.

The deficiency is obviously national not political. Examples here include the Royal Library, the Opera House and the Humboldt University.

868 Palace of Peterhof (Petrodvorets) on the Gulf of
Finland, about 15 miles west of Leningrad.
Designed Le Blond 1716–17; remodelled by
Rastrelli 1747–53. The drawing shows the palace
as it is now, restored from war damaged condition,
largely to the original design

869 Bell tower of the Cathedral of the Assumption,
Riazan Kremlin, 1789–1840, completed Voronikhin

870 Bishop's Palace near the Cathedral, mainly
seventeenth century

871 Cathedral of S. S. Peter and Paul, Leningrad (in the Fortress on an island in the River Neva). Built 1714–25 by Domenico Tressini. Spire nearly 400 feet high. This drawing shows the cathedral as it is today. It is more severe and less Baroque than Tressini's work.

façade immensely, but retained its proportion by adding a new storey. Again, despite the fact that it was not his new project, he infused a more Baroque element into the French classical structure and decorated it with rococo fenestration. The extensive grounds were laid out in French manner with *rond-points* and vistas, parterres, terraces and fountains. These are of engineering interest: the whole scheme is based on a gravity feed system of hydraulics as the great palace is on the brow of a hill and the central cascade descends directly to the sea (**868**). The palace was seriously damaged in the Second World War, but is now fully restored on the exterior. It is all painted in yellow with white decorative features. The sculpture of the fountains and walks has been replaced. These are copies, poor ones unfortunately, of the original subjects and groups, including the central Samson fountain. A number of classical buildings remain in the grounds, for instance *Mon Plaisir* by *Le Blond* (*c.* 1717), where Peter lived while his palace was being built, and Braunstein's Orangery of *c.* 1725. Mon Plaisir was later enlarged by Rastrelli and altered by Quarenghi.

The *Great Palace* of *Tsarkoe Selo* was built in the village of this name 32 kilometres from S. Petersburg. The name means Tsar's (or Imperial) Village, taken from the original Finnish settlement there. It is now re-titled Pushkin. Rastrelli also altered and enlarged this vast palace for Elizabeth. It had a frontage of nearly 1000 feet, rather monotonous on the main elevation but carried out in Rastrelli's rococo style. Further alterations and additions were made under Catherine, notably interiors by Charles Cameron. Tsarkoe Selo was almost totally destroyed in the war but is now magnificently restored.

Empress Catherine II—the Late Eighteenth Century

Catherine the Great (1729–96), remarkable inheritor of the Romanov dynasty, was not a Romanov or a Russian. She was born in Stettin (now Szczecin in Poland), a German princess called Sophia. The Empress Elizabeth approved of her and she married Peter in 1744, Elizabeth's nephew and heir who became Peter III on her death. Within a few months of his accession he had shown himself unsuitable and incapable

the reflections in the waters of the Neva. The Winter Palace has been altered and restored more than once, but Rastrelli's magnificent panache still shows through.

He began enlargement and reconstruction at Peter's *Petrodvorets* in 1747. Elizabeth wanted much more space and large reception rooms for her much greater court. Rastrelli lengthened the

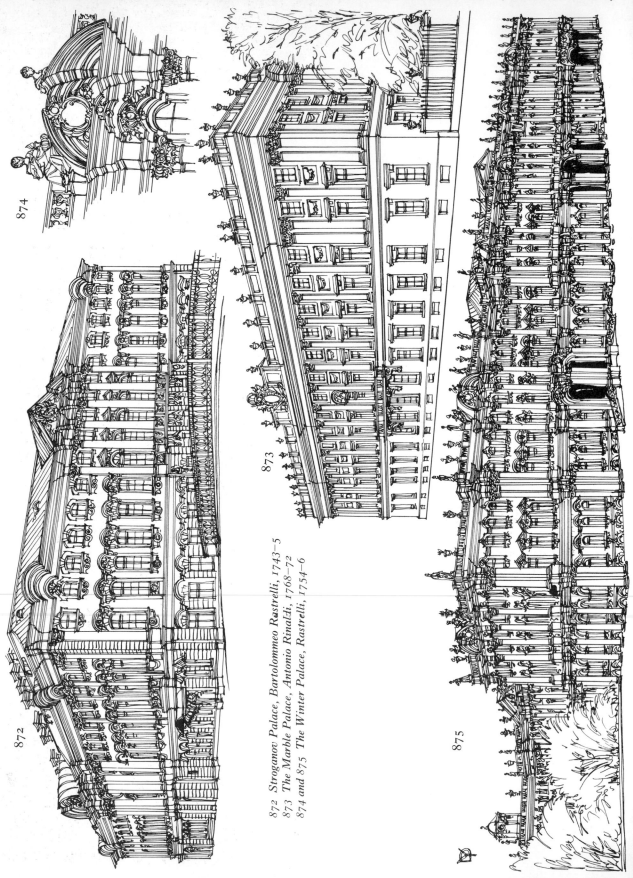

874

873

872

875

872 Stroganov Palace, Bartolommeo Rastrelli, 1743–5
873 The Marble Palace, Antonio Rinaldi, 1768–72
874 and 875 The Winter Palace, Rastrelli, 1754–6

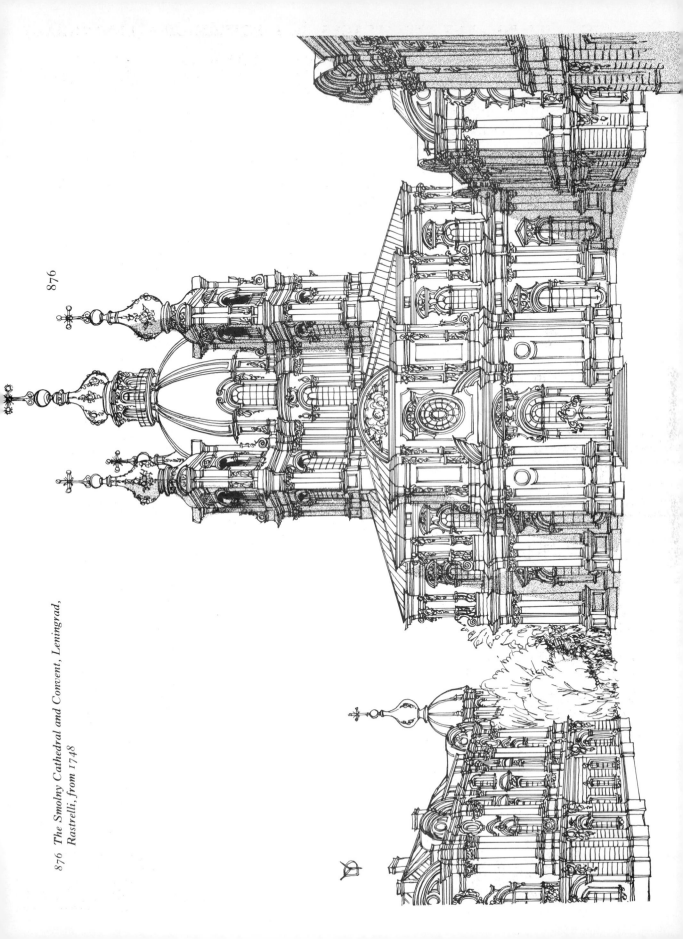

876 *The Smolny Cathedral and Convent, Leningrad,*
Rastrelli, from 1748

for the responsibilities of Tsar. Sophia, who had taken the name of Catherine on her acceptance into the Russian Orthodox Church in 1744, became Empress and ruled for 34 years. She identified herself completely with Russia and its people and became, more even than Elizabeth, natural successor to Peter the Great.

During her reign architecture and the other arts flourished and became completely professional, able to compete on level terms with western European countries. Catherine abandoned Baroque and rococo styles and embraced neo-classicism. This was the trend of the day in Europe as well as her own personal preference. Under her, different architects, foreign and Russian, evolved a pure Russian classical style.

Catherine employed a number of foreign architects, among them the Frenchman *Vallin de la Mothe*, the German *Velten* and the Italian Rinaldi. *Antonio Rinaldi* came to Russia from Rome in 1755. He built two large palaces, of which the *Marble Palace* in *S. Petersburg* survives (**873**). As can be seen, this is a much quieter elevation than Rastrelli's work, with only slight projections and a neo-classical emphasis on the horizontal members. It acquired its name from the red and grey materials with which it was faced. Rinaldi also began the great *Cathedral of S. Isaac*, an impressive design, but the building was not completed; it was finally erected by Montferrand 1817–57 (Volume 2, p. 189).

Of the Russian architects, *Vasili Ivanovich Bazhenov* (1739–99) built the *Arsenal* in *S. Petersburg* and a palace. In *Moscow* he was responsible for the *Pashkov Palace* which is built on an eminence near the centre of the city. It is now part of the Lenin Library (**879**). His *Church of All Mourners* is more classical and of later date (**880**).

In the last decades of the century *Ivan Yegorovich Starov* (1743–1808) built the impressive *Tauride Palace* and the new *Cathedral* for the large *Alexander Nevsky Monastery* in *S. Petersburg*. This, a monument of neo-classical design, was to replace the now decaying structure designed by Tressini.

Catherine then showed a preference for Western European architecture and employed *Charles Cameron* (c. 1740–1812), a Scot, to decorate a new series of private rooms for her at the *Palace* of *Tsarkoe Selo*. Cameron's style of work was after that of Robert Adam and he used this form of neo-classical décor in delicate stucco relief work, marble columns and wood panelling. Some of his interiors, like Adam's, were in Imperial Roman tradition and he employed beautiful materials such as marble veneers, agate, malachite and ceramics to produce a rich, glowing and colourful effect. Cameron was then employed as architect for the Grand Duke's *country house* at *Pavlovsk* (1781–96). Here again his interior work was highly successful, especially the two halls, one Greek, one Roman, which again show a marked affinity to Adam's Roman palace schemes. Cameron also laid out the park here on English (Capability Brown) lines. Catherine preferred such landscaping to the formal French (Versailles) pattern. Unfortunately much of Cameron's work here, as at Tsarkoe Selo, suffered greatly in the Second World War.

The best architect of this period was the Italian *Giacomo Quarenghi* (1744–1817), who worked in Russia from 1780 onwards. He designed the Palladian type structure, called the *English Palace*, at Petrodvorets in 1781–9, as well as a palace at Tsarkoe Selo. In *S. Petersburg*, he built the *Academy of Sciences* (1783–7) on Palladian pattern and, in 1782–5, the *Hermitage Theatre*. Quarenghi's work was on Italian lines but he followed different sources according to commission: Palladio, early Renaissance or Baroque. His buildings were monumental, well-proportioned and designed with taste and quality.

Scandinavia: Denmark

Scandinavia was still too cut off in the seventeenth century from the artistic centres of Baroque Europe to develop her individual approach to this form. On the northern fringe of Europe, Norway and Finland largely went their own way architecturally, using traditional materials and building styles. Sweden and Denmark initiated building programmes under royal patronage, trying to establish cities planned and decorated in contemporary manner, but Italy was too far away for the Baroque forms to percolate other than slowly and the northern cities had little to offer to attract Italian architects. In both countries the work in contemporary manner of the seventeenth and much of the eighteenth centuries was by foreign-born architects, chiefly French

EIGHTEENTH CENTURY CLASSICAL BUILDING IN MOSCOW

877 Entrance porch and 878 Steeple
of the Church of the Archangel
Gabriel, I. P. Zarudny, 1705–7
(restored 1733–80)

879 Pashkov Palace (now part of the
Lenin Library), V. I. Bazhenov,
1784–6

880 Church of All Mourners,
Bazhenov, 1790; rotunda
rebuilt, 1828–33

877

879

878

880

and Dutch. It was certainly the Dutch Palladian style which dominated the earlier classical work.

Typical of this style in seventeenth century Denmark is the *Charlottenburg Palace* in *Copenhagen*, built by the Dutchman *Evert Janssen* (**883**). Severe, symmetrical, restrained in brick, with sandstone reserved for decoration, this is characteristically Dutch Palladian.

A measure of how far the Danes were lagging behind in classical development is seen in the seventeenth century churches in *Copenhagen*. The interior of the *Trinislatis* (Trinity) *Church*, its white and light décor contrasting pleasingly with the dark, gaunt exterior, has classical, octagonal piers and Baroque furniture, but retains a Medieval style vault, despite the late date (**881**). The *Vor Frelser Kirke*, on the other hand, designed by *Lambert van Haven* in 1682, is fully classical. The brick exterior is essentially northern early Baroque with its tall western tower, rather than a dome, and its simple brick mouldings, doorway and fenestrations. (The strange spiral steeple is a later addition by de Thurah and based on Borromini's S. Ivo alla Sapienza in Rome). The interior, in vivid contrast, is sparkling, light and spacious. On Greek cross plan, this is spatial Baroque, northern in its plain, large, round-headed windows, simple Doric piers and broad curving vault, decorated only by restrained stucco work above each pier, but the altarpiece, with complete change of mood, creates a focus, after Bernini, its figure sculpture capturing the instant of movement, live and ardent. Quite different again is the richly carved organ loft at the other end of the church. This is in typical northern seventeenth century style, very fine, but more in the trend of Grinling Gibbons (**884**).

In the early eighteenth century, Frederik IV began a comprehensive building programme. He had been attracted on his travels in Italy to the larger villa type of design and commissioned two such buildings in Denmark. The *Palace of Frederiksberg* was begun in 1699 on the outskirts of Copenhagen (**886**). It was a long, simple block, on Roman pattern, in brick and painted stucco. A succession of architects worked on the palace during the eighteenth century, altering and enlarging so that the present building, now under military occupation, has lost some of its character and charm, particularly in the addition

of the extensive flanking wings. It is a pleasant building but provincial in appearance and standard.

Fredensborg, just south-west of Helsingör, was begun in 1719. Frederik this time commissioned a Palladian villa which was designed on symmetrical plan, with a domed, central hall. On either side of the main block, low wings extend round an octagonal courtyard. This building has also been added to and altered but retains its original design better than Frederiksberg. A pleasant structure, situated in a fine park, it is somewhat mediocre in design and finish. It is still used as a royal palace.

The finest eighteenth century building scheme in Denmark is the street layout in *Copenhagen* centred on *Amalienborg*, called Frederiksstaden (**885**). King Frederik V, on the throne from 1746–66, envisaged a distinguished residential area around Amaliegade and extending on either side from Bredgade to the harbour. The central open space, the Amalienborg Plads, or the Place Royale, was to be an octagon lined by palaces and divided by streets radiating from a central focal point. The scheme was begun in 1749 and the equestrian statue of Frederik, by the French sculptor J. F. Saly, was set in the centre of the piazza in 1768. The blocks around the octagon were designed to be of one scheme. Four of these are set on four of the sides and (later) Ionic colonnades connect the ranges. The scheme was conceived by Marcus Tuscher, but it was put into operation by the King's architect *Niels Eigtved*. He laid down the overall detailed plans for the buildings of the whole area round the Amalienborg as well as the design for the four palaces round the octagonal *place* which were to be occupied by noble families as town mansions. Now, all four are used as the royal town palace.

Facing the equestrian central statue on the chief axis intersection is Frederiksgade at the end of which *Frederik's Church* was to be built to terminate the vista. It was to be based upon Juvara's type of Baroque memorial church, a centrally planned building with a great dome surmounting the centre. Several designs were made, by Eigtved, by de Thurah and others, but that by the Frenchman *Nicolas Jardin* was finally accepted in 1756 and the church was begun. Building was much interrupted and delayed so that the church was not ultimately

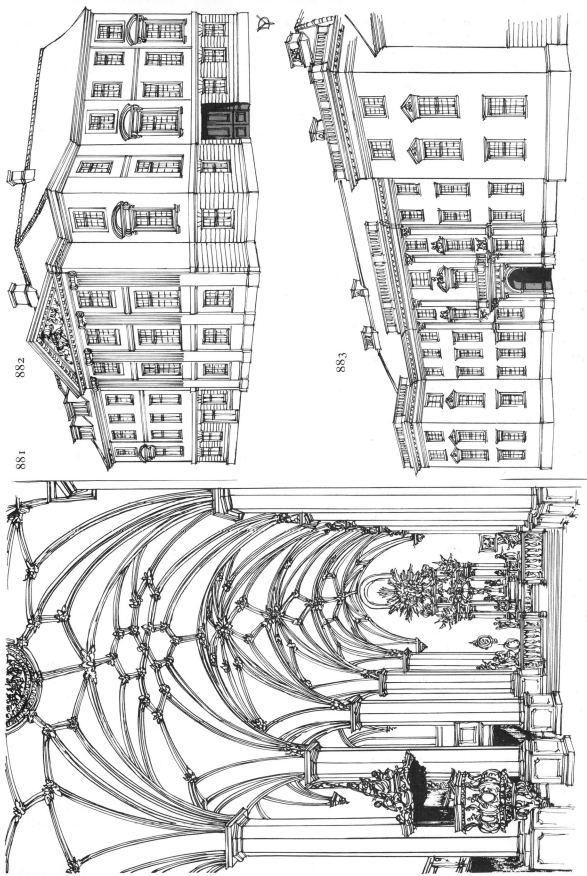

881 *Interior, Trinislatis Church, Copenhagen, 1637–56*
882 *Nos. 3–5, Kongens Nytorv, Copenhagen. House and apartments, C. F. Harsdorff, 1779–80*
883 *Charlottenburg Palace, Copenhagen, Evert Janssen, 1672–83*

884

884 Vor Frelser Kirke (Church of Our Saviour), Copenhagen, Lambert van Haven, 1682

completed until the nineteenth century (Volume 4, p. 67).

A number of country houses on simple, traditional classical pattern were built in the later eighteenth century. That at *Lerchenborg* (**887**) is typical. It is large, long and low, in whitewashed brick. It is unpretentious but well-proportioned and adapted to the flat, pastoral landscape in which it stands.

Town buildings in the later years of the eighteenth century were firstly rococo, of which there are one or two good examples in the Amalienborg area near Bredgade and, then, in line with the times, neo-classical. *C. F. Harsdorff* was an architect who often built in this latter style. His houses and apartments in Kongens Nytorv are one example (**882**), as is his Ionic connecting colonnades in the Amalienborg Plads (**885**).

Sweden

Seventeenth and eighteenth century architecture in Sweden was more distinguished than that in Denmark. Classical design was developed in the first half of the seventeenth century and consolidated in the second. This was largely due to the work of four architects, two families of father and son, of French origin. *Simon de la Vallée*, a Frenchman who had worked in Holland, spent the last five years of his life in Sweden. He died in 1642 but his work was admirably continued and improved by his son *Jean* (1620–96). *Nicodemus Tessin* (1615–81) was also of French origin but passed all his working life in Scandinavia. He became city architect for Stockholm and was the chief royal architect. His *son*, also *Nicodemus* (1654–1728), continued his father's work and inherited his positions. He was in effect Sweden's Christopher Wren. A fifth architect, who contributed considerably to later seventeenth century

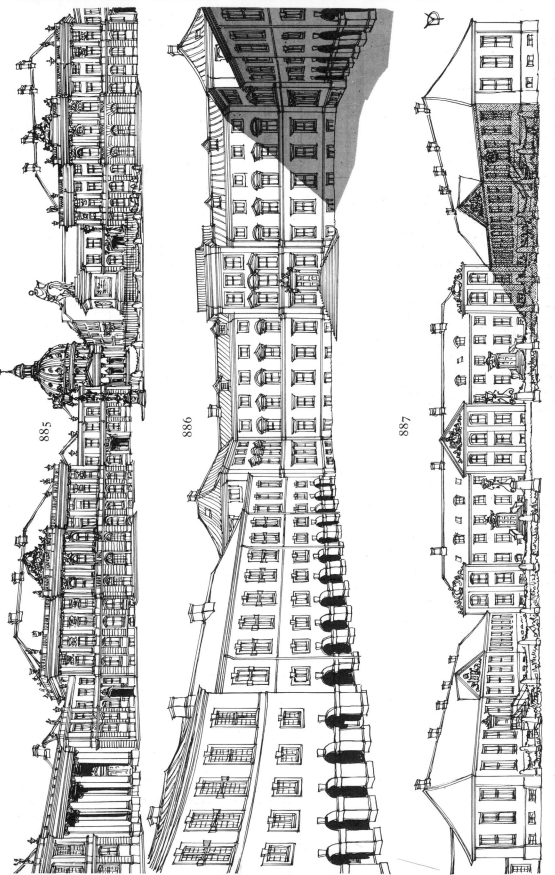

885 *Amalienborg Plads (Place Royale), Copenhagen, begun 1749*
886 *Frederiksberg Palace, near Copenhagen, Italian style, 1699–1730*
887 *Country house, Lerchenborg, later eighteenth century*

work, was *Erik Dahlberg* (1625–1703), Swedish, nationalist and very much an individualist.

A good example of the earlier seventeenth century type of work is the severely plain brick building in *Göteborg* (Gothenburg) the *Kronhus* or Crown House. This has classical doorways and plain windows, but makes no concession to Renaissance decoration, let alone Baroque ornamentation.

The castle or palace at *Skokloster* (**888**), just south of Uppsala, is classical, but in the early Renaissance northern tradition of four-square severity with corner octagonal towers, reminiscent of Aschaffenburg in Germany (**699**).

In this period the Swedish nobility were becoming wealthier and began to build in a more contemporary manner: a Dutch Palladian style. *Joost Vingboons* came from Holland (p. 188) to work on some building projects, one of which was the Nobles' Assembly Hall or House of Lords, *Riddarhuset* in *Stockholm*. This is one of the most perfect Dutch Palladian buildings in Sweden. It was designed by *Simon de la Vallée* in 1641, Vingboons continued the work after the architect's death, but it was completed by Jean de la Vallée (**891**). The strongest influence here was probably Vingboons', as is shown in the simple pilastered front and central pediment though, inside, Jean de la Vallée's fine contribution is the double staircase.

Among the numbers of houses and palaces designed by *Nicodemus Tessin the Elder, Drottningholm Palace* is the most famous. Begun in 1662 as the summer royal palace (for which purpose it is still in use), the palace and gardens were laid out on the island of Lovö in Lake Mälaren about seven miles from Stockholm. The entrance front looks out on to the lake (**893**) while the garden façade (which is of very similar design) faces the park with its imposing terraces and parterres designed in the manner of Versailles. The house itself is very French and inside there is a beautiful hall, saloon and staircase. On Tessin's death in 1681, his son continued the work.

Nicodemus Tessin the Younger was a more cosmopolitan architect, accomplished and with an individualistic style. He had travelled widely in Europe and his best work is modelled on Roman Baroque, especially that in the style of Bernini. Tessin's chief work is the *Royal Palace* in *Stockholm*. This was a castle which the King decided to rebuild. Tessin reconstructed the north wing, but in 1691 a fire destroyed the castle leaving intact only part of the new wing. Tessin continued work, designing a new palace to incorporate the remains. The work proceeded during much of the eighteenth century long after the architect's death. Despite the mixture of styles in classical form resulting from the supervision of several architects, Tessin's Roman Baroque can be seen clearly overall. It is a large palace on Italian plan ranged round a great court. The south façade is vigorously Baroque with monumental Corinthian columned and sculptured centrepiece contrasting with the water elevation, which is severely classical. Equally, the courtyard is monumental and correctly classical while the *cour d'honneur* is boldly rusticated and articulated (**892**).

There is a markedly Baroque flavour about the best of both seventeenth and eighteenth century *churches* in Sweden. A pace-setter was the *Church of S. Katarina* in *Stockholm* by *Jean de la Vallée* (1656), a symmetrical, centrally planned building on Greek cross layout with dome over the crossing and four chapels at the corners each with a smaller cupola over it. Another centrally planned church in the city is that of *Hedvig Eleonora* (**889**), also by Jean de la Vallée. *Nicodemus Tessin the Elder* then designed the *Chapel of King Charles XII* (1671), a centrally planned, octagonal chapel added to the Riddarholm Church in Stockholm. (This was completed by Hårleman in 1743.) Also by Tessin is the imposing *Cathedral* at *Kalmar*. This is on oval, rather than circular plan. The east and west elevations are fronted by a façade, while on the north and south sides, which are shorter, there is an apse. The projected central dome was never built (**894**). The exterior is severe and monumental with good classical detail, while the interior is particularly fine eighteenth century Baroque. A rectangular hall, it has a simply barrel vaulted nave and choir with short barrel vaulted transepts midway. Coupled Ionic pilasters support a continuous entablature. At one end in the apse is the high altar, at the other, the organ. At the sides, in the transepts, seating galleries are carried on Composite columns. The decoration of the church is restrained but of high quality (**895**).

In much simpler vein, the centrally planned

SEVENTEENTH CENTURY ARCHITECTURE IN SWEDEN

888 *Skokloster Castle, Jean de la Vallée and Nicodemus Tessin the Elder, 1646–68*

889 *Hedvig Eleonora Church, Stockholm, Jean de la Vallée, 1656*

890 *Läckö Castle. Medieval fortress enlarged and adapted to a country house in the late seventeenth century by Jean de la Vallée*

891 *The Riddarhuset, Stockholm, Simon and Jean de la Vallée and J. Vingboons, 1641–74*

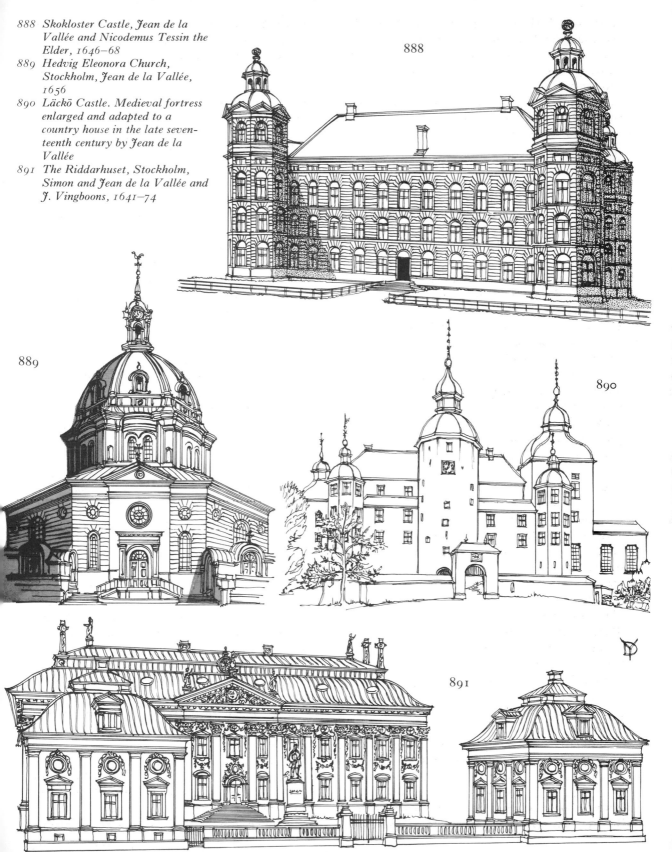

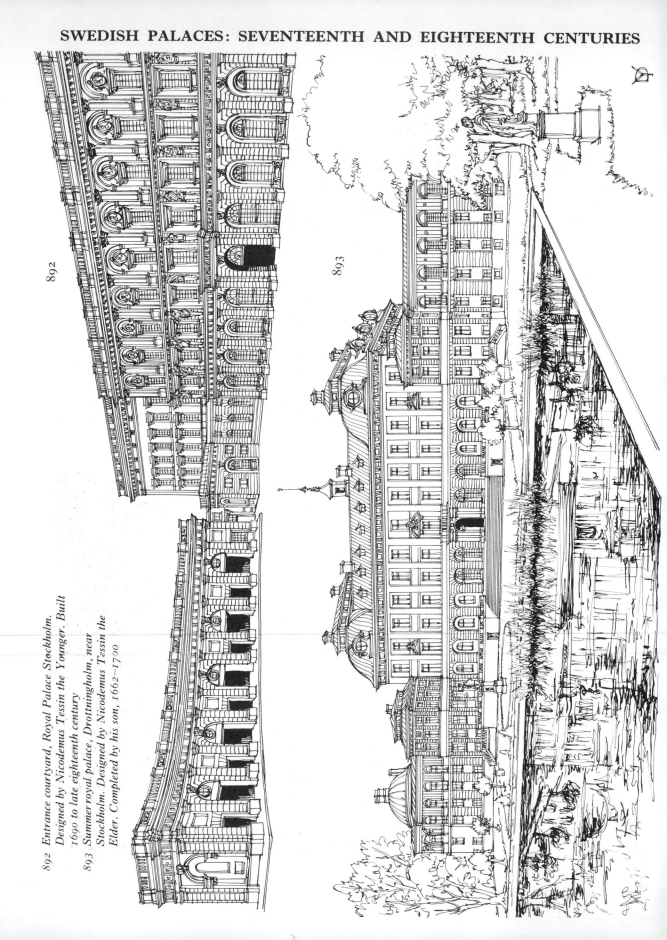

SWEDISH PALACES: SEVENTEENTH AND EIGHTEENTH CENTURIES

892

893

892 *Entrance courtyard, Royal Palace Stockholm.*
Designed by Nicodemus Tessin the Younger. Built
1690 to late eighteenth century

893 *Summer royal palace, Drottningholm, near*
Stockholm. Designed by Nicodemus Tessin the
Elder. Completed by his son, 1662–1700

894

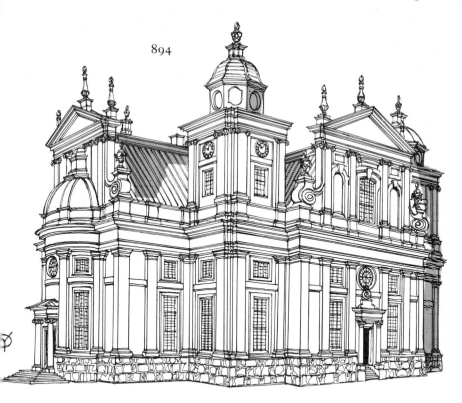

*894 Kalmar Cathedral,
Sweden, Nicodemus
Tessin the Elder, 1660–
1703
895 Interior, Kalmar
Cathedral, Sweden,
Tessin, 1660–1703 (pews
omitted)*

895

church of S. Katarina was also used as a pattern for *Erik Dahlberg* in his late seventeenth century churches at *Karlshamn* and *Laxå*. The latter is entirely of wood, the walls and roofs being covered with shingles. It is octagonal, with four porches symmetrically placed.

Notable among the architects of the later eighteenth century were *Karl Adelcrantz* (1716–96) and *Erik Palmstedt* (1741–1803). Adelcrantz carried out much of the civic planning work, especially in *Stockholm*, where he implemented some of Tessin's original designs for the area round the royal palace. Tessin had planned the palace as a centrepiece for a large scheme. Adelcrantz initiated the *Gustav Adolf Torg* (Square) layout, designing the Opera House there (now demolished), while *Palmstedt* was responsible for the still existing palace which balanced it. The square is on the mainland and opposite to it to the southwards is the large island of Old Stockholm where the royal palace faces the mainland. Between the two is a small island, the Helgeandsholmen. A bridge connects this island northwards and southwards and is the *Norrbro* which was also begun at this time by Adelcrantz. Also in Stockholm, this architect was responsible for the *Adolf Frederik's Church* (1768–83), which is a traditional Baroque design with central dome and lantern. It has a well-proportioned exterior with good detail. Inside, like Il Gesù, it is on genuine Roman Baroque pattern, no aisles or piers and all four arms of the cross barrel vaulted. Typical of *Palmstedt*'s classical work is the *Exchange* in *Stockholm* (1767–76), built on Roman lines.

Norway

The pattern of development in Norway and Finland was different from that of Denmark and Sweden. The former countries were poorer, more remote from the art centres of Europe and in mountain and lakeland terrain which hindered communication and maintained isolation. Until after 1800, the great majority of building was in timber so that, even in the eighteenth century, when contemporary Baroque styles were percolating through, the derivation and adaptation of the time was governed by the medium and climatic conditions. Again, because nearly all structures were of wood, whole streets of buildings, even towns, were periodically ravaged by fire, so that beautiful cities like Bergen, Trondheim and Oslo were constantly replacing their older buildings with new ones.

There is, in consequence, very little left in the towns dating from before 1700. Of eighteenth century work, the most interesting is in *Trondheim*, which was largely rebuilt after a severe fire in 1708. Norway was more prosperous in this century, and, though the new buildings were still of wood, the important ones were larger, more richly decorative and, within the possibilities of the medium, contemporary with design elsewhere. Typical of the best of these is the *Stiftsgården Palace* (**897**). This is the largest wooden building in Scandinavia. It is long, low and built in classical form round three sides of a court. Rather later, but also of wood and very typical, is the *Manor House* at *Lade*, on the outskirts of Trondheim (**898**). Several streets in the centre of Trondheim have a number of fine wooden houses (now sometimes adapted into shops) from the eighteenth and early nineteenth centuries. They are all low and have steeply pitched roofs to throw off the snow. Most of them have classical pedimented window frames and columned porticoes. The best examples are in *Kongens Gate, Munkegata* and *Olav Tryggvasons Gate*.

Other interesting wooden houses in classical style can be seen in *Bergen*, partly in the town and also nearby in Gamle Bergen, at Sandvik. Here, streets of old houses have been preserved as a museum. There are also many examples of domestic and agricultural architecture in wood construction, preserved in the Oslo Folk Museum from these years (Volume 2, p. 155). Particularly interesting structures come from Hallingdal and Heddal.

A few brick houses in *Oslo* date from the eighteenth century. These are more international in design, but are simple, restrained in decoration and with steeply pitched roofs. One such building is No. 2 Olsen's Gate (**896**).

Of especial interest from these two centuries in Norway are the *churches*. New churches built in the seventeenth century were designed for the Lutheran ritual. They were almost all of wood, on cruciform plan and with tall, slender spires. The stave method was abandoned in favour of logs or boarding. A typical and hardly altered example is *Kvikne Church*, standing on

NORWEGIAN DOMESTIC ARCHITECTURE

896 *Mr. Treschow's House. Fred Olsen's Gate, 2, Oslo,*
1740
897 *Stiftsgården, Palace façade, Trondheim, 1774–8*
898 *Garden front, Lade Manor House, near Trondheim,*
1811

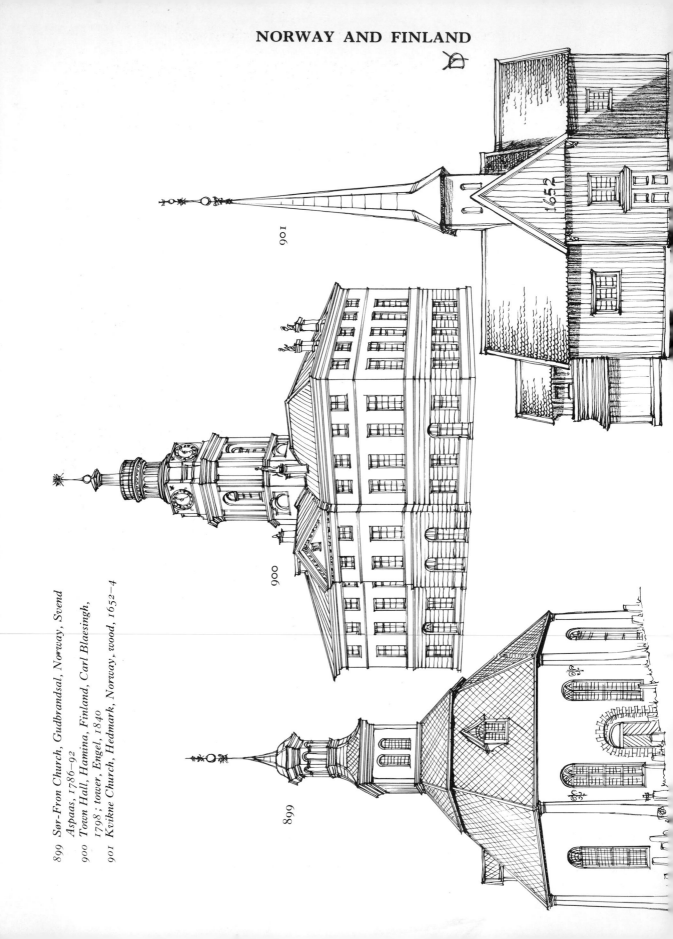

899 *Sør-Fron Church, Gudbrandsal, Norway, Svend Aspaas, 1786–92*

900 *Town Hall, Hamina, Finland, Carl Blaesingh, 1798 ; tower, Engel, 1840*

901 *Kvikne Church, Hedmark, Norway, wood, 1652–4*

901

900

899

902 Sør-Fron Church, Gudbrandsal, Norway, Svend Aspaas, 1786–92

the outskirts of a tiny village in a lonely valley in northern Hedmark (**901**). The exterior is of boarded wood. Inside, the church is painted all over the wood ceiling and walls in acanthus scrolled designs, incorporating panels depicting the Passion and the Life of the Apostles. Both these and the richly carved and painted pulpit are charmingly sophisticated and naïvely attractive—a remarkable testimony to mountain valley craftsmanship in this age. The work has much in common with the equally remote mountain churches of this date in Rumania and Bulgaria.

Though the majority of churches, even in the eighteenth century, were still of this type, after 1740 several examples were built which show a strong Baroque quality. This is clearly national in derivation, but an affinity with Baroque spatial and lighting effects, as well as an adherence to the octagonal, centrally planned form, is notable. Two outstanding octagonal churches are that at *Røros*, not far from Kvikne in northern Hedmark, and that at *Sør-Fron* in Gudbrandsal. Both were

designed by *Svend Aspaas* in the 1780s. Røros Church stands near the summit of a hill at the top of the small town's main street. It comprises an elongated octagon in plan with a square tower at the north-eastern side. It is a large church, painted white and with steeply pitched tiled roofs.

Sør-Fron Church, on the outskirts of a village much further south, is a simple octagon on the exterior, with no tower, only a central lantern (**899**). The interior is fully Baroque in its spatial handling and in altar and gallery detailing. The gallery, supported on columns, extends all round the church, its passage curtailed only by the high altar itself. The illustration in Fig. **902** shows the view from this level. This is a simple church, mainly in carved and painted wood; it is a Norwegian version of Borromini and, as such, charmingly successful.

The *Church* at *Kongsberg* dominates the town from the hillside above. The interior is very like that at Sør-Fron but on a more magnificent scale.

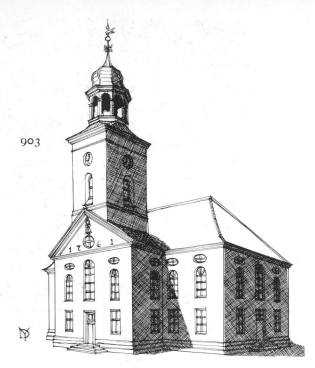

903

903 *Kongsberg Church, Norway, J. A. Stuckenbrock, 1740–61*

Here, though, the church is rectangular, with the high altar in the centre of the long side and opposite are enclosed boxes in the gallery for royal and important guests. It is a large church, with two galleries, one above the other, which can seat 3000 people. The decoration is all Baroque, in wood, carved, gilded and painted to imitate marble and other materials. The church exterior is of brick, large scale but simple in design (**903**).

Finland

Little notable Finnish architecture from these years exists. The great majority of building was in wood, which has perished or been altered during the country's political and military struggles with her larger neighbours. Impressive defence fortifications were built, of which *Sveaborg* was one of the largest. This is an island about three miles south-east of Helsinki. It was completely fortified all round, with strong walling, but the buildings are much altered now. A number of centralised, cruciform churches were built in the eighteenth century, but these were mainly of wood and have not survived well.

Very few civic structures on classical lines were

built in towns until the extensive development of the early nineteenth century (Volume 4, pp. 70, 71). The old *town hall* in *Porvoo* dates from 1764, and is a simple, colour-washed building, now used as a museum. The finest example of such work is the *town hall* at *Hamina* (**900**). This little town, now on the Soviet border, was destroyed during the Russian occupation of 1713–21. After this date it was rebuilt by *Carl Blaesingh*, who laid out the new town on a classical, centralised pattern based on concentric octagons, after Scamozzi's sixteenth century prototype at Palmanova in northern Italy. In Hamina, the streets radiate outwards from the centre of the design where stands the town hall, which is a classical gem. It was built in 1798, but the tower was added later by Engel.

The Low Countries: Belgium

There is a marked difference in the classical architecture of this period in Belgium and Holland. The former, as a largely Catholic area, developed a Baroque style under the leadership of the Jesuits who built many churches. In Holland the trend was similar to that in England and northern Germany.

Seventeenth century work in *Belgium* is mainly ecclesiastical. The towns were prospering less than in the fifteenth and sixteenth centuries and little secular work of interest emerged. Even in the churches the late Gothic structural form was slow to die. Typical is the *Church of S. Michael* in *Louvain*, designed in 1650 by *Willem Hesius* (van Hees). The ground plan is Latin cruciform, transepts and choir are apsidal-ended, while the aisles are formed by free-standing Ionic and Composite columns, not classical piers (**905**). The decoration is Baroque and the columns support an entablature, but above is a Gothic-type ribbed vaulted ceiling. Barrel vaulting decorated with painted panels and stucco decoration is rare in Belgium. The quality of ornament in the interior, and on the exterior façade is good. There is some fine woodcarving and sculpture in the altar rail and confession boxes (PLATE 103).

The *eighteenth century*, on the other hand, is noted for the building of secular structures. The outstanding instance of this is the *Grande Place* in *Brussels*. The guild houses here (**908**)

BAROQUE ARCHITECTURE IN THE LOW COUNTRIES

904 *Nieuwe Kerk, The Hague, Van Bassen and Noorwits, 1665*
905 *Church of S. Michael, Louvain, Willem Hesius, 1650–6*
906 *Nos. 364–370, Herengracht, Amsterdam, Vingboons, 1662–5*
907 *S. Mary's Church, Leyden, A. van 's Gravensande, 1639–49*

908

908 Grande Place, Brussels, late seventeenth and early eighteenth centuries

were rebuilt on the narrow, Medieval sites which they had occupied before their destruction by bombardment in 1695. The treatment of the new buildings is entirely Baroque. Each house differs from its neighbour but they all form a homogeneous unit. The decoration is rich and varied, in gables, finials, columns and sculptured figures; it is a national form of Baroque, characteristic of the country.

After 1750 a more neo-classical style replaced the Baroque. A number of town-planning schemes were carried out in this medium. The most important of these was designed by a French architect, *Barré*. This was the *Place Royale* in *Brussels*, laid out on the site of the old palace. It has a fine position high up in the city, looking down upon the Mont des Arts with its terraced steps and, further away, the town hall and cathedral. *Gilles Barnabé Guimard*, also of French origin, carried out the work with façades round three sides of a square and the equestrian statue in the centre in front of the church portico (910).

Holland

The *seventeenth century*, in particular, was a period of building activity in Holland. There is little Baroque design and this is found chiefly in decoration. Classical architecture is mainly in brick, with correct use of pilasters and ornament. Stone is often used for orders, decoration and facings. Large parts of the centre of *Amsterdam* were built in the seventeenth century, especially in terraces of tall houses along canals like Herengracht, Keizersgracht, Prinsengracht. One of the chief architects was *Philip Vingboons* (1614–78) who built in the same basic style as had been used in the sixteenth century, but replaced the curved, stepped gables with simpler, pedimented ones with curving swags at the sides. Giant orders are used on a number of façades. Doorways are planned in pairs and the whole curved terrace is of one architectural composition. The examples shown in Fig. **906** of the Herengracht are typical. A fine palace at *29, Kloveniersburgwal* (1622) was designed by his brother, *Justus Vingboons*.

Vingboons was designing chiefly in the years 1640–60. In the later years of the century, *Daniel Marot* (1661–1751), a refugee Huguenot, brought a French flavour to Dutch architecture. His work is richer and more Baroque in decoration and structure. It can be seen at *The Hague*, where his *Royal Library* (**912**) and buildings in the *Korte Vijverberg* (such as No. 3), survive. No. 475 in the Herengracht in Amsterdam is also thought to be by him.

909 *Royal Palace (formerly the Town Hall),*
Amsterdam, Jacob van Campen, 1648–65
910 *Place Royale, Brussels, Barré and Guimard, from*
1775
911 *Tower, Town Hall, Maastricht, Pieter Post,*
1658–84

912 No. 34, Lange Vorhout (Royal Library), The Hague, Holland, Daniel Marot, 1734–8

Dutch Palladian architecture was still flourishing, particularly in mid-century. The prime example of this is the large *town hall* in the centre of *Amsterdam* by *Jacob van Campen* (**909**). This immense rectangular block contains two interior courts. A structure designed for prestige, it is one of the few Dutch buildings to be entirely of stone. Of similar style is the *town hall* at *Maastricht* (1658–84) by *Pieter Post* (**911**).

Apart from these specific examples there are many individual houses and, commonly, whole streets of seventeenth and eighteenth century Dutch houses surviving, little altered on the exterior. These are often in towns along the canals. Aside from those already mentioned in *Amsterdam*, there are some elegant, tall façades in the Leidsegracht and round the open Begijnhof, which is a quiet courtyard of unusual shape surrounded by seventeenth century houses. In *The Hague* is No. 74 Lange Vorhout (1760–4) by P. de Swart and in *Leyden* there are several streets, like the Rapenburg Quay and Papengracht, which have many distinguished houses.

The *churches* are also classical in vein though

not very Baroque. Typical is the *New Church* at *The Hague* by *Pieter Noorvits* (**904**), which still has much in common with de Keyser's Amsterdam churches (p. 36). The *Marekerk* at *Leyden* is more Baroque in structure (**907**). It is centrally planned but is in plain brick with a minimum of decoration. It is octagonal and inside has a ring of eight columns supporting the central drum and dome and creating an ambulatory. The *Lutheran Church* in *Amsterdam* (1669–71) still presents a fine exterior and is a landmark in the centre of the city. Also of brick and centrally planned, it is circular with a giant order all round the exterior walls, the columns standing on a stone plinth. Above is an immense dome. The church interior was destroyed in a serious fire in 1882 but was restored in 1888. In 1935 it was deconsecrated due to a diminishing number of church goers and gradually fell into disrepair. Since 1974 the building exterior has been fully restored and the interior adapted as part of a new hotel (Amsterdam Sonesta Hotel), cultural and leisure centre.

Glossary

The bold reference figures in brackets refer to illustrations in the book.

Abacus The top member of a capital, usually a square or curved-sided slab of stone or marble (**665**).

Abutment The solid mass of masonry or brickwork from which an arch springs, or against which it abuts (**669**).

Acanthus A leaf form used in classical ornament.

Acroteria Blocks resting upon the vertex and lower extremities of a pediment to carry carved ornament.

Ambulatory A passage or aisle giving access in a church between the choir, with high altar, and the eastern apse (**661**).

Antefixae Carved blocks set at regular intervals along the lower edge of a roof.

Anthemion A type of classical ornament based upon the honeysuckle flower (**785**).

Apse Semicircular or polygonal termination to a church most commonly to be found on the eastern or transeptal elevations (**776**).

Arabesque Classical ornament in delicate, flowing forms, terminating in scrolls and decorated with flowers or leaves (**818**).

Architrave The lowest member of the classical entablature (**734**)

Arcuated construction Wherein the structure is supported on arches (**711**).

Articulation The designing, defining and dividing up of a façade into vertical and horizontal architectural members (**646**).

Ashlar Hewn and squared stones prepared for building.

Astragal A moulding at the top of a column and below the capital (**648**).

Astylar A classical façade without columns or pilasters (**733**).

Attic In Renaissance and later classical architecture an upper storey above the cornice (**772**).

Baldacchino A canopy supported on decorative pillars, suspended from the roof or projecting from a wall and carried on brackets, set over an altar or throne.

Barrel vault A continuous vault in semicircular section like a tunnel (**662**).

Basilica In Roman architecture a hall of justice and centre for commercial exchange. This type of structure was adapted by the early Christians for their church design. It was a rectangular building usually with an apse at one end. Internally it was divided into nave and aisles by columns rather than piers and these supported a timber roof. There were no transepts. The basilican plan has continued in use for centuries, though somewhat modified. It is especially to be seen in Italy and France (**648**).

Caisson *see* Coffer.

Cantilever A specially shaped beam or other member—for example, a staircase tread—which is supported securely at one end and carries a load at the other, free end or with the load distributed evenly along the beam. A cantilever bracket is used to support a cornice or balcony of considerable projection (**784**).

Capital The crowning feature of a column or pilaster (**773**).

Caryatid Sculptured female figure in the form of a support or column (**701**).

Ceiling cove Curved part of a ceiling where it joins the wall (**690**).

Centering A structure, usually made of wood, set up to support a dome, vault or arch until construction is complete.

Coffer A panel or caisson sunk into a ceiling, vault or dome. Most commonly the coffer is octagonal in shape and decoratively moulded. Its purpose is partly to lighten the roofing structure and partly ornamental.

Conch The domed ceiling of a semicircular apse (**895**).

Console A decorative scrolled bracket used in classical architecture to support a cornice.

Cornice The crowning member of a classical entablature (**713**).

Coupled Columns In classical architecture where the wall articulation is designed with the columns in pairs (**735**).

Crossing The central area in a cruciform church where the transepts cross the nave and choir arm. Above this space is generally set a tower or cupola (**661**).

Cruciform A plan based on the form of a cross (**775**).

Cyma A moulding in a section of two contrasting curves—either cyma recta or cyma reversa—used especially in classical architecture.

Dentil Classical form of ornament.

Domical vault A groined or ribbed vault semicircular in form so causing the centre of the vaulted bay to rise higher than the side arches, as in a low dome.

Drum The circular or poly-sided walling, usually pierced with windows, supporting a dome (**776**).

Echinus A curved moulded member supporting the abacus of the Doric order. The curve resembles that of the shell of a sea urchin after which it is named (*echinos* = sea urchin in Greek) (**662**).

Engaged column One which is attached to the wall behind it.

Entablature The continuous horizontal lintel made up of mouldings and supported by columns characteristic of classical architecture (**657**).

Entasis Taken from the Greek term for distension, is a carefully and mathematically calculated convex curving along the outline of the column shaft. It is designed to counteract the optical illusion which gives to a shaft bounded by straight lines the appearance of being concavely curved. In Greek and high quality Renaissance work, the column sides appear to be straight, so slight is the entasis. In later, especially nineteenth-century, mass-produced buildings, the curvature is often exaggerated, appearing convex.

Fillet A narrow flat band which divides mouldings from one another. It also separates column flutes.

Flute Vertical channelling in the shaft of a column.

Frieze The central member, plain or carved, of the classical entablature (**662**).

Frontispiece The two- or three-stage entrance feature applied to the principal façade of a court or building (**676**).

Giant Order Used in Mannerist, Baroque and later classical architecture where the order spans two storeys of the elevations (**806**).

Greek cross plan A cruciform ground plan in which all four arms of the cross are of equal length (**658**).

Guilloche Classical ornament in the form of an intertwined plait.

Guttae Small cones under the mutules and triglyphs of the Doric entablature.

Intercolumniation The space between columns.

Lantern Structure for ventilation and light. Often surmounting a dome or tower (**794**).

Latin cross plan A cruciform ground church plan where the nave is longer than the other three arms (**775**).

Lintel The horizontal stone slab or timber beam spanning an opening and supported on columns or walls.

Loggia Open-sided gallery or arcade (**662**).

Manoeline Portuguese decorative architectural style of the early sixteenth century named after Dom Manoel I (1495–1521).

Metope The space between the triglyphs of a Doric frieze. Often decorated with sculptured groups of carved ornament (**734**).

Module A unit of measurement by means of which the proportions and detailed parts of a building may be regulated. In classical architecture the column shaft diameter (or half diameter) was used.

Monolithic column One whose shaft is of one piece of stone or marble in contrast to one made up from hollow drums.

Mutule Blocks attached under Doric cornices from which guttae depend.

Necking The space between the astragal of a column shaft and the actual capital.

Pediment In classical architecture the triangular low-pitched gable above the entablature which completes the end of the sloping roof. Pediments are also used as decorative features above doors, niches and windows. In Renaissance, Mannerist and Baroque work these may be broken, open, scrolled or segmental (**753, 707, 806**).

Pendentive Spherical triangles formed by the intersecting of the dome by two pairs of opposite arches, themselves carried on piers or columns (**750**).

Peristyle A row of columns surrounding a court or cloister, also the space so enclosed (**732**).

Piano nobile An Italian Renaissance term meaning literally 'the noble floor'. In classical building it is the first and principal floor.

Pilaster A column of rectangular section usually engaged in the wall (**734, 737**).

Plateresque A form of rich, surface ornament in Spanish architecture used in both Gothic and Renaissance building. The term is derived from platería- = silverwork (**plate 93**).

Podium A continuous projecting base or pedestal (**729**).

Putto From the Italian word meaning child, used to describe cherubs in sculpture, especially in Baroque architecture (**plates 82, 103, 104**).

Retablo An altar piece or framing enclosing painted panels above an altar. A Spanish word used especially when referring to Spanish architecture (**plate 91**).

Rotunda Building of circular ground plan often surmounted by a dome; a circular hall or room (**655**).

Rustication A treatment of masonry with sunk joints and roughened surfaces. Used in classical architecture (**892**).

Shaft The column of an order between capital and base.

Spandrel Triangular space formed between an arch and the rectangle of outer mouldings as in a doorway. Generally decorated by carving or mosaic (**664**).

Strapwork A form of ornament using straps of decoration intertwined and forming panels. The straps are flat with raised fillet edges. Used especially in early Mannerist type of Renaissance work in Flanders, Germany, England and Poland (**plates 83, 90**).

Stucco An Italian word for decorative plasterwork. The Italian *stucco duro* was the hard plaster used by Renaissance craftsmen which, in addition to lime and gypsum, contained powdered marble.

Transept The arms of a cruciform church set at right angles to nave and choir. Transepts are generally aligned north and south.

Triglyph The blocks cut with vertical channels which are set at regular intervals along the frieze of the Doric order (**734**).

Tympanum The face of a classical pediment between its sloping and horizontal cornice mouldings also the area between the lintel of a doorway and the arch above it. Tympana are generally carved and/or sculptured or are decorated with mosaic (**646, 909**).

Vault Arched covering.

Vaulting bay The rectangular or square area bounded by columns or piers and covered by a vault (**662**).

Volute A spiral or scroll to be seen in Ionic, Corinthian and Composite capitals (**664**).

Voussoir Wedge-shaped stones which compose an arch.

Bibliography

A select list of books, classified by country, recommended for further reading.

Europe in general

ALLSOPP, B., *A History of Renaissance Architecture*, Pitman, 1959

ALLSOPP, B., BOOTON, H. W., and CLARK, U., *The Great Tradition of Western Architecture*, A. and C. Black, 1966

BAZIN, G., *The Baroque*, Thames and Hudson, 1968

BENEVOLO, L., *The History of the City*, The MIT Press, 1986

BLUNT, A., *Baroque and Rococo*, Elek, 1978; *Baroque and Rococo Architecture and Decoration*, Granada, 1982

BUSCH, H., and LOHSE, B., *Renaissance Europe*, Batsford, 1961; *Baroque Europe*, Batsford, 1962

CAMESASCA, E., *History of the House*, Collins, 1971

CICHY, B., *Great Ages of Architecture*, Oldbourne, 1964

COPPLESTONE, T., Ed., *World Architecture*, Hamlyn, 1963

FLEMING, J., HONOUR, H., and PEVSNER, N., *The Penguin Dictionary of Architecture*, Penguin, 1977

FLETCHER, BANISTER, *A History of Architecture*, Butterworth, 1987

FOSTER, M., *The Principles of Architecture*, Phaidon, 1983

GOMBRICH, E., *The Story of Art*, Phaidon, 1972

HARRIS, J., and LEVER, J., *Illustrated Glossary of Architecture*, Faber and Faber, 1966

HEMPEL, E., *Baroque Art and Architecture in Central Europe*, Pelican History of Art Series, Penguin, 1965

HERSEY, G. L., *Architecture, Poetry and Number at the Royal Palace at Caserta*, The MIT Press, 1987

HINDLEY, G., *Castles of Europe*, Hamlyn, 1968

HOAR, F., *European Architecture*, Evans, 1967

HONOUR, H., and FLEMING, J., *A World History of Art*, Macmillan, 1982

HUGHES, J. Q., and LYNTON, N., *Renaissance Architecture* (Simpson's History of Architectural Development), Longmans, Green, 1965

JORDAN, R. FURNEAUX, *A Concise History of Western Architecture*, Thames and Hudson, 1969; *European Architecture in Colour*, Thames and Hudson, 1961

KOSTOV, S., *A History of Architecture: Settings and Rituals*, Oxford University Press, 1985

KRINSKY, C. H., *Synagogues of Europe*, the MIT Press, 1986

McANDREW, J., *Venetian Architecture of the Early Renaissance*, The MIT Press, 1987

MILLON, H. A., *Baroque and Rococo Architecture*, Prentice-Hall

MURRAY, P., *Architecture of the Renaissance*, Academy Editions, 1971; *Renaissance Architecture*, Faber and Faber, 1978

MUSCHENHEIM, W., *Elements of the Art of Architecture*, Thames and Hudson, 1965

NORBERG-SCHULZ, C., *Baroque Architecture*, Academy Editions, 1971

NORWICH, J. J., Ed., *Great Architecture of the World*, Mitchell Beazley, 1975

NUTTGENS, P., *The Story of Architecture*, Phaidon, 1983; *The World's Great Architecture*, Hamlyn, 1980

OLSEN, D. J., *The City as a Work of Art; London, Paris, Vienna*, Yale University Press, 1986

PEVSNER, N., *An Outline of European Architecture*, Penguin, 1961; *A History of Building Types*, Thames and Hudson, 1984

PLACZEK, A. K., Ed., *Macmillan Encyclopedia of Architects* (4 Vols), Collier Macmillan, 1982

RAEBURN, M., Ed., *Architecture of the Western World*, Orbis Publishing, 1980; *An Outline of World Architecture*, Octopus, 1973

RICHARDS, J. M., *Who's Who in Architecture from 1400 to the Present Day*, Weidenfeld and Nicolson, 1977

RYKWERT, J., *The First Moderns: The Architects of the Eighteenth Century*, The MIT Press, 1987

SITWELL, S., *Great Houses of Europe*, Weidenfeld and Nicolson, 1961; *Great Palaces of Europe*, Weidenfeld and Nicolson, 1964

STIERLIN, H., *Encyclopaedia of World Architecture*, Macmillan, 1983

SUMMERSON, J., *The Classical Language of Architecture*, Thames and Hudson, 1983

TRACHTENBERG, M., and HYMAN, I., *Architecture from Pre-history to Post-Modernism*, Academy Editions, 1986

WATKIN, D., *A History of Western Architecture*, Barrie and Jenkins, 1986

WITTKOWER, R., *Architectural Principles in the Age of Humanism*, Academy Editions, 1977

YARWOOD, D., *Encyclopaedia of Architecture*, Batsford, 1985; *Chronology of Western Architecture*, Batsford, 1987

Belgium and Holland

GERSON, H., and TER KUILE, E. H., *Art and Architecture in Belgium, 1600–1800*, Pelican History of Art Series, Penguin, 1960

ROSENBERG, J., SLIVE, S., AND TER KUILE, E. H., *Dutch Art and Architecture 1600–1800*, Pelican History of Art Series, Penguin, 1966

Britain

ADAM, R., and J., *The Works in Architecture of Robert and James Adam*, Tiranti, 1959

BALCOMBE, G., *History of Building Styles, Methods and Materials*, Batsford, 1985

BEARD, G., *The Work of Sir Christopher Wren*, Bartholomew, 1982; *The Work of Robert Adam*, Bartholomew, 1978; *The Work of John Vanbrugh*, Batsford, 1986

BRAUN, H., *Elements of English Architecture*, David and Charles, 1973

BRUNSKILL, R. W., *Traditional Buildings of Britain*, Gollancz, 1982

BRUNSKILL, R. W., and CLIFTON-TAYLOR, A., *English Brickwork*, Ward Lock, 1977

CLIFTON-TAYLOR, A., *The Pattern of English Building*, Faber and Faber, 1972; *English Parish Churches as Works of Art*, Batsford, 1974

CLIFTON-TAYLOR, A., and IRESON, A. S., *English Stone Building*, Gollancz, 1983

COOK, O., *The English House Through Seven Centuries*, Whittet Books, 1983

CRAIG, M., *The Architecture of Scotland*, Batsford, 1978

DOWNES, K., *Vanbrugh*, Zwemmer, 1977; *Hawksmoor*, Zwemmer, 1979; *The Architecture of Wren*, Granada, 1982

DUNBAR, J. G., *The Architecture of Scotland*, Batsford, 1978

FLEMING, J., *Robert Adam and His Circle*, Murray, 1962

FRIEDMAN, T., *James Gibbs*, Yale University Press, 1986

GIROUARD, M., *Life in the English Country House*, Yale University Press, 1978; *Cities and People*, Yale University Press, 1985

GUINESS, D., and SADLER, J. T., *The Palladian Style in England, Ireland and America*, Thames and Hudson, 1976

HARRIS, J., *Sir William Chambers*, Zwemmer, 1970, *The Palladians*, Trefoil, 1981

HILLING, J. B., *The Historic Architecture of Wales*, University of Wales Press, 1976

HOOK, J., *The Baroque Age in England*, Thames and Hudson, 1976

ISON, I., and W., *English Church Architecture Through the Ages*, Arthur Barker, 1972; *The Georgian Buildings of Bristol*, Faber and Faber, 1952; *The Georgian Buildings of Bath*, Faber and Faber, 1948

JONES, E., and WOODWARD, C., *The Architecture of London*, Weidenfeld and Nicolson, 1983

LLOYD, D., *The Making of English Towns*, Gollancz, 1984

LLOYD, N., *History of the English House*, The Architectural Press, 1975; *A History of English Brickwork*, Antique Collectors' Club, 1983

PETZCH, H., *Architecture in Scotland*, Longman Group, 1971

SAUNDERS, A., *The Art and Architecture of London*, Phaidon, 1984

SITWELL, S., *British Architects and Craftsmen 1600–1830*, Batsford, 1948

STROUD, D., *George Dance Architect, 1741–1825*, Faber and Faber, 1971; *Henry Holland*, Country Life, 1966

SUMMERSON, J., *Architecture in Britain 1530–1830*, Pelican History of Art Series, Penguin, 1969; *Georgian London*, Barrie and Jenkins, 1962

WILSON, M., *William Kent*, Routledge and Kegan Paul, 1984

WITTKOWER, R., *Palladio and English Palladianism*, Thames and Hudson, 1974

YARWOOD, D., *Robert Adam*, Dent, 1970; *The Architecture of Britain*, Batsford, 1980; *Outline of English Architecture*, Batsford, 1977; *English Interiors*, Lutterworth Press, 1984; *The English Home*, Batsford, 1979

Bulgaria

STAMOV, S., Ed., *The Architectural Heritage of Bulgaria*, State Publishing House Tehnika, Sofia, 1972

Czechoslovakia

KNOX, B., *Bohemia and Moravia*, Faber and Faber, 1962

France

BLOMFELD, R., *A History of French Architecture* (2 Vols.), Bell, 1911

BLUNT, A., *Art and Architecture in France 1500–1700*, Pelican History of Art Series, Penguin, 1957

BOURGET, P., *Jules Hardouin Mansart*, Vincent, Fréal, Paris, 1956

BRAHAM, A., *The Architecture of the French Enlightenment*, Thames and Hudson, 1980

BRAHAM, A., and SMITH, P., *François Mansart*, Zwemmer, 1973

COOPE, R., *Salomon de Brosse*, Zwemmer, 1972

DUNLOP, I., *Royal Palaces of France*, Hamish Hamilton, 1985

GOUVION, C., and PHILIPPE, D., *Châteaux of the Loire*, Thames and Hudson, 1986

TADGELL, C., *Ange-Jacques Gabriel*, Zwemmer, 1978

THOMSON, D., *Renaissance Paris*, Zwemmer, 1984

WALTON, G., *Louis XIV's Versailles*, Penguin, 1986

Germany

REUTHER, H., *Balthasar Neumann*, Suddeutscher Verlag, 1983

RUSSELL-HITCHCOCK, H., *German Rococo: the Zimmermann Brothers*, Penguin, 1968; *Rococo Architecture in Southern Germany*, Phaidon, 1968

WATKIN, D., and MELLINGHOFF, T., *German Architecture and the Classical Ideal 1740–1840*, Thames and Hudson, 1987

Italy

ACKERMAN, J. S., *The Architecture of Michelangelo*, Penguin, 1986

BATTISTI, E., *Brunelleschi*, Thames and Hudson, 1981

BERGÈRE, T., and R., *The Story of St. Peter's*, Dodd, Mead, New York, 1966

BLUNT, A., *Borromini*, Allen Lane, 1979; *Sicilian Baroque*, Weidenfeld and Nicolson, 1968

BORSI, F., *Bernini*, Rizzoli, New York, 1984

BRAHAM, A., and HAGER, H., *Carlo Fontana*, Zwemmer, 1977

BRUSCHI, A., *Bramante*, Thames and Hudson, 1977

FANELLI, G., *Brunelleschi*, Scala, 1980

FAGIOLO DELL' ARCO, M. M., *Bernini*, Mario Bulzoni, Rome, 1967

GANGI, G., *Il Barocco nella Sicilia Occidentale*, De Luca, Rome, 1968

GODFREY, F. M., *Italian Architecture up to 1750*, Tiranti, 1971

GUNTON, L., *Rome's Historic Churches*, Allen and Unwin, 1969

HOWARD, D., *Jacopo Sansovino*, Yale University Press, 1987

LABO, M., *Guarino Guarini*, Astra Arengarium, 1956

LEES-MILNE, J., *Baroque in Italy*, Batsford, 1959

LIEBERMANN, R., *Renaissance Art in Venice*, Frederick Muller

MURRAY, P., *The Architecture of the Italian Renaissance*, Batsford, 1963

PALLADIO, A., *The Architect and Society*, Penguin, 1966

PALLADIO, A., *The Four Books of Architecture*, Dover Publications, New York, 1965

SERLIO, S., *The Five Books of Architecture*, Dover Publications, New York, 1982

SITWELL, S., *Southern Italy Re-visited*, Weidenfeld and Nicolson, 1969

VITRUVIUS, *The Ten Books on Architecture*, Dover Publications, 1960

WITTKOWER, R., *Art and Architecture in Italy 1600–1750*, Pelican History of Art Series, Penguin, 1965

YARWOOD, D., *The Architecture of Italy*, Chatto and Windus, 1970

Poland

DOBRZYCKI, J., *Cracow: Landscape and Architecture*, Arkady, Warsaw, 1967

JANKOWSKI, S., and ROFALSKI, P., *Warsaw: A Portrait of the City*, Arkady, Warsaw, 1979

KNOX, B., *The Architecture of Poland*, Barrie and Jenkins, 1971

KOSTROWICKI, I. and J., *Poland*, Arkady, Warsaw, 1980

STANKIEWICZ, J., *Gdansk*, Arkady, 1971

ZACHWATOWICZ, J., *Polish Architecture*, Arkady, 1967

Romania

CIOCULESCU, S., and others, *Romania*, Meriadne, Bucharest, 1967

Russia

BERTON, K., *Moscow*, Studio Vista, 1977

HAMILTON, G. H., *The Art and Architecture of Russia*, Pelican History of Art Series, Penguin, 1954; *Leningrad*, Aurora Art Publishers, Leningrad, 1977

Scandinavia

FABER, T., *A History of Danish Architecture*, Det Danske Selskab, 1964

KAVLI, G., *Norwegian Architecture*, Batsford, 1958

RICHARDS, J. M., *800 Years of Finnish Architecture*, David and Charles, 1978

Spain and Portugal

BROWN, J., and ELIOT, J. H., *Palace for a King: The Buen Retiro and the Court of Philip IV*, Yale University Press, 1986

DIETERICH, A., and BOGER, B., *Portrait of Spain*, Oliver and Boyd, 1958

Index

WITHDRAWN